WITHDRAWN

Books are to be returned on or before
the last date below.

Also by Paul Kennedy

AFRICAN CAPITALISM: The Struggle for Ascendancy
TO MAKE ANOTHER WORLD (*co-editor*)
GLOBAL SOCIOLOGY (*co-author*)

Also by Catherine J. Danks

RUSSIAN POLITICS AND SOCIETY

Globalization and National Identities

Crisis or Opportunity?

Edited by

Paul Kennedy
Senior Lecturer in Sociology
Manchester Metropolitan University

and

Catherine J. Danks
Senior Lecturer in History
Manchester Metropolitan University

palgrave

First published 2001 by
PALGRAVE
Houndmills, Basingstoke, Hampshire RG21 6XS and
175 Fifth Avenue, New York, N.Y. 10010
Companies and representatives throughout the world

PALGRAVE is the new global academic imprint of
St. Martin's Press LLC Scholarly and Reference Division and
Palgrave Publishers Ltd (formerly Macmillan Press Ltd).

ISBN 0–333–92963–2

This book is printed on paper suitable for recycling and
made from fully managed and sustained forest sources.

A catalogue record for this book is available
from the British Library.

Library of Congress Cataloging-in-Publication Data
Globalization and national identities : crisis or opportunity? /
edited by Paul Kennedy and Catherine J. Danks.
      p. cm.
   Includes bibliographical references and index.
   ISBN 0–333–92963–2
   1. Social change. 2. Globalization. 3. Nationalism. I. Kennedy,
Paul T., 1941– II. Danks, Catherine J., 1956–

   HM836 .G58 2001
   303.4—dc21
                                                      2001016404

10   9   8   7   6   5   4   3   2   1
10 09 08 07 06 05 04 03 02 01

Printed and bound in Great Britain by
Antony Rowe Ltd, Chippenham, Wiltshire

Contents

List of Tables

Preface

The theme for this book emerged from the papers originally given at an interdisciplinary conference organized around the theme of 'globalization and identities'. This was organized by the Institute for Global Studies and the Department of Sociology at Manchester Metropolitan University and was held in the summer of 1999. Although sociologists formed the core of the participants, people from other social science disciplines also made major contributions, including political scientists, art historians, geographers and anthropologists. This spread of scholarship is partly reflected in our choice of contributors to this book so that at least four chapters were written by scholars who, if compelled to do so, would probably label themselves as political scientists – though ones with leanings towards history, political economy and sociology. Indeed, and strange though it may seem, not only did the interdisciplinary nature of the conference present few if any serious problems, it actually proved to be one of the occasion's great strengths. For one thing, our common interest in and focus on global themes linked to the issue of identities proved more than equal to the task of enabling us to engage in a fruitful dialogue across the discipline lines without encountering problems of understanding – or misunderstanding. But, in addition, the very multifaceted nature of globalization – pulling us in its wake as it crosses all boundaries, re-scrambling our experiences and exposing us endlessly to new connections – is such that it compels most of those who become embroiled in its study to gain at least some familiarity with other disciplines to the mutual benefit of everyone working in this field.

We would like to express our sincere gratitude to all those who attended the conference: both those who gave papers and those who attended the sessions and showed such a lively interest. Everyone who came contributed towards making the 1999 conference a truly rewarding and enjoyable experience. However, we would especially like to thank Martin Albrow for his inspirational address and warm encouragement.

CATHERINE J. DANKS and PAUL KENNEDY
Manchester Metropolitan University

Notes on the Contributors

Ioannis Armakolas is a Doctoral candidate in the Faculty of Social and Political Sciences, University of Cambridge. His research is on identity transformations in the Yugoslav conflict. His general research interests include, conflict analysis, international theory and Balkan affairs. He has previously been the 1998–99 Tip O'Neill Fellow in Peace Studies.

William Berthomière is a post-Doctorate student at the French Research Centre of Jerusalem and the Avraham Harman Institute of Contemporary Jewry at the Hebrew University of Jerusalem with the support of the Lavoisier grant from the French Ministry of Foreign affairs. He is also an associate member of Migrinter (UMR6588–CNRS). He is co-editor of the special issue of *Revue Européenne des Migrations Internationales* about 'The New Faces of Imigration in Israel', 1996, vol.12–13.

John W. Books is Associate Professor, Department of Political Science University of North Texas. His publications include 'Contextual effects on individual political attitudes: the impact of the state and local economy on retrospective economic evaluations', *Political Behavior* (March 1999) and co-authored with Charles L. Prysby *Political Behavior in the Local Context* (1991).

Catherine J. Danks is Senior Lecturer in the Department of History and Economic History at Manchester Metropolitan University and a member of the Institute for Global Studies (MMU). She is the the author of *Russian Politics and Society* (Prentice Hall (2001)).

G. Honor Fagan is Lecturer in Sociology at the National University of Ireland, Maynooth. Her current research interests include social theory, gender and development, cultural politics, and globalization and culture. She has done field research on early school leavers in Dublin for her book *Cultural Politics and Irish Early School Leavers: Constructing Political Identities* (1995) and on women in South African townships. She is currently researching for a book to be titled 'Globalization and Culture: Placing Ireland' and is Convenor of the Globalization and Democratic Development Research Group, NUIM.

Patricia Hogwood is a Lecturer in the Department of Politics, University of Glasgow. Her research interests are comparative European politics, German politics (particularly issues of state and popular identity), devolution in Scotland and Wales, and coalition theory. She is co-author, with Geoffrey Roberts, of *European Politics Today* (1997) and is currently working on a companion reference volume and writing a book on the initial consolidation of the unification process in Germany.

Paul Kennedy is Senior Lecturer in Sociology at MMU, and Director of the Institute for Global Studies at MMU. Most of his research has been concerned with Development and African Studies and has now broadened into the study of global social change and social problems. Among his recent publications are *African Capitalism* (1988) and *Global Sociology* (Macmillan, 2000 co-authored with Robin Cohen).

Lauren Langman is a Professor of Sociology at Loyola University in Chicago, USA. He is a critical theorist whose research interests are concerned with identity in the post-national, globalized worlds of consumer capitalism. His publications include 'Neon cages: shopping for subjectivity', in Rob Shieds (ed.), *Life style Shopping* (1993) and 'Suppose they gave a cultural war and no-one came: Clinton and the carnivalization of political culture', in *American Behavioural Scientist*, February 2000.

Asawin Nedpogaeo is a Doctoral candidate at the Centre for Communications and Information Studies, University of Westminister researching 'Glocalization and Thainess'. He has worked in both print and broadcast journalism and in 2000 will become a Lecturer in the Faculty of Communication arts, Dhurakipunditn University in Bangkok, Thailand.

Darren J. O'Byrne is Lecturer in the School of Sociology and Social Policy, University of Surrey Roehampton, Southlands College. His research interests include citizenship, globalization and human rights. His publications include the co-authored *Local/Global Relations in a London Borough* (1994) and *The Dimensions of Global Citizenship: Political Identity Beyond the Nation State?* (2001) and *Human Rights: an Introduction* (2001).

Julie F. Scott is Lecturer in the Sociology of Religion in the Department of Sociology at Liverpool Hope University College. Her research interests include Protestant fundamentalism in the USA, apocalyptic worldviews and contemporary trends in religiosity in the UK and USA.

Glen Segell is Director of the Institute of Security Policy in London and has been the chair person of the BISA Workgroup on Globalization and International Relations. He is also an elected member of the Governing Council of the International Security Studies Section of the ISA. He has published widely on globalization and civil–military issues.

Elizabeth Stanley is Lecturer is Critical Criminology at the Centre for Studies in Crime and Social Justice, Edge Hill College, UK. Her research interests include human rights and crimes of the state, transitional justice, storytelling and truth commissions.

List of Abbreviations

ANC	African National Congress
CDU/CSU	Christian Democratic Union/Christian Social Union (Germany)
CIS	Commonwealth of Independent States
CPSU	Communist Party of the Soviet Union
EC	European Community or European Communities
EU	European Union
EURO CORP	European Corps: Combined French, German and Belgian military force
FRG	Federal Republic of Germany
GATT	General Agreement on Tariffs and Trade
GDP	Gross Domestic Product
GDR	German Democratic Republic
GNP	Gross National Product
IBRD	International Bank for Reconstruction and Development – usually known as the World Bank
IDA	Irish Development Association
IFP	Inkatha Freedom Party (South Africa)
IMF	International Monetary Fund, founded together with the World Bank
INGO	International Non-Governmental Organization
IPEG	Independent European Programme Group
KFOR	Kosovo Force
MNC	Multinational Corporation
NATO	North Atlantic Treaty Organization founded in 1949. A transatlantic military organization led by the USA
NGO	Non-Governmental Organization
NP	National Party (South Africa)
NUPI	Norwegian Institute of International Affairs
OECD	Organization for Economic Cooperation and Development
PDS	Democratic Socialist Party (Germany)
PRIO	Peace Research Institute, Oslo
PTT	Petroleum Authority of Thailand
RCP	Communist Party of the Russian Federation
ROC	Russian Orthodox Church

RSFSR	Russian Soviet Federative Socialist Republic
RSI	Rationalization, Standardization and Interoperationability of Policies, Strategy and Equipment
SA	South Africa
SED	Socialist Unity Party (Germany)
SNP	Scottish National Party
TNC	Transnational Corporation
TRC	Truth and Reconciliation Commission
UN	United Nations
UNIFIL	United Nations Interim Force (in Lebanon)
USSR	Union of Soviet Socialist Republics
WTO	World Trade Organization

1
Introduction: Globalization and the Crisis of Identities?

Paul Kennedy

The literature on contemporary identities and social change abounds with terminology and images of radical transition, disorientation, turbulence, confusion, rootlessness and constant motion. The possibility of crisis or even the chaos of a Humpty-Dumpty world where no amount of trying will ever succeed in putting things back together again, seems an ever-present reality. Thus, societies are fragmenting and disintegrating; their internal structures are becoming dis-assembled and merged into the maelstrom of the 'global post-modern' (Hall, 1992: 302). The boundaries of societies and cultures are being breached by vast, criss-crossing flows of ideas, images and information, their former impermeability lost forever. Communities, once invested with deep meanings and encapsulating close-knit relations, are becoming de-localized – torn from familiar and particular places (Albrow et al., 1997). Everywhere the once-separate items in the global mosaic of cultures are leaking, merging into one another (Friedman, 1994), losing their distinctiveness. Meanwhile nations have become 'unbound' and experience deterritorialization as multinational corporations (MNCs) weave chunks of local economies into their own global empires, as migrant diasporas refuse permanent assimilation, preferring to develop transnational 'networks . . . that span their home and host society' (Basch et al., 1994) and as global social movements embed national citizens in worldwide commitments. Everyone on the planet, it seems, is being propelled into a life of perpetual mobility, whether of the imagination, the body or both (Rapport and Dawson, 1998: 4).

This book explores some of the issues raised by just such a theorization of a 'world-in-turmoil' through a selection of case studies drawn from the conference outlined in the Preface. A key theme running through these chapters is that in many situations the nation-state and nationalism continue to provide a pivotal axis around which individuals and collectivities frame their sense of cultural affiliation and feelings of belonging. Other kinds of cultural identity also figure in these accounts, especially those relating to regional, ethnic, religious, racial and class affiliations along with lifestyles. However, not only were issues surrounding nationality and national identity invariably present somewhere in the narrative, they normally assumed the central place and so it is with the implications of such questions – whether for societies, institutions, groups or individuals – that our contributors are mostly, though not solely, concerned.

Understanding identities

Social scientists invariably reject essentialist notions of individual, national or other collective identities as determined by fixed properties derived from common origins which define the distinctiveness, solidarity and inclusiveness shared by members. This is not to say that major differences do not exist between collectivities and do not inform the actions and beliefs of their members. Thus, Hall (1998) argues that ethnicity is a particularly 'strong, well-bounded version of cultural identity' precisely because it is based not just on shared meanings but also generations of intermarriage and descent coupled to long-standing residential ties to particular places. In such circumstances ethnic identity is 'experienced as if it were a part of our biological nature' (Hall, 1998: 181). Similarly, modernizing nation states usually drew upon common characteristics of language, historical heritage, ethnic origins and geographical location that preceded the modern era. During this process the ideology of nationalism came to embody the 'belief that national identity is fundamental and natural' (Basch et al., 1994: 37). However, all this is a very different thing from claiming that the very existence and identities of modern nation-states depended on an inner core of immutable characteristics inscribed in immemorial time.

In decisively rejecting such 'common sense' notions, social scientists have insisted that identities are constituted and validated through ongoing interactions. Because the process of identification always involves construction it reveals additional characteristics. Firstly, it is 'a process never completed – always "in process" ... conditional, lodged in contingency' (Hall 1997: 2). Similarly, identity is not 'permanently given' (Melucci, 1996: 159). Rather, identity formation involves construction and reconstruction throughout 'the life-course of individuals and groups and through their different faces, roles and circumstances'

(Melucci, 1996). Identity looks more towards an uncertain future than it harks back to a clearly defined past. Secondly, though identity may encompass some difference within itself it also 'entails...the binding and marking of symbolic boundaries, the production of "frontier effects"' (Hall, 1997: 2–3). Indeed, all identity construction requires the summoning of difference, the relativization of the self as against the 'other' imagined as separate, outside – and perhaps also as marginal, inferior and dangerous. Thus, drawing on Anderson (1983), Hannerz (1996: 21) observes how shared commonality within the nation is paralleled by a strong sense of cultural and linguistic discontinuity with respect to outsider-nations. In Europe, this condition was profoundly shaped by the growing ability of people to 'engage in a common intelligibility' within each nation assisted by the spread of print. Here, too, Said's pathbreaking study, *Orientalism* (1995), remains illuminating. Thus, he showed how the Orient became a mirror in which Europe saw its own reflection, revealing both its objective but also its imagined differences from the Orient. The largely mythical Orient invented by European artists, explorers and later colonial officials was mysterious, decadent and barbaric. This tells us far more about the fears and desires of Europeans than about the objective realities of the world they attempted to depict.

Thirdly, rendering collective identities meaningful and viable requires representations or structures of meaning. In the case of the nation-state, Anderson's (1983) argument has been enormously influential. Modern nationhood was not only invented through the 'imagined community', but this was the only vehicle capable of unifying vast numbers of dispersed citizens, divided by class and other interests, into the unit of belonging we call the nation. Thus, the prime ingredient which makes a national or any other kind of community viable is 'the idea we have of it,...the meanings we associate with it, the sense of community with others we carry inside us' (Hall, 1998: 182). Among the representations crucial in bringing modern nationhood to life as a rallying point for citizen loyalty were the following: the ability through art, popular culture or the media to relate the 'narrative of the nation', its turning points, defining features and past glories; the emphasis on its continuity with a distant past, aided by traditions and ceremonies which speak of an ancient lineage; the existence of a 'foundational myth' of national origin; and the idea of a pure 'primordial folk' from whom all are descended (Hall, 1992: 294–5). However, as many writers have suggested, historical reflection soon reveals a very different story; centuries of violent civil wars, the forced amalgamations, exclusions or

oppressions of peripheral peoples, periods of inward and outward conquest and frequent migrations bringing new cultures to unwelcoming
shores. Such realities belie the fiction of unified national communities
enjoying centuries of unbroken solidarity and purity of purpose.

Finally, most observers insist that power relations are invariably central to the construction of representations of identity; certain groups
and individuals exercise more influence over this process than others. As
Gupta and Ferguson (1992: 14) suggest, when it comes to constructing
such representations the key question is to enquire who has defined 'the
"we" that keeps coming up in phrases such as "ourselves" and "our own
society"'. Similarly, we need to question the determination to separate
so decisively 'the unity of the "us" and the otherness of the "other"'.
However, as Gupta and Ferguson (1992: 17) also point out, the 'politics
of otherness' is not just about control over the formulation of representations; the ability to determine differences of identity between people
and places also resides in power over military, economic and legal
resources – as, for example, in the case of laws and rights pertaining to
immigrants.

Turning to individual identities, we find that economists and psycho-
logists regard individuality and individual identities as separate
and distinctive from social identities. Here, there appear to be two selves
with the individual/personal unique self being regarded as more real,
more significant and quite different from the socially learned or social
self (Jenkins, 1996: 15). How these two entities may be linked is unclear.
Reviewing twentieth century sociological thinking on this topic, and
adopting a starkly different viewpoint Jenkins (1996) argues that
'individual identity – embodied in selfhood – is not meaningful in
isolation from the social world of other people. Individuals are unique
and variable, but selfhood is thoroughly socially constructed' (20)
through early socialization and everyday social interactions. Individual
and social identity are 'entangled' with each other, they are produced
by 'analogous' processes and they are both 'intrinsically social' (19).
According to interactionist theory (for example, Mead, 1934), what
guarantees this overlap between individual and social identity is the
fact that the self is constituted through interactions with significant
others who provide us with various definitions of ourselves. Indeed,
we are unable to know ourselves except through our perceptions of
how others see us and how they respond to our characteristics
and actions. The wider set of ongoing and organized social relationships – or the generalized other – provides actors in micro-relationships
with an agreed interpretation of characteristics and actions and thus

gives an overall coherence and confirmation to shared interactive experiences.

In all this there are close but not perfect parallels with the way in which collective identities are formed. Thus, at the core of the self there is a lack, a deficit. The contrived identity which emerges to fill this gap arises largely from our interactions with different others whose responses enable us to focus more clearly on who we are in relation to them. Indeed, neither the 'I' – Mead's formulation of the ego, the individual self – nor the 'me', as 'the organized set of attitudes of others which one himself assumes' (Mead, 1934: 175) can be formed except through the impact of external forces coming from our social world. Moreover, though the internalized 'I' possesses a capacity for autonomy it is one that is largely informed by involvement in social life. This theorization enables us to ' "bridge the analytical gap" between the individual and society' (Jenkins, 1996: 25) – agent and structure, object and subject – that has formed such a central part of the twentieth-century sociological debate.

In this widely employed sociological-interactionist formulation, social identity simultaneously becomes synonymous with 'collectively shared' identity (19) and 'the way in which we more or less self-consciously locate ourselves in our social world' (Preston, 1997: 168). Thus, the individual has to invest in the social positions and cultural identities – nationhood, ethnicity, vocation, class and so on – offered by society. This is the process of identification whereby we 'align our subjective feelings with the objective spaces we occupy in the social and cultural world' (Hall, 1992: 276). Identification, therefore, 'stitches...the subject into the structure' (276). When this occurs, social identity 'marks the ways in which we are the same as others who share that position and the ways in which we are different from those who do not' (Woodward, 1997: 2).

This seems straightforward enough. However, returning to Hall, in a later discussion (1997) he hints at the existence of two different and contradictory ways of thinking about identification. On the one hand, identities are something we are 'obliged' to assume and they involve 'attachment to the subject positions which discursive practices construct for us' (6). Here, a compulsive element seems to be paramount. Yet, in taking on these identities, the 'knowing' subject is also quite aware that they are 'representations...(which are)...always constructed' (6). Accordingly, we need to theorize why, when and how subjects 'fashion...these positions...struggling with, resisting, negotiating and accommodating...the rules which they confront and regulate themselves' (14). This second scenario seems to open the door to a rather different interpretation of individual identity, one that endows the self with more capacity to act autonomously. It also seems to accept that social identity does not always occlude individual personal identity. Thus, the 'balance of power' between society and social actor, structure and agent is tipped more decisively towards the latter. Other writers have been prepared to go somewhat further in recognizing not only the agent/actor's scope for autonomy but also the capacity to activate this through the individual's personal rather than his/her social self and identity.

Albrow (1996: 151), for example, insists that 'the transformations of structure which the multiplication of worlds has created' means that we need to distinguish self from personal identity. While the former is constructed out of the membership of social groups and everyday social life, the latter is 'forged out of individual experience' and enables individuals to give 'accounts of themselves'. What is expressed by personal identity is not membership of particular social groups but 'the unique identifier' to which everyone is entitled' namely, 'the universality of the right to be a distinct human being'. Giddens (1991), too, believes that under the condition of late modernity individuals exercise much greater control over whether, when and how to assume a given social identity. Indeed, he believes that the individual is more or less compelled to take charge of the self as a reflexive project given the weakening hold of once-powerful solidarities such as class, occupation, church, locality, gender and family and their declining ability to define and confine our life experiences. Beck (1992) develops a similar argument, though he sees greater individual self-determination partly as a response to the additional risks caused by the environmental devastation associated with industrial modernity.

Returning to Giddens, 'self-identity becomes a reflexively organised endeavour' (1991: 5) which requires the construction of a biography and a striving for coherence in the face of growing exposure to a multiplicity of global influences. Accordingly, as the collective cultural identities prominent during the period of modernity and the high point of nation state power diminish in significance, so the 'tightly confined personal realm' (209) where lifestyle choices abound becomes 'increasingly important in the constitution of life-planning and daily activity' (5). In short, although the individual has almost certainly been valued in all previous cultures and epochs (75), in late modernity, 'the self undergoes massive change' (80) and it is choice and 'self-actualization' that are central to this transformation. Later in this chapter we return to this theme.

Globalization and competing explanations for change

Many observers continue to doubt the significance and uniqueness of globalization as a force for change in human affairs. Nevertheless they might concur with the groundswell of opinion which asserts that we are indeed living through a period of rapid change even turmoil. Here – as the contributors to this book are well aware – there is no lack of competing explanations for the universal and multidimensional changes we face at the turn of the millennium. Major geopolitical events are surely significant: for example, the unravelling of regimes following the end of the Cold War; the determined moves towards regionalization, especially in the European Union (EU), and the challenge this poses for nation-states; and the rise of new industrial nations each armed with their own version of modernity and contributing to the 'dehegemonisation' of the West (Friedman 1994: 41). According to Laclau (1994) the end of the Cold War helped to bring other consequences. Thus, it has eliminated any further possibility for ideologies, countries or movements to claim that their project offers 'a fulfilment of a universal task... a mission predetermined by universal history' (Laclau 1994: 1). While this has opened the way for a flowering of 'particularistic political identities' it also added fuel to the postmodern bonfire of philosophical, political and moral certainties that was ablaze long before the period 1989–1992. Meanwhile – and boosted by the feminist assault on patriarchy and gender relations and the green movement's message that environmental destruction calls into question the project of modernity itself – postmodern sensibilities have also eroded all the boundaries, expectations and certainties that once structured everyday social and cultural life. Here, perhaps the most momentous shift in social life has been the apparent disintegration of class loyalties, work and occupation as central forces that once gave shape, meaning and solidity to identities and affiliations.

Accompanying all these sources of uncertainty there has been a series of seismic shifts in economic life. In large part, these come under the general heading of economic globalization: the worldwide penetration of capitalism into every social and geographical crevice; the rise of apparently unaccountable global corporations and instantaneous, unregulated – and perhaps uncontrollable – financial markets; the ability of corporate interests, at one and the same time, to superimpose their own changing grids of multifaceted activities regardless of national borders onto certain world regions while marginalizing and starving others of capital; and the pressures and worldwide insecurities associated with growing economic rivalry between industrial/izing nations. Here, some writers (for example, Burbach et al., 1997; Martin and Schumann, 1997; Bauman, 1998; and Sassen, 1998) seem to blame globalization for most of these problems – whether this is understood primarily as an economic phenomenon or in broader terms. However, as we have already seen, the changes associated with economic globalization have been accompanied by several parallel transformations including geopolitical change, a shift in ontological orientation, at least in the industrial societies, and the worldwide shift towards post-Fordist flexible labour regimes involving widespread casualization at the workplace. Though globalization is presumably implicated in these changes, each also needs to be seen as driven partly by its own logic and momentum. In any case, both economic globalization and post-Fordist insecurities have been massively bolstered by the triumphalist ascendancy since the late 1970s of one particular variant of capitalist economics – namely the ethos of neoliberalism. By the late 1990s, and with its tendency to equate individual freedom and happiness almost entirely with private economic decision-making and its blatant celebration of inequality, neoliberalism had come to dominate the policies of most governments as well as the agendas set by powerful intergovernmental organizations (IGOs) such as the World Bank. Together, post-Fordist practices and neoliberal ideology have further tightened the screws of economic insecurity experienced by millions in North and South.

Economic uncertainties have been further compounded by technological change especially 'the information technology revolution' and the rise of the symbolic economy as the major source of wealth and power (Castells, 1996: 470–5). The latter has strengthened capital but individualized labour, especially in manual work. It has also split the world between those who have ready or easy access to the spaces where information and knowledge flow along the lines of communication that make up the network society and those excluded from it. The shift of power towards the global symbolic economy and network society also undermines democracy since the activation of civil society and electoral politics dwindle in significance now that government policies exercise diminishing influence over national affairs (Castells, 1997: 11).

We turn now to the question of globalization – as a multi-dimensional and not just an economic force – and its special contribution to the radical uncertainties of the current era. Here, as we have just seen, any attempt to unravel and lay bare its essential features and effects as compared to the other parallel transformations of our time is bound to be speculative and contentious. In addition, we need to ask what, if anything, is new and distinctive about globalization today compared to the past. Thus, Albrow (1996: 7) suggests that the era of modernity, spearheaded by the nation-state, and marked by the struggle to 'extend human control over space, time, nature and society', is now coming to an end. Moreover, the era into which we are now moving is not the result of powerful globalizing tendencies that have suddenly been invented from scratch since the impulses to modernization and capitalism evident from the early nineteenth century were inherently globalizing from the outset (Giddens, 1990). Partly, this was because nation-state rivalry and capitalist competition compelled the first industrializing nations and their bourgeoisies to incorporate the whole world into their commercial spheres through imperialist ventures. In addition, the orientations at the heart of the modernizing process facilitated the spread of resources, meanings and collaborative social networks across the world. Giddens identifies three such orientations: the separation of time from space; the increasing proliferation of disembedding mechanisms and expert systems which release actors from their dependence upon relationships involving specific others; and the increasing application of reflexivity to every life experience.

Thus, what is different about the present compared to the recent past is that globalization processes have intensified and accelerated during recent decades, they have become autonomous and self-sustaining – no longer dependent upon leading or hegemonic countries, as in the case of America's postwar multi-dimensional leadership of the West – and they have undergone qualitative change. We now explore this claim by highlighting six mutually reinforcing aspects of globalization – though in doing so we make no claims to offer a definitive interpretation.

Drawing on Magatti's useful analysis (1999), we argue, first, that in recent decades, the economic, cultural, political and social spheres of the social system have become more and more disconnected and autonomous from each other. These can be regarded as roughly approximate to the four institutional sub-systems once identified by Parsons (1951) as clearly differentiated from each other, but also operating as vital and functionally interdependent parts of each society or nation At the same time there is a 'diminishing spatial coincidence' between these spheres 'within the boundaries of the nation state' (Magatti, 1999: 10). In other words, this detachment from the nation-state framework has been accompanied by the absorption of these spheres as components into global structures or realities – whether of worldwide cultural flows, transnational social exchanges, supra-state political loyalties or the economic power over regions and nations super-imposed by MNCs. Each of these spheres, moreover, is increasingly integrated around its own needs, rules and values.

Although none of this necessarily means that nation-state power has declined, these detachments have massively deepened the overall fragmentation existing at the national-societal level, calling into question 'the very idea of society as a unitarian . . . cohesive and institutionally organized system' (Magatti, 1999: 11). Like other observers, Touraine (1998: 129–30) insists that these changes are most advanced in the economic sphere. While he believes that what is often referred to as 'economic globalization' actually consists of several technological and economic strands which operate partly independently of each other – as we have also suggested – he nevertheless argues that it has 'destroyed and come to replace . . . the mobilizing state' while causing 'the breakdown of social and political constraints on economic activity' (130). This amounts to 'the most radical rupture ever observed between the actor and the system' (130) and given that it signals not only the declining ability of social actors to influence economic life, except as consumers, but also other changes including: 'cultural fragmentation'; the return of issues such as ethnicity and religion to the centre of public life; and a form of extreme individualism marked by the collapse of normative control in many areas of social life (Touraine, 1998: 130–1).

Secondly, like most observers, we note that it has been the unparalleled advances achieved by worldwide capitalism in the economic sphere – in transport, communications and information technology – which have largely underpinned the 'great leap forward' in the transnational interconnectedness and interdependencies we associate with globalization. The latter, of course, are the other side of the coin to the dwindling internal coherence of individual societies. Thus, ultimately global linkages rely upon the greatly enhanced opportunities for innumerable social actors to stretch and intensify social relationships across the world as time–space compression slices through boundaries, gobbles up territory and distance, speeds up exchanges and facilitates the much greater mobility of people, goods, ideas, images and much else besides.

Thirdly, and from the perspective of individuals, globalization exposes us to a bewildering proliferation of influences and experiences. Of course, sociologists have always been alert to the ways in which modernization profoundly altered social life. Thus, medieval communities – based on intersecting social allegiances grouped around blood ties, friendship and unquestioned loyalty – shared a 'common life-world' which bound localities and different social groups together (Berger et al., 1973: 63). In contrast, modern societies are highly differentiated, impersonal and specialized. Not only is the public world of work, the economy and bureaucracy sharply separate from the private world of family, leisure and friendship but both sectors are subject to increasing complexity with growing knowledge and proliferating choices. This 'plurality of life worlds' (62) means that modern individuals need to engage in 'long range life-planning' (71) and increasingly have to 'define themselves' (73) and their own identities while coping with 'widely discrepant ... meaning systems' (75). Consequently 'the subjective realm of identity is the individual's main foothold in reality' (74). But since it is always changing in response to the increasing pluralization of life-worlds, modern individuals also experience a condition of 'homelessness' (77). They are always in migration; never at home. Globalization has further radicalized this subjective experience of a disjointed and homeless life because it has massively increased the available life-worlds (Magatti, 1999). This multiplication in the flows of pluralizing influences has been so considerable that it amounts to a quantum leap in human experience.

Thus, along with money, goods, people and information, cultural experiences of all kinds – abstract knowledge, aesthetic preferences in everything from cuisine and music to designer goods and TV soaps, marriage customs, religious beliefs and so on – exhibit a growing capacity to break loose from their original moorings in particular societies. Through these often disjointed, incomplete yet powerfully evocative 'landscapes', individuals and groups carry their different 'imagined worlds' (Appadurai, 1990: 296), weaving them into criss-crossing patterns of meaning and social exchange spanning cultures and nations. Such 'landscapes' are disseminated through a multiplicity of overlapping sources. Here, the role of the mass media and the dissemination of popular cultural forms are absolutely crucial because they provide abundant and seductive resources for the construction of 'imagined worlds'. Furthermore, and linking to our earlier argument about the technological underpinnings of globalization, the mass media also constitute perhaps the single most powerful force responsible for bringing cultures and societies into constant juxtaposition but without the necessity for 'actual bodily movment' (Smith and Guarnizo, 1998: 14). Nevertheless, 'real' transnational personal encounters are also increasing rapidly and contribute strongly to the pluralization of life worlds and the greater opportunities for cultural hybridity associated with globalization in general. Important, here, are tourist flows – nearly 600 million international visitors in 1996, worldwide – various kinds of corporate, professional or political collaboration in the pursuit of global goals but especially the transnational cultural, business and political links being forged by many ethnic diasporas 'from below' (Portes, 1997).

Fourthly, the different dimensions of globalization coupled to geo-political changes such as the end of the Cold War are increasingly generating a syndrome of interconnected world problems from whose consequences none can escape and which require global collaboration if solutions are to be found. The spread of industrialization to many countries accompanied by the relative marginalization of other regions (Hirst and Thompson, 1996) is perhaps the most obvious case. Here, we see environmental pollution caused by overheating in the industrial regions but coinciding with the devastation to forests, soils and climates, linked to poverty and destitution, in the marginalized ones. The prospects may be bleak: a world community which must not only face the present and future burdens associated with climate change and the costs of amelioration but which also needs to deal with the unrest caused by mass migrations or wars, triggered by conflicts over scarce resources – especially water – and large-scale environmental deteriorat-ion in particular regions. It is easy to point to many additional problems which are truly global in scope: drug trafficking; the dissemination of technologically advanced weaponry, including nuclear materials, asso-ciated with the globalization of the nation-state system, persistent region-al quarrels and the disintegration of the former Soviet Union; growing global inequality; how to stabilize the deregulated global financial mar-kets and encourage more even investment flows; and dealing with the abuses of media power and information technology.

A fifth and qualitatively distinctive feature of globalization – one of the key themes highlighted in Robertson's crucial contribution to this field – concerns the emergence of what he refers to as 'globality'; the 'consciousness of the (problem) of the world as a single space' (1992: 132). Our internalized experience of globalization includes the capacity to begin thinking about ourselves collectively. Our shared concern with 'humanity', as expressed, for example, through the United Nations and its numerous humanitarian organizations and declarations, has begun to extend our loyalties beyond an affiliation solely to people of the same national, ethnic or religious identities as ourselves. Arguably, this marks a clear break with the past. Perlmutter (1991: 898) adds flesh to the bones of this newly emerging subjectivity, by claiming that now, for the first time in history, we are increasingly prepared to value diversity and the right of every culture to occupy a space in the world and to share in the common human endeavour on equal terms. Thus, we are seeing an end to the long era of one-sided cultural and political flows where societies engaged with others primarily in order to dominate them.

Lastly, the global problems shared by once-separate nations and allied to the capacity to think about ourselves collectively, seems to be contributing towards the creation of an 'embryonic global civil society' (Shaw 1994: 23). Partly, this consists of the proliferation of international non-governmental organizations (INGOS), whose members increasingly collaborate transnationally in order to pursue goals concerned with human rights, green, women's, aid, alternative development and other issues, but also overlaps with churches, trade unions, student groups and others. Certainly, if some observers had failed to find such activities especially noticeable before, 1999 was the year in which it became virtually impossible to ignore such pressures and demands. These were especially focused on two campaigns. The Jubilee 2000 campaign involved the attempt to persuade the G7 nations, the World Bank and International Monetary Fund to act decisively with respect to the issue of Third World debt relief. The second, directed at the World Trade Organization, attempted to link the goal of trade liberalization much more firmly to those of fairness and environmental safety and to find ways to exercise more control over the juggernaut of corporate capital. But global civil society is also being formed by the extension and the 'convergence' (Shaw, 1994: 23) of many nation-states' civil societies in global space. This is being facilitated by such changes as the formation of active regional economic/political groupings, especially the EU, the increasing reach of key intergovernmental organizations and their tendency to become focal points for local and global pressure group activity, the growing range of transnational community networks and lifestyles and the shared values carried by global communication, sports, educational, arts and entertainment systems (21–3).

There are many reasons for scepticism about the ability of a 'medley of boundary-eclipsing actors' to successfully reshape 'the political architecture of international relations' and to act as 'an unambiguous force for democratization of a global society' (Pasha and Blaney, 1998: 418). Not least among these are the continuing power of (and deep inequities within) the nation-state system, the authoritarian and predatory nature of many states, so that the prospect of autonomous and viable civil societies and NGOs operating within – never mind between – some countries remains highly dubious (437–8), and the fact that consensus between INGOS concerning what exactly constitutes the 'global "common good"' (436) is rarely assured and sometimes blatantly absent. Nevertheless, a multi-stranded global civil society is springing up, it is striking ever-deeper roots into the social life experienced by even the poorest people and nations, and so long as we live in a world of intricately linked problems of great magnitude, it is likely to remain a major actor on the world's stage.

Globalization and society: a crisis of identities?

Multi-dimensional changes, including globalization, presumably mean that like societies, nations and communities, individuals too, are facing a condition of acute anxiety, perhaps even crisis. Thus, as Hall (1992: 303) points out, marketization, migration, communications, time–space compression and the 'cultural supermarket' effect, among other influences, are 'fragmenting the cultural landscapes of class, gender, sexuality, ethnicity, race, and nationality and it is these which previously gave us firm locations as social individuals' (275). These structures and certainties also defined and shaped our social and personal identities. Because they are now disintegrating, so individuals, too, are losing the feeling they once experienced of having a 'place in the social and cultural world'. It follows that 'our sense of ourselves as integrated subjects' is also becoming dislocated and de-centred. Indeed, in the view of many writers (for example, Hall, 1992; Woodward, 1997; and Castells, 1996, 1997), the de-centred self faces a crisis of identity.

Castells (1997: 1) outlines the dilemma in no uncertain terms: 'Our world, and our lives, are being shaped by the conflicting trends of globalisation and identity.' But 'when the world becomes too large to be controlled, social actors aim at shrinking it back to their size and reach' (66) while engaging in a search for meaning. Individuals attempt this 'not around what they do but on the basis of what they are, or believe they are' (Castells, 1996: 3). In short, identity becomes our 'only source of meaning'. But there are great dangers here, as many writers have suggested. The most obvious is that many people may be tempted to cluster around the primary identities and meanings derived from religion, ethnicity and nationality. This, in turn, may lead to extreme forms of identity politics. Indeed, wherever globalizing forces lead people to seek 'protective strategies' involving the attempt to 'salvage centred, bounded identities for placeless times' we are likely to find the revival of 'patriotism and jingoism' (Robins, 1991: 41). Constructing 'defensive' (Castells, 1997: 9) identities as 'trenches of resistance and survival' (8) around such territorial and primary affiliations is particularly likely as a response to stigmatization and social exclusion, whether this is experienced by minorities living within host societies or by the majority populations inhabiting nations that feel themselves to be marginalized within the world polity. Here, Barber (1995), for example, points to the dangers of an ethnic, religious or nationalistic resurgence or jihad, in various parts of the world, as a backlash against the trivializing, commercialized 'McWorld' ethos associated with hegemonic western values and economic power.

Other writers believe that the desire to re-establish traditional identities as a bulwark against the forces of globalization is as likely to affect sections of the majority host populations living in wealthy, established nations as the excluded minorities or the new and/or ethnically fractured countries and/or marginalized and impoverished countries of the Third World (Hall, 1998: 200). Thus Robins (1991: 41) describes the uncertainties facing the Europeans as they learn to live with the minority cultures imported from their former colonies, to cope with American and Japanese influences and to construct a new continental identity around the European Union (EU). The alarming ascendancy of right-wing, authoritarian and anti-immigration parties across the EU, for example in France and Austria, and the increasingly restrictive 'fortress Europe' policies adopted by the EU with respect to refugees, asylum seekers and immigrants during the 1990s bears sad witness to the power of such pressures (see, Okojie, 1999). More generally, Melucci (1996: 158) observes that the fragmentation brought about by the organizational complexity of modern life and intensified by globalization has undermined 'the stability of belonging' that once defined most people's lives. This has forced identity concerns to centre stage and encouraged the revival of nationalist, ethnic and linguistic particularities as a way both of re-asserting difference and of re-discovering a lost sense of identity.

On the face of it, the claim that we are faced with a crisis of identities intensified by globalization seems sensible and difficult to refute. Yet, we are surely entitled to ask certain questions; what kind of crisis are we are dealing with?; is it of manageable proportion?; and do the transformations linked to globalization constitute a crisis for everyone and in equal proportion? Unravelling these doubts involves dealing with two sets of issues. One concerns the need to ask questions about theory. How useful are the foundational concepts and the underlying assumptions about social life upon which sociologists and other social scientists have tended to rely at least until recently? Secondly, there is a substantive or phenomenological dimension – namely, how do humans at this historical juncture actually experience the changes we have been discussing? What evidence, for example, is there to suggest that in their personal lives social actors perceive these changes as entirely threatening and disempowering, and does this vary as between individuals and situations?

Theoretical difficulties

When thinking about the impact of globalization on identities much more is at stake than the increasing fragmentation of those structures and processes which supposedly create fully socialized actors by enabling us to 'align our subjective feelings with the objective places we occupy in the social and cultural world' (Hall, 1992: 276). Rather, it is their very existence which is increasingly being thrown into doubt. A list of the problematical entities now in question would have to include the following:

- Society as a bounded unit which can be mapped quite literally on to a nation-state located in a fixed territorial space, both coinciding with a more or less self-sufficient economy and carrying its own distinctive culture of 'Thainess', 'Britishness' or whatever;
- The operation of a 'generalized other' of master rules, sufficiently coherent to be able to offer a template for guiding and reinforcing the overlapping webs of social exchanges as these extend to the furthest micro-extremities of social life;
- A largely self-contained, consistent and inclusive flow of shared cultural meanings moored to 'definite places' and where any differences there may be are negated or neutralized by vague references to 'multiculturalism' or 'subcultures' (Gupta and Ferguson, 1992: 7); and
- The existence of flourishing communities as small-scale units of belonging which are rooted in known, fixed localities and built around persisting social relations between particular social actors based on the recognition of mutual ties, obligations and loyalties.

Secondly, therefore, it appears that the categories and assumptions which apparently served sociology and other social science perspectives well in former times now require drastic re-thinking. Touraine, for example, claims that ultimately 'the idea of society has lost its significance' (1998: 132) and that a fundamental reappraisal of sociology is therefore necessary. In a similar vein, the writers from the Roehampton Institute who explored London as a global city and who contributed to the book edited by Eade (1997: especially chapters 2, 3 and 4) have questioned much of our existing repertoire of sociological assumptions and models. Partly this is because the latter derive from nineteenth-century anxieties concerning the replacement of traditional communities by the complex, impersonal Gesellschaft structures of urban-industrial, capitalist societies – an era of state-led nation-and society-building which has now past, at least in the West. But in addition, globalization is causing deep changes which further undermine conventional sociological categories (Albrow et al., 1997).

Thus, it 'detribalizes' community and culture while disaggregating these entities into disparate elements and relocating the fragments into new locations and flows (34). It also de-links community and culture from specific locations along with both individual and collective identities. In addition, intellectuals themselves, including sociologists, are travelling the world and are encountering 'decontextualized knowledge' which does not depend upon fixed locations or commitments (31). In fact, sociology is becoming as fragmented as the societies it tries to understand (35). But we also need to recall out earlier discussion. If recent changes, including globalization, have virtually demolished the coherence of the social collectivities, structures and systems of meanings that once created the fully socialized actor – as most observers seem to agree – then presumably the latter, too, must have become severely dysfunctional, or much more self-reliant and distinctive – or perhaps both. In either event, living with late modernity's plurality of life worlds, now magnified and multiplied by globalization, requires the person who is skilled in the task of continuous self-construction and re-construction and able to deal with the ever-changing particularity of experiences which assail him/her alone. This contemporary social actor desperately needs his/her core personal identity and the scope for autonomy that goes with it in order to navigate the now much more perilous uncertainties associated with being a social being. Similarly, the same resource makes it possible to cope with life in a globalizing world so that it is experienced sometimes as a challenge rather than a constant crisis.

Thirdly, it may be possible to go one step further and argue that the central concepts employed by sociologists and others were never as valid or useful as we once supposed even when applied to traditional societies and the earlier phases of modernity. Rapport and Dawson (1998: 4), for example, claim that the 'localizing image of separate and self-sufficient worlds' demonstrated in much earlier anthropological work was 'never more than a useful ideology that served the interests of (some) local people, and . . . was animated by the practices of (some) anthropologists'. Perhaps this is an unduly harsh evaluation. Be this as it may, at least since the mid-1980s anthropologists and others have increasingly re-evaluated what earlier scholars understood by such terms as 'culture' and 'tradition'. Thus, neither of these entities can be regarded as totally fixed and internally coherent forces which are programmed into social members through childhood learning, once and for all. Nor are they simply reinforced in later life by unchanging and unchallengeable external social pressures. Moreover, culture and tradition do not have clearly defined boundaries. Instead of invading and then dominating social actors from outside, culture provides 'a "tool kit" of symbols, stories, ritual and world views, which people may use in varying configurations in order to solve different kinds of problems' (Swidler, 1986: 273). It provides scope for inventiveness and negotiation by its members. It evolves continuously and overlaps with alternative cultures (Clifford, 1988).

In conclusion, it may that the very notion of an identity 'crisis' linked to globalization may sometimes tell us as much about the challenges confronting some established sociological concepts and modes of thinking as it does about the changes underway in the existential world and the way they affect people's actual lives. Alternatively, what is really being threatened by globalization, perhaps, is the need – both by citizens and some social scientists – to believe in the idea of bounded, coherent, distinctive and separate societies, nations, cultures and communities, tied to familiar, concrete locations, even though our actual daily experiences mostly tell us that these once closely entwined but now 'lost' entities are neither possible any longer – nor are we necessarily always harmed by their departure.

Living with globalization: crisis or challenge?

If there is indeed a crisis of identities augmented by globalization, then for whom does it matter, how much and why? There is surely a possibility that for some nations, collectivities and individuals, globalization is perceived and experienced less as something innately threatening and disempowering and, rather more, as a force offering challenges which can be met and managed to advantage. Presumably, we can suppose that responses as between these two polar positions are likely to vary considerably. Any attempt to think seriously about such questions is seriously hampered by the relative dearth of detailed case studies. Much more empirical work needs to be done. Nevertheless, the following writers provide useful ideas pointing us in some interesting directions.

We begin with Robins' (1991: 22) observation that the citizens of older nations such as Britain not only should heed Bhabha's call (for example,

1990) for a new sense of responsibility 'in our recognition of other worlds... other cultures, other identities and ways of life', but that the inclination to cling to older notions of an inclusive, closed British identity imposes a 'burden' because while such attempts may still be possible they are certainly decreasingly meaningful (40–3). More positively, Hall (1992) argues that while many people fear and resent the disintegration of national and other collective identities and try desperately to restore closure and cultural purity, others 'accept that identity is subject to the play of history, politics, representation and difference' (Hall, 1992: 309). They learn to live with the kaleidoscope of fragmented, ever-changing and plural realities brought by immersion in a global culture and the need to live in a multicultural society. Such capabilities are likely to be especially evident among migrant communities living within often hostile host societies. The continuous journeys of self- and collective discovery in which some Caribbean people as well as many black minorities living in Britain have been engaged, represent just one interesting case (Hall, 1991). Often such projects involve not just a search for roots but also the rediscovery or tracing of numerous, intertwining cultural and historical 'routes' based around the Black Atlantic diaspora (Gilroy, 1994).

Other diasporic groups also seem to find little difficulty in moving continuously across boundaries and cultures while juggling identities and maintaining permanent transnational networks, loyalties and interests (for example, Basch et al., 1994 and Chan, 1997). Moreover, most display at least some elements of the cosmopolitanism defined by Hannerz (1990) as the ability to coexist comfortably with cultural diversity or even to actively seek immersion in other cultures (241). Again, the London research carried out by colleagues at the Roehampton Institute suggests that whether such migrants are 'voluntary' or 'involuntary' cosmopolitans they have the capacity to make themselves feel at home wherever they are currently located (Albrow et al., 1997: 24). In doing so they construct 'locality' – and, presumably, a sense of collective kinship-ethnic-national identity – by activating communication technologies and the media but also by utilizing global social networks tied primarily to family and ethnic affiliations. 'Community' has become independent of specific places. Over time and for second-generation migrants, identities and affiliations become even more malleable as they stretch to include members, values and meanings drawn both from the host society and from a burgeoning transnational community. In fact, a growing number of scholars have celebrated the confident expressions of 'cultural hybridity, multi-positional identities (and) border crossing' on the part of numerous diasporic, transnational groups across the world (Smith and Guarnizo, 1998: 5).

However, coping with cultural fluidity or even the inclination to lean towards it is not confined to diasporas and ethnic minorities. Thus, according to Albrow (1996: 151), globalization may be undermining our ability to make sense of national and other kinds of collective identity but it is likely that most people do not wish to engage in such activities anyway. Some writers are even more upbeat on this subject. Drawing on the recent work of many anthropologists, Rapport and Dawson (1998: 6) declare that 'movement has become fundamental to modern identity, and an experience of non-place (beyond "territory" and "society") an essential component of everyday existence'. Indeed, they suggest that it is the perpetual need to manoeuvre between the 'global inventory of ideas and modes of expression' which enables people to 'make sense to themselves and others' (25). Consequently, for many individuals, and not just those with a strong cosmopolitan bent, living in the global mainstream is not only perfectly amenable but 'that movement can be one's very home' (27).

Again, the London research (Eade, 1997) supports this claim because it demonstrates the numerous ways of coping with the de-localization of community, social fragmentation and pluralization of meanings brought partly by globalization. For example, some white residents remain isolated in the face of large-scale overseas migrant communities, mourning the loss of the older, native community and resenting multiculturalism. Others participate in global friendship networks through holiday visits, letter and phone and/or maintain regular ties with other elderly people through local amenities. Meanwhile, yet other white residents embrace the opportunity to participate in migrant life through neighbourhood, school or other connections while others feel neither loyalty to any group nor resentment arising from their relative social isolation with respect both to white and migrant inhabitants because for them the borough is simply a site offering temporary accommodation while their significant relationships lie elsewhere. More or less the same wide range of possible affiliations to local and global networks are displayed by migrants.

Further, the London study (Eade, 1997) elaborates several concepts designed to help scholars understand how individuals living in de-localized communities navigate the global realities to which they are exposed while making sense of their relationships and identities. For example, Albrow (1997: 51–3) employs the idea of 'sociosphere', viewed from the perspective of each individual's own network of social relations. The degree to which each individual's sociosphere either over-laps with those of others or remains more or less entirely separate, will vary considerably but either way locality is engendered when and where any given sociosphere is acted out in physical space. This formulation enables us to understand how individuals can experience thoroughly globalized lives and multiple identities, participate in rich, diverse and satisfying relationships, and yet live more or less completely outside a community in the traditional sense.

Coming to terms with globalization: case studies

We have presented the debates surrounding globalization and identities in terms of a dichotomy between the reality of crisis and threat as contrasted with the possibility of challenge and opportunity. This has also provided us with a modus operandi for presenting our case studies such that the chapters are arranged into three sections. The first section (Part I) deals with nations or with groups for whom globalization appears to present extreme difficulties such that the words 'crisis' and 'threat' fit their situations rather accurately and do not unduly exaggerate their current plight. In stark contrast, the second section (Part II) examines four case studies where 'opportun-ity' and rather successful 'adaptation' to change seem to offer a more accurate depiction of the prevailing situation. Here, global-ization seems to offer – or promises to do so in the near future – a set of resources for empowering the reconstruction of identities in ways that enhance problem-solving and genuine hybridization without jeo-pardizing integrity or autonomy. Finally, in Part III our four contributors explore situations where those involved confront 'difficult and uncer-tain challenges' where it is even more difficult to predict future outcomes.

Clearly our mode of presentation involves an essentially contrived format. A different range of examples might generate very different forms of presentation, themes and key issues. In any event, the situation currently facing the countries included in our study is highly provi-sional; their circumstances may alter dramatically in the future. Finally, identity questions are not necessarily the sole or even the most critical issues pertaining to our case studies. Nevertheless, we believe that our selection and form of presentation does relatively little injustice to empirical reality while providing a useful framework for thinking about the issues of identity formation, and its tensions and dynamics, at a time of rapid globalization.

Part I deals with two nations (Russia and Serbia), one former nation (the former German Democratic Republic, now east Germany) and a small fundamentalist Christian sect in the USA. Though they are not all locked into 'crisis' situations of the same magnitude, each appears to have been severely problematized by recent exposure to globalization and other worldwide changes. Here, internal divisions and nervous, angry dealings with external interests all indicate that leaders and citizens perceive their identities to be in crisis and desperately in need of re-inventing for the sake of national pride or even survival.

In Chapter 2, Catherine Danks examines the historical circumstances that help to explain the attempts by Russia's leaders and internal political groupings to cast around for an identity that can help to revive its severely wounded national pride in the aftermath of the Cold War, economic collapse and the humiliations inflicted by dependence on western financial handouts. Simultaneously, they are endeavouring to generate citizen support for a project of national revival. In pursuing these tasks Russia's political groups have tried to forge a new national identity out of various traditional ingredients by insisting on such timeless sources of cultural uniqueness as the peasant commune, the ancient bonds of blood and soil and the idea that the Russian Orthodox Church remains the repository of the national soul. Similarly, there have been attempts to manipulate representations of the western 'other'. This is depicted not just as different but also as evil and likely to undermine Russian spirituality and communality given the West's obsessions with material progress and hedonistic individual self-realization. Such concerns are understandable but may constrain the development of a healthy civil society.

A similarly picture of stark alternatives and risky confrontations intensified by global pressures is explored by Ioannis Armakolas in his study of Serbian nationalism from 1990 to the middle of the decade (Chapter 3). He suggests that the consolidation of an aggressive Serbian national identity and the crystallization of clear and hardened ethnic divisions among ordinary citizens only became apparent following the unparalleled upsurge of global interest associated with the 1990 elections in Bosnia and the growing external pressures to find solutions to ethnic conflict by separating the Croatian, Serbian and Muslim communities. Until this time, ethnic cultural identities were not especially problematic for most ordinary people and there was relatively little popular support for the nationalist projects pushed by some political leaders. Normally, we associate the global civil society of humanitarian observers, journalists, media specialists and international non-governmental organizations (INGOS) – dispensing aid, protecting the rights of oppressed minorities, informing an alarmed global public and galvanizing reluctant governments into supportive action – as major players in the frontline struggles against injustices. In this case, however, the unprecedented scale of intervention by global civil society, accompanied by escalating western government interest, led to a growing perception on the part of Serbian citizens that a formidable and hostile 'global other' was unfairly representing them as a barbarian, pariah people. Moreover, because this gargantuan labelling process by the world community offered few avenues of escape it also seems to have helped foster a spiralling process of deviance amplification. Governments and the agents of global civil society need to take careful stock concerning their role in this and similar events elsewhere.

In Chapter 4, Patricia Hogwood's study of how the former citizens of the German Democratic Republic (GDR) are struggling to cope with the reality of post-Cold War absorption into a united Federal Republic of Germany (FRG) contains strong echoes of the same sense of national and personal identities-in-crisis that we encounter in Danks' and Armakolas' studies. A key factor underpinning such anxieties is the perception by eastern citizens that the majority FRG members and the inhabitants of the wider European Union find it all too easy to disparage their previous situation and current predicament. This barely concealed contempt further problematizes the difficulties of coping with the new and much larger scale of German and European identity. The new situation has also exposed east Germans to the globalizing images rampant in a thoroughly postmodern and Americanized economy much more intensively than ever before. Many have responded by seeking refuge in a reactive 'identity of contrariness' based on 'Ostalgia' and 'Ossi' pride for the former GDR. Here, alternative representations celebrating such former virtues as community solidarity have been rekindled in popular east German cultural exchanges.

The last chapter in Part I by Julie Scott (Chapter 5) traces the ways in which the different overlapping changes associated with modernity, postmodernity and now globalization have progressively undermined the once-stable sense of personal and national identity experienced by many white Christians in the United States of America. By offering an ever-greater scope for exercising personal freedom and hedonistic lifestyles, uncluttered by moralizing pressures, postmodernity has provoked panic and fear among many American Christians. Various aspects of globalization, from the rise of powerful rival economies across the world to the growing proportion of Hispanics, Asians and other non-white residents who claim American citizenship rights, have accentuated these uncertainties. The community members believe that being 'chosen' by God promises them personal sanctuary in a society threatened by satanic forces. This perception is often linked to another – namely, that the USA is a country which once enjoyed the status of being God's 'chosen' nation. This particularity was based on a pure, racialized national identity. But in the absence of religious conversion it is now equally in jeopardy from contamination by dangerous internal and external forces.

In marked contrast, Part II examines two nations (Thailand and Ireland), a major institution with strong historical loyalties to nation-hood (the military) and a tiny sample of citizens living in Britain for whom globalization has so far brought certain creative opportunities for re-constructing a sense of identity but in ways that are potentially beneficial rather than threatening or dangerous. Instead of undermining identities, global influences have provided various resources, which have been utilized in the attempt to find creative and empowering responses to the challenges constantly posed by a fast-changing world.

Asawin Nedpogaeo's chapter (Chapter 6) examines how over time the manipulation of media and cultural resources by Thailand's political elites and professionals has resulted in the construction of a modern national identity partly by relying on the power of representations. Central to this process has been the employment of images of the Occident as 'other'. These have provided a vehicle for distilling those unique ingredients that constitute the essence of 'Thainess' and in much the same way as the West has relied on the reverse process. His research also offers interesting examples of the universal process of 'glocalization' highlighted by Robertson (1995) through which global influences are selected, indigenized and so turned into locally accessible and relevant resources by active national agents. Using examples taken from recent Thai adverts he shows how comical representations of westerners are used to render harmless and comprehensible what might otherwise be perceived as the dangers of western dominance while accentuating what is positive and special about a thoroughly modern yet continuously re-Orientalized Thailand.

Focusing mainly on Ireland's cultural and media industries, Honor Fagan (Chapter 7) evaluates the content and validity of the claims, which have accompanied the 'Celtic Tiger''s rapid economic ascent and re-invention. Whereas most observers insist that globalization has so far proceeded furthest in the economic and technological spheres

Fagan argues that globalizing forces have actually penetrated deepest into our everyday lives at the social and cultural levels. This chimes strongly with the increased significance of issues concerning the self, subjectivity and personal identity which appear to dominate the lives of most postmodern citizens – at least in the advanced societies. But it also helps to explain Irish cultural confidence and creativity. Thus, Ireland's ability to re-invent itself in recent years has involved drawing on its history and ancient culture. However, the national identity which has been re-imagined is not pure, local and authentic. Not only is such a thing impossible, given that all culture is contrived and perpetually in movement, but the momentum for reconstituting Irishness has partly arisen as a response to the demands of global markets which it helps to feed. Global culture also provides some of the ingredients which sustain the essentially hybrid nature of all cultural processes.

In Chapter 8, Glen Segell considers the changing nature of the relationship between the civil and military authorities within nation-states, given the declining autonomy and even sovereignty they are experiencing in the face of regional economic and defence arrangements – especially in Europe – and the pressures of globalization. Among the many indications of declining state power are the dependence of national defence needs on strategic inter-state alliances and the growing number of international and especially internal disputes which require the joint deployment of national military forces at regional or world level. Such changes are creating dilemmas not just for nation-states but also for the military as an institution and for its individual serving members since they call into question the latters' sense of patriotic, national identity which until now has always been strongly instilled into military forces. Change is also imposing new professional duties and obligations such as providing humanitarian and relief aid, acting as buffers between warring civil factions and the need to collaborate closely with troops from other countries – services for which few serving members been properly prepared or trained. Despite these problems, Segell agues that in most countries the military are proving to be surprisingly adaptable in coming to terms with the changes generated by globalization.

Arguing from the standpoint that globalization has de-linked society and culture from politics and the nation-state, Darren O'Byrne (Chapter 9) explores the implications this has for individual citizens living in London today. Once, the nation-state could either disregard cultural pluralism or suppress any such manifestations while insisting upon the coalescence of political and cultural identity into one unambiguous national identity. However, the pluralization of life worlds and multi-culturalism, both augmented and intensified by globalization, have progressively called into question the very possibility of a universally acceptable and clearly understood image of nationhood. In short, recent changes have finally exposed the underlying multi-ethnic character of most nations leaving citizenship much freer than before to become a formally abstract entity, devoid of specific cultural content. In the British case, individual strategies for coping with these changes vary enormously but for many, far from being perceived as disorientating and traumatic, the situation seems to have fostered or underpinned a pragmatic journey of self-discovery empowered by the reflexive exercise of personal choice.

In Part III, our contributors examine four cases where rapid change, partly brought about by globalization, is challenging identities and in ways that are deeply uncertain with respect to possible outcomes. Here, there are opportunities as well as threats and so there is much for social actors to play for.

In Chapter 10, the role of the 'other' in the construction of Israeli national identity is explored by William Berthomière. He argues that until quite recently Israel was able to remain largely self-absorbed in the internal enterprise of national consolidation and so was rather insulated from the globalizing forces which have compelled most countries to question their national identity. This possibility was strengthened by certain circumstances – especially the ability to rely both on returning Jewish emigrants and on the flow of Palestinian workers as sources of skilled/professional and unskilled labour, respectively, for Israel's expanding economy. However, from the late 1980s, Palestinian revolt, the 'Intifada' and the closure of the Occupied territories cut off most of Israel's Palestinian labour supplies. This has forced Israel's employers to rely increasingly – and for the first time – on a rising flow of semi- and unskilled immigrant workers from across the world. These new workers bring with them a new multiculturalism and a variety of religious identities. Coinciding with growing internal divisions between neo- and post-Zionists, these escalating global influences are helping to push Israel into a long-delayed but challenging era of identity reconstruction.

Elizabeth Stanley (Chapter 11) explores the issues raised by the deliberations of the Truth and Reconciliation Commission (TRC) in the new, Post-apartheid South Africa. While many nations are finding it necessary to forge a new identity in the face of radical globalizing forces, few have been compelled to engage in such wholesale re-invention as a matter of very survival while remaining under the full glare of a largely sympathetic global spotlight as South Africa. Here, and unlike the Serbian case, the involvement of global civil society has been largely positive not least by helping to legitimize the process of national renewal and identity reconstruction. As with our other case studies we encounter the central role of processes of representation. However, in the South African case these have taken the form of deeply harmful ethnic categorizations and myths of exclusion and separation, once inscribed dangerously into the national psyche and political structures, but now being painfully re-constituted with the support of the TRC.

Working within the sociological tradition of critical theory, Lauren Langman (Chapter 12) observes that we now live in an age of cyberfeudalism and technocapitalism – conditions characterized by ever more extreme inequalities of wealth alongside extremely sophisticated technologies from whose influence few can escape. Not only does this condition require a globalized mass consumerism, it also generates thoroughly commoditized mass produced cultural spectacles, closely tied into the world tourist industry. Building his discussion around the two cases of Brazil's annual carnival and US football as expressed through superbowl, Langman shows how these examples of global carnivalization offer their spectators opportunities for individual realization and escape from the destructiveness and divisions of late capitalism. In addition, both of these events are forums for projecting Brazilian and US national identity into the global arena. Thus, they offer examples of the process of glocalization in that each originated in the cultural orientations imported by European Catholic and Protestant settlers in Brazil and the USA, respectively, long ago. Langman is highly critical of global capitalism, and its apparent ability to depoliticize us by 'colonizing' our desires. Yet he also argues that new forms of effective resistance to the destructive impact of globalization are emerging in the shape of numerous groups of cyberactivists who are opposed to world inequality, environmental destruction, human rights abuses and so on.

In our final case study, which explores the character of Scottish nationalism, John Books argues that several theoretical approaches throw light on this phenomenon. Moreover, each points to the significance of certain key causal factors – for example, the long history of Scotland's economic dependency whether as a peripheral extension of the core English economy or as a location for the investment by MNCs. It remains an open question as to whether globalization – as the most recent of those forces which have helped to galvanize support for greater national autonomy and the desire to refine a special identity – will eventually prove to be the most powerful. Nevertheless, the resources and opportunities generated by EU regional economic policies combined with the economic uncertainties brought by wider globalizing tendencies, do seem to have enhanced Scotland's economic and cultural viability. The preference on the part of voters, until now, for greater autonomy rather than political independence may, however, swing more decisively toward the latter should Scotland's industrial policies and the uncertainties and pressures brought by globalizing forces create a situation where the goal of continued economic modernization becomes derailed.

Acknowledgement

We would like to thank our colleagues, David Francis and Phil Mole, for their useful and constructive comments on this chapter.

Part I
Globalization: Crisis and Threat

2
Russia in Search of Itself

Catherine J. Danks[1]

In December 1991 Russian President Boris Yeltsin signed the Belovezhs-kaia Forest Accords with the presidents of Ukraine and Belarus – an act which consigned the USSR to history. At the time it was unclear whether Russia was liberated from an imperial burden or damaged by the loss of an empire that over centuries and in various forms had been a vital component of Russian identity. Among Russia's westernizing liberals there was a very strong sense that Russia could only successfully reform without an empire. Reformers argued that Russia needed to embrace the forces of globalization, to develop a Russian civic identity and to reject Imperialism. Such an undertaking is particularly difficult at a time of the rebirth of national identities and economic hardships within Russia. The disintegration of the USSR and the foundation of the new Russian Federation has focused the attention of Russia's politicians, intellectuals and people on what it means to be Russian today. This raises a range of questions about who belongs to the Russian nation, where Russia's borders should rightly lie and the nature of Russia's relations with its neighbours. The Russians are having to simultaneously rethink their place within their own country and within the world. Internationally, Russia is the rump of a former superpower and of a multinational empire. Reform has entailed an opening up to the rest of the world that would have been inconceivable during the soviet period. Russia's reformers have depicted the ending of Russia's seclusion as a positive move vital to Russian regeneration. Other voices are also being raised which now see Russia as stripped of its protective geographical empire and powerless before alien forces which are fatally weakening Russia and its people.

Background

Globalization and identity: the nemesis of the USSR

The USSR was finally destroyed by the twin forces of globalization and identity politics. The soviet leadership had tried to isolate its people and economy from the capitalist world but with diminishing success. Modern communications technologies made it difficult to isolate the population from the ideas, trends and cultural phenomena that were sweeping the rest of the world. The jamming of foreign radio stations was costly and not wholly successful. From the 1960s there was also an illegal market in books published abroad (*tamizdat*) and illegally imported into the USSR. The USSR also started to encourage tourism in order to augment the country's hard currency earnings. The soviet economy suffered from profound systemic and structural problems which successive leaderships had proved unable to address. From the late 1950s the USSR started to export gas and then oil to the capitalist world. Increasingly soviet raw materials export earnings were used to finance imports of the food stuffs and technologies that its own economy was unable to provide. The internationalization of the global economy proved difficult to resist. It was when world oil prices plummeted in the 1980s that the USSR was finally forced to address reform under first Yury Andropov (1982–84) and more decisively under Mikhail Gorbachev by a programme of Reconstruction (1985–1991). Gorbachev's 'New Thinking' revealed the influence of western social science ideas – for example, he talked about the USSR's interdependence with the rest of the world. Gorbachev believed that the USSR had to open up its economy in order to develop trade, attract investment, bring in new technologies, management skills and know-how.

Learning from the failure of earlier attempts to reform the economy in the 1960s, Gorbachev believed that economic reform would only succeed if supported by democratic reforms and greater openness, or *glasnost*. Gorbachev's elite-sponsored democratization, his 'revolution from above', was supposed to mobilize and harness the support of the people for Reconstruction. Democratization, however, revealed the scale and depth of nationalist discontent within the USSR. The USSR was formally a federation of 15 union republics each taking their name from their majority population – for example, Ukraine, the republic of the Ukrainians. After the 1917 Revolution the Bolsheviks had divided the country into ethnically designated administrative units as a counter-balance to potential Russian chauvinism and its imperial aspirations. They also believed that they could create a 'New Socialist Man' for whom proletarian internationalism rather than national identity would be of primary importance. When in the 1980s they were given a genuine choice at the ballot box, however, the republics elected nationalist leaderships who pushed for secession from the USSR.

Russia within the USSR

Nationalist sentiments also spread within the Russian Soviet Federative Socialist Republic (RSFSR). Russian Nationalists questioned whether the maintenance of what was in reality a multinational empire was in their interests. In the 1960s the village prose literary movement had idealized traditional Russia, implicitly challenging the whole project of soviet internationalism and modernization. In the 1980s the Russian Writers' Union provided a forum for Russian Nationalists such as Valentin Rasputin (a village prose writer) who argued that Russia was being damaged, culturally, economically, socially and spiritually by remaining at the centre of the USSR. In a similar vein the Russian Nationalist writer Alexandr Solzhenitsyn (1995: 83–4) has argued that the Russians bore the chief burden of the soviet economy, its resources such as oil subsidized the whole Union, while the villages of central and northern Russia were abandoned for want of investment. All the USSR's union republics except the RSFSR had their own communist parties, academies of science, national encyclopaedias, radio and television services – the Russians had to make do with the All-Union institutions. While this might seem to demonstrate the Russian domination of the USSR, to many ethnic Russians it was further evidence of their degradation within the USSR. During the late 1980s, opinion was divided as to whether Russia would be damaged or liberated by the disintegration of the USSR. For example, the National Salvation Front argued that Russia would be devastated by the loss of the other republics. To this day the Communist Party of the Russian Federation (RCP) under Gennady Zyuganov would also prefer to see the restoration (in some form) of the USSR. Boris Yeltsin, the new RSFSR President, harnessed Russian nationalist sentiment in support of a pro-western programme of marketization and democratization. Under the slogan 'Russia First' Yeltsin championed Russian independence from the USSR.

Defining Russia's borders

Russia's borders and the Russian diaspora

Russia has never existed within its current borders, they are neither tsarist nor soviet. The debate about where Russia's borders should properly lie is part of the broader debate about what it means to be Russian. At the time of the collapse of the USSR 25 million ethnic Russians were living outside the RSFSR in the 14 other Union republics. The Union republics are now independent countries but Russia insists on referring to them as the 'Near Abroad', which implies that Russia views them as having limited sovereignty compared to the 'Far Abroad'. Advocates of an Imperial concept of Russia argue that Russia's boundaries should at the very least enclose all the ethnic Russian people – and preferably all the people who consider themselves to belong to the Russian civilization. Both of these definitions would mean that Russia's borders should be changed to incorporate the Russian populations in the 'Near Abroad'. The existence of Russian diaspora populations also means that the Russian Government believes it has the right to intervene in other countries to protect Russians and that the Russian Federation is the historic homeland of all Russian communities abroad. Russia's neighbours have been troubled by Russia's aspirations throughout the former USSR and Russian peace-keeping missions in Tajikistan and Georgia are viewed as Russian attempts to promote their Imperial ambitions. Some Cossack communities straddle Russian Federation borders, such as the Russia–Kazakhstan border. Not surprisingly, Yeltsin's support for the Cossacks and their military formations has raised alarm in the countries of the 'Near Abroad'.

A slavic union?

While Russian Nationalists typically do not mourn the collapse of the USSR, the loss of their fellow eastern Slavs of Ukraine and Belarus is more contentious. For example, Solzhenitsyn argues that the Russians, Ukrainians and Belarussians share linguistic and cultural similarities and have a common history stretching back to the mediaeval principality Kievan Rus. For such Russian Nationalists the fact that Kiev is now the capital of an independent country means that Russia is separated from a vital part of its historical and cultural heritage. Once it became clear that the USSR could not be reconstituted, Russian Imperialists began to focus their aspirations on the creation of a Slavic Union. In the summer of 1993 the National Opposition broke away from the National Salvation Group (which continued to advocate the reformation of the USSR) and instead focused on the creation of an eastern Slav state. President Lukashenko of Belarus has been particularly keen on a Union of eastern Slavs – although probably more due to his political ambitions than through a genuine sense of slavic identity. Presidents Yeltsin and Lukashenko first signed a union treaty in 1997. This was followed in

December 1999 by a new union treaty which committed Belarus and Russia to the formation of a conferation. Ukraine has strong historical and cultural ties with Russia, including predominantly Russian-speaking populations in its eastern and northern regions. Ukraine has, however, consistently resisted any moves towards union or integration which it sees as prompted by Russian imperialism rather than by a shared slavic identity.

Russians were rather taken aback in April 1999 when the Yugoslav (southern Slav) parliament voted to join the Russian–Belarus Union. True, these are slavs and Orthodox Christians and Russia is currently promoting the Serbian cause, but that is more to do with Russia's 'sense of betrayal by the West than fraternity between eastern and southern Slavs' (Reeves, 1999: 22). In one of its usual rather theatrical gestures, the Russian State Duma (parliament) voted in favour of the Union. Opinion polls have found, however, that 70 per cent of Russians did not favour a union with Yugoslavia, and there was a general feeling that Slavic brotherhood was nonsense, more to do with propaganda than the real aspirations of the Russian people (ibid.).

Russian identities

Ethnic Russians as an Imperial people

The Russian state developed in the course of imperial expansion over many centuries. In the Imperial Russian empire '...Russian national identity tended to be subsumed in that of the empire, whose values were in principle multinational' (Hosking, 1997: 41). While nation-states developed in Western Europe in the course of the nineteenth and twentieth centuries the Russians remained part of a multinational empire. Following the 1917 Bolshevik revolution soviet ideology lauded the creation of a new community of soviet people and once again ethnic Russians were part of a multinational empire. In contrast to the Bolshevik leaders in the 1920s, Stalin stressed the Russian rather than the International-Proletarian or Soviet identity of the USSR. Great heroes from Russian history such as Ivan the Terrible and Peter the Great reappeared in school textbooks, classical Russian literature such as the works of Fedor Dostoevsky and Alexandr Pushkin also became part of the national curriculum. Local party-state officials throughout the country were purged and replaced mostly by Russians. Similarly, Russian specialists and manual workers spread out throughout the USSR to do Moscow's bidding in the name of soviet modernization

(Hosking, 1997: 483). In the course of soviet history, therefore, for many ethnic Russians the concepts of Russian and Soviet became synonyms.

Another feature of both Imperial Russian and soviet rule was the absence of political freedoms and the limited development of civil society – factors which frustrated the development of a civic identity during the nineteenth and twentieth centuries. People in Imperial Russia and the USSR were subjects not citizens with inalienable rights and freedoms, government was not based upon their consent. Within the USSR there were people such as Galina Starovoitova who championed western-style democratic reforms on the basis of a civic identity shared by all the peoples of the USSR, even if this meant the break-up of the USSR. As we have seen during Gorbachev's democratization, however, people mobilized and organized around their national identities and challenged the legitimacy of soviet rule and the existence of the USSR from this basis. The result was that in 1992 ethnic Russians acquired their own state but still had a very poorly developed sense of an ethnic Russian national identity, shorn of its soviet overlay. There was also only a limited understanding of what was meant by a civic identity that included all the peoples of the new Russian Federation and not just for the ethnic Russians.

Russian as a multinational federation

The preamble to the 1993 Constitution of the Russia Federation states 'We, the multinational people of the Russian Federation, . . .'. There are 89 units of federation, including 21 republics named after their main (non-Russian) nationality known as the titular nationality. The reality is more complicated than this might appear to suggest. In Buryatia, for example, the titular nationality (the Buryats) constitute only 24 per cent of the population and Russians 48 per cent. Similarly, half of the people living in Tatarstan are ethnic Russians and approximately two-thirds of Tatars live outside Tatarstan. The Russian Federation has more than 120 ethnic groups, ethnic Russians constitute about 85 per cent of the population and in certain parts of the country such as Tuva and Chechnia ethnic Russians are in the minority. There are millions of citizens of mixed ethnic background and many Russian citizens have multiple ethnocultural identities. A Cossack might identify him or herself as a Cossack but also as a Russian or a Ukrainian. This is therefore a state in which there is not an exclusive link between Russian ethnic identity and citizenship and yet the Russian people, their language and civilization lie at its heart.

Because Russia was born out of the collapse of the USSR there was a very real fear in the early 1990s that the forces that had torn the USSR apart would destroy the Russian Federation as each nationality and ethnic group demanded self-determination. The Reconstruction period saw not just a growing national-ethnic consciousness in the Union republics but also within the RSFSR itself. The late democratic Duma deputy and ethnographer Galina Starovoitova talked about the 'Matrioshka effect' of the Russian Federation coming apart like a nest of Russian dolls. Russia's other peoples, the non-Russians, have good reason to believe that they were damaged by their experiences first in the Tsarist empire and then in the Soviet Union. They were subjected to forced Russification and Orthodox evangelism at the end of the nineteenth century and then subjected to accusations of anti-soviet 'bourgeois nationalism' and anti-religious campaigns under soviet rule. Twelve ethnic groups, including the Crimean Tatars and the Chechens, were accused of collaboration with the Germans during the Great Patriotic War (1941–45) and were deported from their homelands. In the early 1990s the Russian Federation was trying to create a sense of civic national identity that could be shared by all its peoples, at a time when they are each stressing their own distinct identities and do not wish to be subsumed within yet another Russian empire.

Civic identity: democratization or russification?

The Russians have two words which are translated into English as Russian. *Russkii* refers to the Russian language and ethnicity, while *Rossiiskii* refers to the Russian state and citizenship. A Russian citizen is a *Rossiianin* from *Rossiiskii*. In the first two years of state building Yeltsin stressed this civic concept of Russian (*Rossiiskii*) identity for all the peoples of the Russian Federation. For example, the 1991 Russian citizenship law does not specify Russian nationality, nor does it establish even a basic knowledge of the Russian language as a condition for citizenship. Russia's liberal democrats (not Zhirinovsky's fascist Liberal Democratic Party!) are the strongest advocates of a civic national identity in their search to create a western-style democratic state. The concept has been opposed from two main sources. Firstly, the so-called Red–Browns have resisted this idea. This loose alliance of nationalists, fascists and communists reject Russia's pro-western course and share a largely empire-building and imperialist concept of who are the Russians and where Russia's rightful borders lie. Secondly, there has been opposition from Russia's ethnic minorities, who fear that the creation of a civic Russian identity is merely covert Russification.

In soviet times every adult had an internal passport which recorded both citizenship (*grazhdanstvo*) and from 1932 in the unpopular fifth point their nationality (*natsional'nost'*). The soviet state used nationality data to enforce quotas and to underpin discriminatory policies against whole nationalities. For Russia's reformers, even before the collapse of the USSR, removing the fifth point was seen as a great liberal prize and a major step in the development of a civic concept of Russian identity. The Yeltsin government did not therefore anticipate the furore that broke out in October 1997 when they began to issue new identity cards without the fifth point. Russia's non-Russians now fear that if their nationality is not officially recorded their identity will be subsumed within a Russified identity. The backdrop to these fears include renewed calls by Russia's Red-Browns to abolish Russia's ethnically based republics such as Tatarstan and to return to the pre-revolutionary Imperial Russian practice of dividing the country into territorially based provinces (*guberniia*). In this atmosphere what looks like a liberal move is feared as heralding new forms of discrimination. The parliament in Tatarstan with the support of their president Mintimer Shamiyev simply stopped issuing the new identity cards (Meek,1997b: 12).

Tatarstan: language, identity and globalization

Within the Russian Federation the Republic of Tatarstan has been able to use its oil wealth to extract favourable terms (on subsidies and tax revenues) in return for agreeing to stay within the federation. The Tatars are keen, however, to reassert their identity within Russia as demonstrated by the identity card dispute. Language, and particularly the alphabet used, has also emerged as an issue around which the Tatars seek to stress their identity. Within the USSR speakers of Turkic languages were forced under Stalin to adopt the cyrillic alphabet. Following the collapse of the USSR, the now-independent states of Uzbekistan, Turkmenistan and Azerbaijan have adopted the latin alphabet. This language reform marked a deliberate move to distance themselves from Russia and to resist further russification. In 1997 Tatarstan began a similar process of replacing the cyrillic with the latin alphabet. Within Tatarstan proponents of language reform argue that the latin alphabet better conveys Tatar phonetics than the cyrillic. It is significant that they have chosen the latin alphabet as the Tatars used arabic script from the ninth century until 1927 when they briefly adopted the latin alphabet until forced to use the cyrillic alphabet in 1939. Significantly, one of the arguments used to support the adoption of the latin alphabet was that it would facilitate the computerizing of the Tatar language and the Tatarization of computer programmes (Khasanova, 1997). The Tatar assertion of their national identity and the rejection of russification does not reflect a narrow parochialism. The Tatars are keen to embrace the new technologies that promote globalization and see them as a way of asserting their Tatar identity.

Russian identity: the russian idea and Eurasianism

The Russian Idea (see Berdyaev, 1947) and Eurasianism provide concepts of Russian identity which stress Russia's distinctiveness from the West with its materialism and individuality. They therefore provide analyses of who the Russians are and who are the alien 'other'. The essence of the Russian Idea is a conviction of Russia's uniqueness (*samobytnost'*). Advocates of the Russian Idea point to Russia's rich heritage based on the Russian Orthodox Church (ROC), the peasant commune and a powerful state (McDaniel 1996: 11). They stress that Russia is a great power and that this power is linked to the idea of empire with its strong sense of patriotism, statehood (*gosudarstvennost'*) and spirituality (*dukhovnost'*). The Russian Idea provides an intellectual foundation for the rejection of western culture, political systems and models of modernization. For advocates of the Russian Idea Russia can only be saved by following its own unique historical path and by extension by rejecting the globalizing forces that will distort Russia's development. The rejection of individualism and the stress on ethnic Russian institutions, empire and the ROC makes the development of a civic Russian identity more difficult. Within the Russian Federation the Russian Idea not only leads to the rejection of the Yeltsin-led westernizing model of political and economic development but also to the primacy of ethnic Russians within a multinational state.

The concept of Eurasianism was first developed in the 1920s to challenge Bolshevism by Russian émigrés Prince Nikolai Trubetskoi, George Florovskii and Piotr Savitskii. As its name suggests Eurasianism does not stress the ethnic Russianness of Russian identity but rather its multi-ethnic origins. Eurasianists such as the late Lev Gumilev stressed the difference between the Russian and European civilizations and argued that Russia is a unique historical and cultural fusion of Slav and Turkic, Orthodox and Moslem elements. Gumilev used the term 'ethnos' for a nation, arguing that five hundred years ago the eastern Slavs, Mongols and Tatars fused to form a superethnos (Gumilev, 1992: 10–11). A thousand years before that a Teuton-Latin superethnos had formed in Western Europe and since then had presented a constant threat to the Slav–Tatar–Mongol superethnos. In contrast to the idea that Russia saved Europe and Christendom from the Mongol hordes Gumilev argued that it was the military prowess of the Mongols that saved the eastern Slavs from the predation of the West. Eurasianists define an ethnos in terms of a link to ancestral lands rather than in racial terms. For Gumilev and his adherents there are also parasite states (such as the USA) and parasite ethoses (such as the Jews in Russia) who have lost contact with their ancestral lands and survive as a parasites on another ethnos.

During Reconstruction Gennady Zyuganov, who later became the leader of the RCP, worked with Russians within the Communist Party of the Soviet Union (CPSU) to elaborate a Russian-oriented form of communism combining anti-westernism and anti-capitalism. Curiously it was these communists who helped to revive Eurasianism and in the mid-1980s the CPSU's publishing services began to publish a wide range of non-communist Russian thinkers, including Lev Gumilev. Zyuganov worked closely with Alexandr Prokhanov the editor of the Russian Nationalist weekly *Den'* (renamed *Zavtra* in 1993) which had a page devoted to Eurasia, providing a forum for Russian Nationalists but also for Russia's Muslims. Within the Russian Federation Eurasianist ideas have been used by the Russian Party under Nikolai Bondarik and the National Republican Party. Eurasianism was believed to have the potential to provide the new Russian state with an anti-western identity which could embrace all its Slav, Tatar and Mongol peoples, but not Jewish people. Eurasianism has been employed to support claims that at the very least Russia should have good relations with its Turkic and Asian neighbours and even that these peoples together with the Russians, might rightly belong in a unified Eurasian state.

In the mid-1990s Eurasianism has tended to be superseded by more narrowly focused Russian Nationalist ideas which are anti-western, anti-asian and anti-Semitic. The humiliation of the Russian armed forces in the first Chechen war (1994–96), continuing instability in the Caucasus and fear of Chinese expansionism have provoked a reappraisal of attitudes towards the Islamic world and China. By September 1996 Alexandr Prokhanov was no longer such a devoted Eurasianist and was now arguing that it would be the Islamic and Chinese worlds which would really enjoy the dissolution of Russia (Shlapentokh, 1997: 12). Moscow's mayor Yuri Luzhkov has promoted the work of the artist Ilya Glazunov whose painting *Russia Awake!* shows a Slavic soldier with a Kalashnikov in one hand and a New Testament in the other. The slogan 'Russia for the Russians' appears on the drummer boy's drum. In Glazunov's painting *The Call of the Devil*, a woman sits naked except for a shawl decorated with a Star of David across her knees. A scaly tail peeps out from beneath her knees (Reeves, 1999: 20). In addition to these attacks on Russia's domestic enemies Glazunov regularly attacks western popular culture. Luzhkov, an ardent economic modernizer, has nonetheless also called for all advertisements on Moscow streets to be in the cyrillic rather than the latin alphabet as part of a rejection of the creeping westernization of Moscow.

Globalization: Russia under attack?

Russia and the West

Russia's struggle with the West is a long and bitter one. Russia's modern-izers, whether Peter the Great, Mikhail Gorbachev or Boris Yeltsin, have typically sought to bring Russia closer to the European mainstream, to adopt western technologies and forms of organization, to embrace western ideas and to generally open up to the West. For many Russians these periods of opening up to and copying the West are associated with tremendous hardship and pressures upon society. Gorbachev talked about Russia's place in the Common European Home and stressed Russia's cultural, political and trade links with Europe. He declared: 'We are Europeans. Old Russia was united with Europe by Christianity. [...] The history of Russia is an organic part of the great European history' (Gorbachev, 1988: 190). For many Russians today this was when the rot set in. Gorbachev squandered the great territorial gains of empire in 1989 and set in train the events and processes that reduced the USSR and by extension Russia from a superpower to an impover-ished and weakened state.

A key problem for Russia is that the very institutions that act as the 'gatekeepers' to the world economy – the International Monetary Fund (IMF), World Bank and World Trade Organization (WTO) – are domin-ated by the USSR's and Imperial Russia's traditional adversaries in 'the West'. Under the tutelage of the Harvard Professor Jeffrey Sachs on behalf of the IMF, President Yeltsin introduced economic 'Shock therapy' that was supposed to propel Russia into a market economy. The immediate result was that the value of peoples' savings was wiped out overnight; hyper-inflation, rising unemployment and the collapse of certain sectors of the economy soon followed. Grigory Yavlinsky of the liberal Yabloko party succinctly summed the situation up as 'Too much shock and not enough therapy'. According to data collected by the All-Russian Centre of Public Opinion Studies in 1997, 60 per cent of

Russians reject the western capitalist model for their country and believe that in the 1990s Russia was set on the wrong course (Shlapentokh, 1998: 209).

Outside of Russia's political elite the impact of shock therapy fanned the flames of anti-westernism and anti-capitalism. The reformist social-ist Boris Kagarlitsky for example writes of 'dictatorship by the IMF' in Russia:

> The foreign trade of the Russian Federation has taken on all the features of colonial subjugation. The country exports fewer and fewer industrial products and more and more raw materials. Mean-while, it imports low-quality mass consumption goods, obsolete and hence cheap technology, luxury items and radioactive waste.
>
> (Burbach, Núñez and Kagarlitsky, 1997: 120–1)

There is a general sense in Russia that the West wants it to be weak. For Nationalists this is part of the West's centuries-long struggle to dominate Russia. Typical beliefs expressed to the author by Russians are as follows: that the West wants access to Russia's mineral riches and to destroy their domestic industries; that the West has destroyed Russian agriculture by undercutting Russian farmers and now exports food to Russia con-taminated by chemical additives; that the West wants to use Russia as a dump for its toxic and nuclear waste; and that the West is trying to steal Russia's best people in an orchestrated 'brain drain'. Russian ballet and opera companies spend much of their time touring abroad to earn money and in return the Russian people get Hollywood action films and pornography. The message is clear: the West wants to be able to exploit Russian resources, debase Russian culture and generally to 'dumb down' the Russian people. Little wonder then that 61 per cent of Russians agreed with the proposal that, 'The United States is utilising Russia's current weakness to reduce it to a second rate power and pro-ducer of raw materials' (cited by Shlapentokh, 1998: 209). The expan-sion of NATO to include the former soviet allies Hungary and Poland, reinforces a sense that the West wants to subjugate Russia. Distrust of the West has resulted in 85 per cent of Russians wanting Russia to regain 'military parity with the United States' (ibid.).

Religion: combating spiritual colonization and creating a Russian state

The 1993 Constitution establishes Russia as a secular state and recog-nizes the plurality and equality of religious organizations (Article 14).

The preamble also talks about 'reviving the sovereign statehood of Russia'. The conversion of Prince Vladimir of Kiev to Orthodoxy in 988 is seen as the defining moment in Russian culture and the birth of the Russian state. Orthodoxy was the Russian state religion from 988 until 1917. To many ethnic Russians, both believers and non-believers, the Russian Orthodox Church (ROC) is not just a religion; rather, it is the cradle of Russian history and culture, a repository of art, music and architecture. The ROC played the defining role in the development of Russian national consciousness and isolated Russia from those major developments of Western European history: the Renaissance and the Reformation.

The ROC shares its abhorrence of western culture and consumerism with the Red–Brown alliance. Vyacheslav Polosin, the Chairman of the Supreme Soviet Committee on Religious Freedom, claimed in a 1993 *Pravda* article that some 200 000 preachers from the United States had invaded Russia to found new religious societies. While this was untrue it fell on willing ears given the general sense that Russia had capitulated to and was being colonized by the West (Krasikov, 1998: 77). For Yeltsin, a former communist who has been accused of selling out to the West, association with the ROC helped to strengthen his 'Russia First' credentials. In return for ROC support Yeltsin granted them a form of religious protection by signing the 'Law on the Freedom of Conscience and on Religious Associations'. The law severely restricts the educational, publishing and charitable activities of any religious organization which cannot prove that they have existed in Russia for at least 15 years (Meek, 1997a: 20). The target of this law were foreign missionaries, but any religion denied official recognition under soviet rule, such as the Pentecostal Church and the Jehovah's Witnesses were also caught up by the restrictions. Similarly, Baptists and Seven Day Adventists, who have existed in Russia since before the 1917 Revolution, have been particularly hard hit. Roman Catholics were also initially caught out by the law but have since been granted recognition – although the activities of the Jesuits are still restricted. It was Russia's non-Orthodox Christians who were caught out by the law. The ROC seems to classify all ethnic Russians whether believers or not as 'theirs' and do not want foreigners coming in and 'poaching' in their territory. Russia's Islamic, Buddhist and Jewish communities were granted the status of long-established religions and so their activities, have not been restricted by this particular law.

Russia's other religions do have cause to be concerned by the creeping 'Orthodoxization' of Russian state structures. In 1994 the ROC signed various agreements with the Ministry of Defence, Ministry of the Interior, the Federal Border Service and the Federal Agency for Governmental Relations which gave the ROC a privileged status within these organizations. The very bodies charged with preserving Russia's integrity from internal and external assaults are now Russian Orthodox. In 1989 Russia's Tatars celebrated the 1100th anniversary of their conversion to Islam – they had their own state from the eighth century until their conquest by Ivan the Terrible in 1552 when what they call their 'Russian yoke' began. It was Islam that enabled the Tatars to preserve a sense of Tatar identity through the centuries of Russian domination. The Russian state is becoming increasingly identified with the ROC as part of its search for identity and resistance to perceived western pressures. The growing status and role of the ROC is not only unconstitutional, it also promotes a sense of Russian identity which is ethnically Russian and increasingly confessionally Orthodox. This development contradicts the idea of creating a Russian civic identity and only serves to alienate Russia's many atheists and adherents of other religions.

Conclusion

Since 1992 the Russian Federation has been described as being 'in transition' from Soviet socialism to a liberal-democratic market economy. This has been a disorienting time which has led to the pauperization of the majority of the population. Little wonder then that the Russians describe themselves as 'humiliated and degraded' and that there is a widespread belief that outside forces have both promoted and are taking advantage of Russia's weakened condition. Militarily, economically, socially and culturally this is a country that feels deeply damaged and there is a widespread belief that Russia was set upon a wrong course in 1992 by westernizing elites led by Boris Yeltsin in collaboration with the IMF. In this view Yeltsin's programme of marketization and democratization does not correspond to Russian culture and traditions. Alexandr Rutskoi, who served as Yeltsin's vice-President (1991–93), argues Russia is a Eurasian rather than a European country and so a form of state capitalism such as that pursued by Russia's fellow Asian country South Korea and by the nineteenth-century Tsars is appropriate to Russia's unique historical mission. American-style capitalism is simply alien to Russia and has fatally weakened Russia before its historical adversaries in the West.

The soviet legacy and the problems generated by the transition from soviet socialism to a capitalist democracy have created a weak Russian state that is unable to take and implement consistent policies, combat rampant crime and corruption, provide its people with social and economic well-being, or protect its people from the impact of globalization on their economy and culture. Russians feel under assault and many yearn for the protection of a strong authority and social cohesion:

> A strong national identity still provides the simplest way to achieve both. It will not be created in Russia, however, without turbulence which will affect neighbouring countries. Minimising this turbulence without insulting and belittling the Russians remains one of the major problems facing the international community today.
>
> (Hosking, 1997: 486)

Without some economic success to encourage a sense that Russia's reforms are bringing tangible dividends it will be difficult to develop the civic sense of Russian identity necessary to strengthen Russia's democracy. This problem is exacerbated by the nature of contemporary Russian politics: formal powers are concentrated in a Super-presidency which is in conflict with a recalcitrant and obstructionist parliament and the heads of major financial-industrial groups known as the Oligarchs who have an undue influence on government. Such developments do not help to promote a popular, substantive belief in liberal-democratic politics and will also frustrate the development of a civic Russian identity. A wide range of politicians (including Zyuganov, Luzhkov, Zhirinovsky and Lebed) are advocating Russian identity politics, playing on Russian disorientation, loss of status and one might even say loss of mission in their bids for power. Boris Yeltsin found it useful to court the ROC and following his re-election in 1996 called for the elaboration of a National Ideology, even though this is expressly forbidden in the 1993 Constitution. A new National Ideology has not yet been elaborated and it remains to be seen whether it will be possible to have such an ideology that incorporates all Russia's peoples.

Note

1   The title of this chapter is taken from an article by Sergei Stankevich.

3
Identity and Conflict in Globalizing Times: Experiencing the Global in Areas Ravaged by conflict and the Case of the Bosnian Serbs[1]*

Ioannis Armakolas

Introduction

> Bosnian Serbs are at the moment perhaps the most hated group of people in the Western world. (BBC documentary *Serbian Ethics*, 1992)

> Bosnia, Bosnia, Bosnia is now everywhere. It is an ongoing series in our newspapers, a sound-bite on our television sets . . . we can be there by going to a U2 concert, clicking on a computer screen, by dialling up Sarajevo OnLine or netscaping to the Bosnia HomePage.
> (O'Tuathail, 1996: 171)

These are reminders, of the debates, emotions and awareness that the Bosnian conflict attracted. This chapter analyses Bosnian Serb identities and argues that there has not yet been a full examination of the influence of the 'global constituency', created as a result of the Yugoslav war, on the identities of the warring parties in Bosnia. The materials used in this chapter include interviews and informal discussions with Serbs from Sarajevo and other localities which were gathered during a field trip to Bosnia-Herzegovina (hereafter Bosnia) in spring 1999. The research was carried out in a small town in eastern Bosnia, close to Sarajevo, belonging to the Serbian Republic of Bosnia (hereafter Republika Srpska). The town's population has grown four- or five-fold since the

---

* The Chapter reflects the situation at the time of writing.

war. It has been a popular temporary or final destination for Serb refugees from Sarajevo in two different waves – one during the first days of the war and the other after the Dayton Agreement which allocated some of the Serb-controlled parts of Sarajevo to the Muslim-Croat Federation. The town, unlike other areas in eastern Bosnia, did not experience the violent ethnic cleansing of Muslims and had minimal experience of frontline warfare.

Following, among others, Stuart Hall (1992) identity is treated in this chapter as non-stable, non-unitary and contingent. The focus is shifted from any 'essential' content of identities to the continuing process that constructs, reconstructs and transforms them. The analysis in this chapter draws on previous works on the identity element in the Yugoslav conflict, but attempts to extend these to incorporate the element of global involvement. The argument put forward here is that in order to understand Bosnian Serb identity transformations we need to include in our analysis not only the Serb nationalist discourse or the urban–rural element, but also the experience of the global involvement in its entirety.

The global and the local

Globalization and the question of identity in the Yugoslav conflict

This chapter will not examine whether the argument that the strengthening of local identities is a response to the process of cultural globalization (Hall, 1992) is relevant to the Yugoslav case. Instead, the focus here is on the strain put on local identities by an often disregarded factor of the global political transformation that is linked to globalization. What is scrutinized here, therefore, is the indirect link between globalization and identities in conflict areas that has resulted in the Yugoslav conflict attracting the interest of millions of people abroad, a concerned 'global constituency'. In this respect, the present analysis shares features with and is influenced by the growing literature on global civil society (Frost, 1998; Lipschutz, 1992; Macdonald, 1994; Shaw, 1992, 1994; Walzer, 1995; a critical review in Pasha and Blaney, 1998). The pressure from world public opinion for involvement in the Yugoslav war was one of the first manifestations of the sense of a global responsibility that lies at the core of a global civil society (Shaw, 1992, 1994). It is important to stress here that although in its classic form the global civil society discourse refers to movements 'working on a global scale via advanced telecommunications' (Pasha and Blaney, 1998: 425), in this chapter the media and telecommunications, through their discourses on the

Yugoslav conflict, are considered as an integral part of the global involvement in the Yugoslav crisis.

Global or International? The case for a conceptual 'blurring'[2]

One of the difficult tasks in this discussion is to delineate the 'global' and the 'international' in the Yugoslav conflict. The obvious solution would be to attempt a conceptual distinction and differentiate between the agents and features of the international, like states' and international organizations' diplomacy, and those of the global, like non-governmental activity and other transnational networks. In this case the former would be excluded from this analysis and the latter included. There are two problems with such an approach. The first is that it would leave outside, or rather 'in-between', a whole range of features that played a very important role in the conflict. These are the foreign media and the wider public involvement. The media, for example, cannot be easily put in the global basket unless we talk about the so-called 'CNN effect' cases and that would also limit the analysis to the very few media that have 'global reach'. It can hardly be argued that only large media corporations had an impact on the debates about Bosnia. The role of the wider public involvement would also be minimized by this approach. As it has been shown, especially by Martin Shaw (1992, 1994), the distinctive feature of the Yugoslav war is that it became an issue for a global public, far beyond the narrow circle of the people involved in non-governmental groups and specialized networks. The second problem with such a distinction is that, no matter its intellectual coherence, it would be a distorted view of how the foreign is experienced in the field. Field research in Republika Srpska left no doubts that at least for the Serbs the global and international are interlinked – and more often than not 'blurred'. Thus, all the features of foreign involvement, be they global or international, form parts of a single narrative and so this is how their impact on identities will be considered.

The global involvement as constituting identities in the Yugoslav conflict

Among the analyses that advanced an understanding of identities in the Yugoslav conflict as flexible, few have tried to show how the foreign involvement contributed to the identity dynamics. One notable exception is Cornelia Sorabji (1993, 1995), who argues that the international reaction to the Yugoslav conflict was itself constitutive of the conflict as we know it. The understanding of ethnic identity was very different before and in the early stages of the war. The conflict was reduced to an urban–rural divide. The exclusionist projects advanced by nationalist leaders had initially received little support among the population. However, the outside world perceived the conflict as an 'ethnic war' – and, more importantly, international diplomacy proposed solutions, such as the Peace Plan, that treated the three groups as separate, bounded communities. Therefore,

> ... through its insistence on an essentialist treatment of ethnicity, in which Serbs, Croats and Muslims have immutable identities, Europe has played a part in legitimating nationalist leaders, highlighting the ethnic boundaries, and creating the sort of ethnic war (one based on mutual and compelling hatred and fear) which, so it claims, had been there all along.
>
> (Sorabji, 1993: 35)

Sorabji further argues that in this continuing process of identities formation of the warring parties, the western unwillingness to intervene and stop the war (the article was written before the later active military involvement in Bosnia) contributed' to a decreasing identification of Muslims with Europe and its values. In short, international reaction to the war not only legitimated the nationalist leaderships and produced an ethnic conflict that was not there in the first place, but further contributed to the formation of a specific type of identities among the Bosnian Muslims. Sorabji's (1993) article was influential especially among intellectuals and was indeed one of the most striking examples of the break with the commonsensical and stereotypical early readings of the conflict as involving medieval, irrational hatreds (see Kaplan, 1993; Hansen, 1998; and Godina, 1998). It managed to present an alternative view of the war and brought in the picture identities and experiences that were obviously marginalized by the discourse on Balkan animosities.

Experiencing global involvement in the field: Bosnian Serb identity transformations

This second part of the chapter focuses on the identities of the Bosnian Serbs. It examines the global dimension in their discourse about the conflict and how it has affected their identity transformations, their construct of versions of reality and how their identity was influenced by the experience of global involvement. The first task is to establish the impact of the global involvement in its entirety. Only after it is clear that in this conflict something has changed in the way the world responds to a civil war shall we be able to grasp also the potential impact on identities. Sorabji's views (outlined above) are too restrictive to fully address this issue. The next section challenges analyses of identity in the Yugoslav conflict that concentrate only on the nationalist discourse. Following this, the features of the involvement that play a role in identity are presented and also the potential variations in discourse and identity. This leads to the question of the urban–rural divide and the issue of the 'identity project' of the international community in Bosnia both of which are critically assessed.

Involvement and impact on identities: incorporating the global in its totality

As shown above, Sorabji has tried to address the reaction to the war in Bosnia as an element that influences identities; this was done as a supplement to other arguments and not in a fully-fledged manner. Following Sorabji's thought one would draw the conclusion that the early western military 'inaction' (read: non-intervention) or the later 'action' (limited intervention) was the only element of foreign involvement that shaped identities. What such an approach does not grasp is the fact that the Yugoslav conflict was not unlike other conflicts in which foreign powers did or did not intervene militarily or in any other way. What needs to be comprehended is the extent to which millions of people got involved in the conflict. Thus, at the same time as Sorabji laments the lack of interest on the part of Europe, or the West in general, a different kind of interest and emotional involvement sprung up all over Europe and North America. Hundreds of non-governmental organizations (NGOs) rushed to Bosnia; hundreds of thousands of people became involved indirectly through fund-raising, networking, organizing activities and transmitting information relevant to the conflict. The media kept the conflict on the front pages for years. Numerous journalists tried self-consciously to alter the perceived wrongdoings of international politics with their reports (O'Tuathail, 1996 and O'Kane's reports in *The Guardian*). Others wrote books, some of which have become extremely influential in the construction of the image of the war as we know it (see Gutman, 1993). Cyberspace was flooded by appeals of all kinds to press for a more active policy on Bosnia. Academics, intellectuals and artists became involved in heated debates on how to save Bosnia, organized themselves into influential pressure groups and participated in all kinds of awareness-raising activities.

Especially in the West's generalized discourses, the backdrop of the global emotional and active involvement in the conflict, it is clear that Serbs occupy the place of the 'absolute evil'. In her thorough study of the western debates on the Bosnian conflict and their security implications, Lene Hansen (1998: esp. 168ff) identifies two distinctive discourses: the 'Balkan' or 'Bosnia as Other' discourse, and the 'Bosnia as Western Self' discourse. In this mapping of the debates, the Bosnian conflict is represented in the former discourse as a civil conflict based on ethnic hatred and in the latter as a war of aggression against an independent state and a multicultural society. It is interesting that in both discourses, which cover a wide range of political positions, the Serbs are being damned as the barbarians, aggressive and violent. The 'Balkan' discourse is 'Othering' the Balkans as a whole and is assigning the conflict to the violent history of the area drawing a clear line between the civilized West and the primitive Balkans. This discourse would not deny that the Serbs are violent and aggressive but it would advance realpolitik reasoning against any military intervention, and would also try to make a more balanced assessment of where the responsibility for the war lies. On the other hand the 'Bosnia as Western Other' discourse, which increasingly dominated political, intellectuals' and media debates after the first year of the war, assigns responsibility for the war to Serbian aggression and plans to create a Greater Serbia out of the ruins of Bosnia. This discourse also draws a clear line between civilization and multiculturality on the one hand and nationalism and ethnic segregation on the other; only this time the line runs parallel to the mountains surrounding Sarajevo. It is clear that in both cases, and of course especially in the latter, the Serbs are portrayed as the 'evil Other' or as Hansen calls it the 'radical Other' (1998: 169).[3] It is interesting to note here that Serb distrust of academic discourses about the Bosnian conflict is enormous. Towards the end of the field trip, Vojka (a 23–year-old university student) told me that she knews that now that I was going abroad I would write critically of the Serbs. I replied that although I did not necessarily agree with the Serbs (something that was clear from other discussions I had with her) I had nothing against the Serbs, therefore I could not write 'against them'. She was convinced; being a Greek I had the 'correct references' anyway. But then she told me that even if I wanted to write something good about the Serbs, my academic supervisor would not allow me to do so!

Going back, one would legitimately wonder why the only thing that counts when it comes to the impact on identity is formal military intervention. I would suggest instead that if involvement is to the extent described above, it has to be taken into account. For example, even though the Muslim identities in Bosnia are not the focus of this chapter, I would suspect that the much-feared Islamic radicalization of the Bosnian Muslims had not come about partly due to the support (by all means except early intervention) that Western European and North American societies provided. In the end, what I suggest here is not different from Sorabji's critique of essentialist conceptions of ethnicity: 'ethnic identities are [not] set in stone and hence immutable... they are [not] constructed in isolation without reference to other identities' (1993: 33). In fact, it should be clear that no ethnic group constructs its identity isolated in a laboratory and, since this is also true for Bosnian ethnic groups, the enormous scale of global involvement did and still does play its role in the construction of all Bosnian identities.

The flexibility of Bosnian Serb identities: not simply the discourse but the experience of involvement

As stressed throughout this chapter, identities cannot but be conceived as contingent, non-necessary and constructed. Naturally, people's identification with various images of the collective produce real-world effects, but that does not make these identities less constructed or more 'real'. This is no less true for the Bosnian Serb identities. Not surprisingly, approaches to the Yugoslav conflict that treat identity as a timeless property of groups and advance the age-old hatreds thesis would not be concerned to show the fluidity of Bosnian Serb identities. The problem, however, lies with works that share a constructivist outlook and treat identities as flexible, non-necessary and constructed in discourse. Some of these works demonstrate an inexplicable uneasiness with Serbian identities as if these alone, in their violent, exclusionist form, are less constructed or, to put it better, more 'real' than other identities. Sorabji, for example, despite her commitment to analysing the non-essential and constructed character of ethnic identities, informs us that '...greed and barbarity are frequently regarded as essential aspects of Serbian ethnic identity' (1993: 33). Others correctly assign central importance to the construction of the new Serbian identity by the semi-official and later official nationalist discourse deployed from mid-1980s by the Serbian political, intellectual and religious leadership (Bowman, 1994, 1999; Salecl, 1993, 1994; Sofos, 1996a, 1996b). Most of these works incorporate the element of violence as an important dimension in the construction of identities either before the real war started (Bowman, 1999; Eide, 1997) or after (Campbell, 1996; Sorabji, 1995). To pause just there though would mean that from some point on Serbian identities ceased being influenced by other discourses and experience. In contrast I want to argue that the official nationalist discourse that constructed the exclusionist Serbian identity in the first place, is not autonomous but has interacted with the foreign involvement in the Yugoslav crisis, in constituting these identities. Furthermore, as argued in the previous section, this involvement has to be incorporated in the picture in its totality, including not only military action/inaction but also all diplomatic activity, foreign media discourses, NGO activity and any manifestation of the global civil society.

A lot of things have been written about the discursive element in Serb nationalism. The ideological basis for the nationalist discourse deployed by the Serbian leadership was presented in its most official form by the Serbian intelligentsia in the Memorandum of the Serbian Academy of Sciences. Written in 1986, only a few years after the death of Tito, it was a direct attack on the Titoist legacy of the multiethnic Yugoslavia (Dragovic-Soso, 1997; Magas, 1993) and notoriously challenged the taboo of nationalist discourse in Yugoslavia. The memorandum was preceded by literature and other intellectual activity in Serbia which had created fertile ground for such moves (Popov, 1994; Ramet, 1996b). This fertile ground was exploited by the Serbian political elite, namely by Milosevic and his proxies, who gave a death blow to the ideology of 'brotherhood and unity' by fully endorsing a nationalist agenda. A series of discursive attacks followed – first against the Kosovo Albanians and later against virtually everybody. The details of the Serbian nationalist discourse need not be presented here since they have been painstakingly analysed in the literature about the conflict. The important point to stress is that 'the articulation of a Serbian discourse ... served to reconstitute "Serbia" as a locus of identity and "Serbian interests" as a focus of concern' (Bowman, 1994: 153; also Popov, 1994: 47ff). The Serbian leadership (as did the other nationalist leaderships) answered the question 'Who are the people?', posed due to the collapse of the federal system, by constituting their national subjectivities/constituencies and at the same time scapegoating the 'national Other' (Bowman, 1994: 144–8).

The impact of these developments on the identities of the Bosnian Serbs was nevertheless supplemented by the subsequent global involvement as described above. First of all it seems that in Bosnia the impact of this discourse was differentiated. In my interviews it appears that, at least for the Serbs residing in Sarajevo, the discourse itself was not so salient until the three nationalist parties won the 1990 elections in Bosnia and especially until Bosnia declared its independence. In this respect, the initial and crucial confirmation of the discourse was provided by international support for the Bosnian declaration of independence and recognition of the new state. Since then, the increasing siding of international diplomacy, non-state actors and western media with the Muslim side has contributed to the defensive aspect of Bosnian Serb identities. The whole of the Bosnian Serb population was homogenized to a very exclusionist form of identity. More moderate voices, people estranged by violence, even Sarajevans fully endorsing the values of multiculturality of old Bosnia and Yugoslavia, were forced to fully integrate ideologically in a country whose image as an 'evil force' was constructed not only by the atrocities and the ethnic cleansing but also by the perceptions of the whole world. This demonization of Serbs was more often than not a standard feature in my interviews and discussions in Republika Srpska. In such cases, identification with that image would even replace a serious reflection on the violent excesses and the incidents of ethnic cleansing; or as Vojka put it when responding to a question about a violent episode: 'Isn't that what you expected from Serbs?' (informal discussion, May 1999). As analysed by Bowman with reference to the case of Slovenia, experience has the potential not only to inflate exclusionist identities but also to deflate them contrary to efforts to maintain the nationalist enemy discourse: ' . . . with the loss of an enemy perceived as common, the nationalist community that [the] enemy's violence made possible simply dissolved and people began to enunciate their encounters with frustration and violence in situational terms rather than in terms of a global antagonism' (Bowman, 1999: 12).

What this makes clear is that nationalist discourse itself is predicated on a reality or a representation of this reality that confirms its 'truthfulness'. In this line one would expect a substantial opening in the Serb identities. It is not only the fact that the war has been over since 1995, but also that other 'favourable' conditions, such as a considerable shift in the Serbian political leadership during the last two years, were apparent. The new or 'reformed' leadership has collaborated with the international community and, to a certain extent, with the other ethnic groups. At the same time it has attempted to isolate the extremist political forces. A subsequent shift in the Serb discourse about the war was also attempted. By trying to tie the 'excesses' of the war with the previous leadership and its 'criminal mafia', a project of considerable 'moderation' at the discursive level was advanced. In addition to these, the 'identity project' of the international community in Bosnia has been deployed in full force, something that will be analysed later in this chapter. Despite these 'favourable' conditions the much-hoped-for and expected change in Serb identities and opinions did not happen, at least not at any substantive level. A minimal substantive split with past attitudes was apparent and an equally limited popular support for the isolation of the extremists was gained. The Bosnian Serb people still seem a solid and defensive whole and the continuing power of the radicals was made more than clear in the 1998 elections. All the above clearly indicate that the shift in the Serb nationalist discourse is not enough to significantly change Serb identities. One could legitimately argue that this is to a large extent due to the continuing influence of the foreign element. The international community's continuing confrontation with the Serbs and their accusations of sole Serb responsibility for the war, maintained the image of the Serbs as a nation hated by all, encircled by enemies and maltreated by the big powers.

Of course, the argument here could very well be that global involvement did not really alter identities but rather that what is constructed currently as a very defensive Bosnian Serb identity is a self-fulfilling prophecy. This is a legitimate claim since the path followed by the agents of the Serbian nationalist discourse could only lead to some kind of a dead-end. As early as 1989 a Serbian journalist stressed:

> If I did not read those Serbian newspapers I would not know that you Slovenes hate us Serbs and that the Croats also hate us, as do the Albanian, Vojvodinian, Montenegrin, and Bosnian-Herzegovinian leaderships, that the West and the East also hate us, and that practically the whole world hates us.... [E]everyone hates us except our wonderful leadership.

> (quoted in Posa, 1998: 75)

But what is important to acknowledge here is that this process that produced a self-fulfilling prophecy was not devoid of foreign influence; that the international reaction to and involvement in the conflict facilitated this process. The question here is not whether foreign involvement could have been different, or whether it would have been just to treat Serbs differently. What is important for analysis, for policy and for the response to similar future situations, is to acknowledge the part that foreign involvement played in this process. Once this is put in the picture then one can decide on an appropriate hierarchy of values, outcomes and policies. If this is not acknowledged in the first place we simply receive a completely distorted idea of the identities engaged in the conflict and the place of foreign involvement.

Features of the global involvement that influence Bosnian Serb identities

The features of global involvement that play a role in influencing the Bosnian Serb identities are either the experience of diplomatic and military intervention or the discourses on the Yugoslav conflict. What counts here is the population's perception of both and not whether we would consider such intervention and discourses as legitimate and justified. More specifically, such features are first and foremost the break-up of Yugoslavia and the recognition of the new states; the perceived double standards of the international diplomacy shown in a series of issues affecting the Serbs (Krajina, the bombing of Bosnian Serbs, the Dayton Agreement, the Brcko decision, the ousting of President Poplasen, the bombing of Federal Republic of Yugoslavia, Kosovo and others); the generalized discourse of the western media blaming the Serbs for the break-up of Yugoslavia and the war; and finally the demonization of the Serbs. Concerning this demonization, certain features constantly appear in the Serbian discourse about the conflict. The most common feature apparent in ordinary Serbs' conversations is an uneasiness with the portrayal of Serbs as barbarians, responsible for a genocide in Bosnia, perpetrators of slaughters and rape warfare. It is usually argued that western media have been prejudiced against the Serbs, overstating the responsibility of the Serb side and overlooking that of the other parties in the conflict (on the impartiality of the western media see Petras and Vieux, 1996). Another feature that often appears is the perceived neglect of Serb concerns – the fact that the international community supported the break-up of Yugoslavia without taking into account the fears of the entrapped Serbian minorities. Finally, considerable significance is assigned to the indictment of the Bosnian Serb leadership.

Variations in discourse and identity

Amongst the various different subcategories often suggested by researchers to detect variations in identification (namely age, gender, class/occupation, education, place of origin) only age seemed to make the difference. As Laclau (1990: 3) points out, 'every age adopts an image of itself – a certain horizon, however blurred and imprecise, which somehow unifies its whole experience'. In that sense the younger generation of Bosnian Serbs had little difficulty in presenting a coherent exclusionist narrative; lacking significant experience of coexistence with the 'ethnic other' it seems to be more extreme and to hold clearer and more consolidated views of the conflict. Middle-aged and older people are generally more ambiguous or even confused. Although these categories and divisions should not be considered as too rigid, it is clear that the minimal experience of coexistence and collaboration with the other ethnic groups has influenced the opinions of the younger generation. As for other categories such as gender and class/occupation, I observed minimal variation in the reception of the nationalist message amongst them. It is interesting to note the intricate way in which the previously salient urban–rural distinction is currently involved in the ethnic identifications.

Additional issues related to the identities of the Bosnian Serbs

The case for the urban–rural divide: putting the argument in its context

The 'urban–rural division' thesis has been very influential among analysts of the Bosnian war who resisted the easy and stereotypical explanations of ancient hatreds and Balkan animosities. It was a source of hope that in the end not everything was as black as the early analyses of the conflict had painted it; that if one is patient enough to scratch the surface of the easy representation of the conflict as an ethnic nationalist war then it will be revealed that other identifications were much more salient than the ethnic ones. In this view the conflict in Bosnia was a revenge of the countryside, with its traditional values and its backwardness, against the civility, the progress and the civilization of the city. Reports of Serbs remaining in Sarajevo to defend their city along with their Muslim, Croat and Jewish neighbours, and not joining the nationalist forces led by the leader of the Bosnian Serbs Radovan Karadzic – a person notorious in the West for his declarations in favour of ethnic segregation contributed to an image of Sarajevo and consequently of Bosnia as the perfect example of a multicultural society. These reports also contributed to the construction of a negative image of the Serbian nationalist forces which were depicted as having a backward rural mentality, reviving memories of previous wars and genocides.

In its crude configuration this argument was elaborated by the eminent expert on Yugoslavia Sabrina Ramet (1996a). She contends that the current brand of Serbian nationalism is the ultimate revenge of the Serbian countryside against the urban culture imposed by the Titoist regime. In fact, following Ramet it would seem that the rural traditions and values and 'rural nationalism' are the essential characteristics of the Serb identity. Throughout her article this 'rural nationalism' is analysed through a series of negative features in contrast to the supposedly more 'positive' urban nationalisms. Of course, distinctions between 'good' and 'bad' nationalisms can be criticized. As Kathryn Manzo (1996: 19) would point out, discourses on nation and ethnicity are always built on a latent racial foundation; for in them difference (even in its more tolerant form) is always constructed as unfamiliar, alien, 'a problem to be solved'.

However, beyond such excesses the urban–rural argument still seems a legitimate point of departure in analysing the conflict. The problem is that it is very likely to have lost its explanatory power once the war got well under way. Although extremely important and useful for under-standing the early stages of the conflict, ten years on it is perhaps naïve to continue to assign to it such significance. To be sure, superficially it is still an important consideration. In fact, during an initial exposure to the current situation in Republika Srpska might easily lead one to conclude that the rural–urban divide is the main cause of the conflict. During my field trip I was continuously 'informed' by my Serb interlocutors who had fled Sarajevo and found sanctuary in the small town of eastern Bosnia that there is huge cultural difference between them and the local inhabitants. Older people would often talk with nostalgia about 'the big city'. Many of them would even visit Sarajevo from time to time, their old neighbourhoods, if they felt secure enough, or at least the old part of the city, the Starigrad and Bascarsija. The younger people would be more radical – they would describe the 'villagers' as backward and they would avoid socializing with local youngsters because they had a completely different conception of friendship or relationships than the one they had been used to in Sarajevo. All these I have to admit in the beginning of my field trip led me naïvely to consider that the urban–rural chasm is still the crucial point of reference. It was only after I started to scratch the surface of their arguments and tried to draw more general conclusions from their remarks about the 'villagers' that I realized that, at least for the Serbs of Republika Srpska that I have met, the divide had a completely different context after the war.

Cornelia Sorabji has described the complexity of the national identi-fications in Yugoslav Bosnia, which provided the context in which the urban–rural divide could perfectly fit. In the post-Second World War multi-ethnic Bosnia there were three different but supplementary con-cepts of what in Serbo-Croat is called the *narod*. This is rather inad-equately translated into english as 'nation' or 'people', but has a much richer meaning than either of these two words suggests. Firstly there are the Muslims, Serbs and Croats as separate *narods*; secondly all the inhab-itants of Bosnia as a joint *narod* and lastly the Muslim, Serb and Croat *narods* joined through Yugoslavism and 'brotherhood and unity' (Sorabji, 1995: 87–91). This complex web of interwoven ethnic identifications and also the fact they were conceived in positive terms meant that they were loaded with inclusionist meaning and provided a fertile ground for people to assign importance to local identities. Hence, in urban centres, and especially Sarajevo, a very distinct urban civility and pride in comparison to the countryside people and their culture had developed (Sorabji, 1993, 1995). This is largely the meaning of what we call the urban–rural divide in Bosnia.

Therefore, the urban–rural divide was predicated upon a specific context set by other identifications and most importantly by representations of the ethnic/national question. In addition, it functioned smoothly and without disruption all the way from the locality to the Yugoslav state level. Once the context was changed, the urban–rural was likewise re-articulated. It continued to play a role, but a different one corresponding to the transformed context of the ethnic identifications. In fact, Sorabji provides an insightful analysis of the shift in the web of identifications that the creation and maintenance of ethnically pure territories required: 'the first view of *narod* [had to] be retained and reinforced while all others... jettisoned' (Sorabji, 1995: 90). Thus, in three ways the context upon which the urban–rural divide was predicated has changed. Firstly, and most importantly for Serbs, the Yugoslav state that provided the backdrop for multicultural projects dissolved. Secondly, on the discursive level new ideologies contradicting the previously multicultural Bosnia emerged, and thirdly, physical conflict erupted and it was often systematized in such a way as to destroy previous memories of peaceful multi-ethnic coexistence in the locality.

Whereas the discourse element, as shown above, has been central to the analyses of the conflict and the violence element is also well acknowledged (for example, Sorabji, 1995), what is often neglected is the role of the break-up of Yugoslavia and interestingly what it has been replaced with. This is no unimportant issue. Firstly, it is central to the Serb discourses; according to which the Great Serbian project was developed as a 'remedy' to the 'dangers' presented for Serbs being left outside of the remaining Yugoslavia after the break-up of the federation (Bowman, 1999). Secondly, it has deprived people of the backdrop of Yugoslavism, which supplemented other more inclusive identities, as Sorabji has shown. Thirdly, and importantly for our discussion, the fact that Yugoslavia had been brought to an end by the recognition of the new states, provided the first and crucial rift with the global/international involvement for all those still associated with the dream of a common state – namely the Serbs, the Montenegrins and a few others. Finally, what has replaced Yugoslavia is important, and particularly the fear and insecurity produced by the collapse of the state and the lack of authority (for example, Ignatieff, 1994, 1995). What has not yet been fully evaluated is the effect that the quick replacement of these authorities had on people's options and in fact on people's identities. In the Bosnian context, the Bosnian Serb leadership has managed rapidly to present an alternative authority within the territories that it claimed, as have other leaderships. This narrowed down the options to almost nothing. Those that did not identify with their nationalist leadership had no other option than to stay in a predominantly Muslim Sarajevo. The choice was either/or, there were no chance for people to be able retain their old ways of living and their old habits. In an interview, for example, it was described to me how a Serb from Sarajevo, now living in Republika Srpska, struggled for days to continue to work in his job in the Muslim sector of Sarajevo and live with his family in Serb-controlled areas (interview with Anastazija, 23 May 1999). In the end he had no choice other than to leave his old job and be fully incorporated in the body of the new physical space created in eastern Bosnia. This would also be the case with people who attempted to resist the separation. More disheartening were the effects on those who quickly identified (out of habit or conviction) with the new authorities. During my interviews phrases like 'what could we do if our authorities decided so', 'our government told us to . . .' and so on appeared again and again. An interviewee even told me that he doesn't blame his old Muslim neighbour in Sarajevo for anything that happened because he 'had to do what his government told him' (interview with Ilija, 14 May 1999).

From all the above it is obvious that the context of urban–rural divide has changed. This element continues to play a role but now in the context of the dominating ethnic divisions and within the new symbolic and physical space that violence and nationalist elites' discourse have created. Within this context the current conception of the urban–rural divide can vary. In the best of cases, and I have to make clear that I have not in this trip encountered such a person, someone would be so nostalgic as to hope for the reintegration of Bosnia. Others, people in their forties and fifties, would lament old Sarajevo but be convinced that they will not live there again. Some of them would feel sorry about the three–year siege of their city by the forces of their own nation, but most of them would rationalize this by saying that 'Sarajevo after the war started was no longer what it was' or 'What can you do? It was a war'. Others like Anastazija, a 24–year-old student, would feel nostalgic about

Sarajevo but they would still want to join the remaining (New) Yugoslavia even though that would mean that in the new geography their place would become a little border town, many hours, drive away from the capital (interview, 23 May 1999). However, it can even take extreme forms, completely opposed to the hopes of those who stress the urban element as a remedy for the nationalist fervour. For example, Grozdana, 23, expressed her urban identity by saying 'we should have conquered Sarajevo', or Draginja, 28, who contested the peace agreements on the grounds that they gave the most important urban centres to the Muslim–Croat Federation (various informal discussions, May 1999).

The limitations of functionalist 'identity projects' in Bosnia

At this juncture a few points should be mentioned concerning the policies of the international community in Bosnia. These policies are predicated on a specific conception of how identities should be in the area and how one could legitimately refer to an 'identity project' put forward by the international community in Bosnia. This issue is relevant for our topic firstly, because this project is implicitly premised on an understanding of identity and ethnicity in Bosnia as flexible, and secondly, because this project is the inevitable follow-up to an involvement in which the international community, and especially the western countries and societies, projected their image and values. The argument here is that this 'identity project' has specific limitations. The basic idea behind this 'identity project' is that increased interaction among the three groups will result in the much-celebrated opening-up of identities that will allow the reintegration of the country. This functionalist approach underlies the measures taken by Carlos Westendorp as the High Representative of the international community in Bosnia. Many of these actions aimed at increasing the interaction and freedom of movement between the two entities, but also within the Muslim-Croat Federation. Although no one could doubt that such moves do have some impact on identities, it is doubtful whether they do in fact have the hoped-for salience. My interviews and informal discussions with young people, educated, speakers of foreign languages and often working for international organizations, NGOs and other agencies, revealed that opinions hardly change even though these young people had experienced prolonged exposure to different environments and multi-ethnic settings They had had discussions with foreigners and might even have met young people from other groups. In fact, these young people remain much more extreme and uncompromising than their parents. The lack of a long experience of coexistence with the other groups and the minimal exposure to the Titoist discourse of 'brotherhood and unity' is detrimental to any opening-up of their identities. Functionalist ideals about bringing these people together with the other groups have first to address the fundamental mentality of suspicion, defence and closure at the discursive level. It is clear to me that these people are not attracted by the discourse of the international community in Bosnia because they cannot find their place in it. One can debate the extent to which a balance at the discursive level can be found or real concessions can be given, considering the fact that the international community has a very clear and partisan view about the responsibility for the war. Nevertheless, the fact remains that, if there exist real intentions about the reintegration of the country, the project has to address at the discursive level the fears, the opinions and the mentalities of all the constituent groups.

Concluding remarks: self-reflection for the sake of the future

Is there a potential for future coexistence among the south-Slav groups? And is there a potential for more inclusive identities? I would suggest that there is potential for both the best and for the worst. There are possibilities for coexistence and multiculturality but also for new conflicts. The seed for the best and the worst is incorporated in the current identities of all three groups. It is important that arguments about the existence of age-old hatreds are not confirmed. At the same time Serbs mostly blame foreigners for the war and less their fellow south-Slavs. In fact, it would be quite surprising for someone used to the media reporting of ancient hatreds in Bosnia to find out that even after years of war, Bosnian Serbs do not seem to hate Muslims and Croats. Most of my interviewees, even the holders of the most extreme views, would have some good word for Muslims and Croats – and some of them would even talk about them as if nothing has happened. This is in stark contrast to their views on Albanians. Even though very few Bosnian Serbs have ever met a Kosovo Albanian they would typically hold very negative or even racist representations about them. This feature, shared even by moderate interviewees, reveals the place of Albanians as the 'pure evil' in the Serbian nationalist discourse (Salecl, 1993), but also demonstrates the fact that stereotypes against 'backward southerners' were a more generalized feature of the former Yugoslav society (see Bakic-Hayden 1995, and Hayden, 1992). On the other hand, moderate voices and ordinary Muslims and Croats blame the Serbian leadership instead of demonizing the Serbian nation as a whole. This situation of blaming either the foreigners or a leadership may seem helpful in the short term, but can prove disastrous in the longer run. Real catharsis, self-reflection and self-criticism are needed for all sides if future conflicts are to be avoided. On the other hand, the global constituency created by the Yugoslav conflict also needs to self-reflect. This conflict has revealed the potential for stereotyping that we all share and which was demonstrated in the various discourses about the conflict. It is also evident that this global civil society has created a force with unprecedented global reach and political influence. If this force is to be used, and used properly, in future conflicts, we need to understand its power, its political implications, and its immense moral responsibility.

Notes

1 I would like to express my gratitude to the American Ireland Fund and the Initiative on Conflict Resolution and Ethnicity (INCORE) for awarding me the 1998–99 Tip O'Neill Fellowship in Peace Studies that funded a six-month period of research at INCORE (Northern Ireland) and a field trip to Bosnia. Thanks also go to Mervyn Frost, Manos Marangudakis, Roger McGinty, Michelle Pace, Catherine Danks, Paul Kennedy and the participants in the panel. 'Globalizing influences and the implications for regions in turmoil' for their comments on earlier drafts of this chapter. Naturally, I remain solely responsible for any mistakes.
2 This 'blurring' is not employed by the proponents of a global civil society as they see it as laying clearly beyond state limits. The concept is used flexibly here for the sake of the general outlook and argument of this chapter (see Pasha and Blaney, 1998).
3 The fact that the Bosnian Serb leadership seemed to prefer the first discourse as it secured more convenient (for them) western policy prescriptions (Campbell, 1996 and O'Tuathail, 1996) does not undermine the argument in this chapter that the general discourses in the West confirmed the Serb nationalist discourse.

4
Identity in the Former GDR: Expressions of 'Ostalgia' and 'Ossi' Pride in United Germany

Patricia Hogwood

East Germans Between East and West

Given its dual orientation throughout the postwar period as a socialist state and one of the rival German states and part-nations, the former communist East Germany (GDR) is in a unique position in confronting contemporary globalization. The collapse of state socialism and the unification of Germany on terms set by the West Germany (FRG) has left the GDR community exposed to globalizing cross-pressures and accelerated societal change. This chapter identifies some of the forces of change and discusses the way in which these might impact on eastern German identity.

1989–1990: the GDR's unique path to democracy

In the context of the eastern European democratic transitions and process of 'marketization', the experience of the former GDR was unique. The countries of central and eastern Europe followed a pattern of transition carried by internal opposition forces, often under negotiation with the communist leading forces. Following the mass protests of the GDR 'peaceful revolution' in the last months of 1989, the GDR deviated from this pattern. The peaceful revolution became the first step in the process of German unification (1989–90). As the former FRG progressively marginalized the former GDR in setting the terms for unification, the process of transition became secondary to, and eventually almost synonymous with, the western-directed unification. Contrasting this experience with the eastern European model, Offe (1994, 1996) characterizes the GDR transition as a 'transformation from the outside'. He argues that the mode of decision-making within the process reduced the GDR to an object of the political strategy of the FRG. In the central and eastern European transitions, the subject and object of the transformation were one and the same, with each country conducting its own transformation on its own terms. In the German case, though, the FRG was the subject of the transformation and the GDR the object.

The First State Treaty on Currency, Economic and Social Union (1 July 1990) removed the GDR's economic order and replaced it with the West German model. The Unification Treaty of 3 October 1990 formally erased the territorial integrity of the former GDR. One of the most striking features of the 'transfer paradigm' (Lehmbruch, 1993, 1994) characterizing the unification process was its extensiveness. So complete was the integration of the former GDR into the pre-existing structures of the FRG that formal German language allows for no way of distinguishing, as a self-contained entity, the territory – and, by extension, the social and political community – of the former GDR from that of the FRG (Offe, 1996: 156–7). The most common official forms of terminology are the 'new Länder' or the 'area of accession', both of which relegate the former GDR to part of the pre-existing federal polity of the FRG. The transfer paradigm has proved controversial,[1] not least in its implications for identity in the former GDR. Did the mode of German unification effectively deny east Germans the opportunity to complete their democratic revolution? In (re)associating the former GDR with the cultural norms of the FRG, did it prevent an independent east German cultural regeneration? Certainly, the forms of east German identity which have begun to develop since unification have been influenced by perceptions of the negation of a community (see below). To what extent has unification by transfer accelerated the process of westernization in east Germany, compared with the countries of central and eastern Europe? Transition from the outside brought about incomparably abrupt and radical social changes in the GDR community. What does this concentration of transition effects with its associated social dislocation imply for the community's identity?

A multi-German, multi-ethnic society

On unification, the former GDR found itself in the new position of a receiving country for refugees and would-be immigrants. In 1990, the GDR's foreign population was negligible. Resident foreigners were largely limited to the Vietnamese workforce, which, segregated from the German community, had remained virtually invisible. In comparison, the proportion of resident foreigners in the population of the FRG was relatively high, standing at 8.4 per cent in 1990 (SOPEMI). The FRG had long been a favoured migration destination, for a number of reasons: its territorial position; its sound economy; its exceptionally liberal asylum laws; and its well-established immigrant communities, which had drawn in additional family members and acted as a base for further 'chain migration'. In the early 1990s these factors were compounded by the collapse of border restrictions in the former central and eastern European countries and by the civil war in the former Yugoslavia. The numbers of foreign entrants, particularly asylum seekers, soared. In 1992 the number of asylum claims registered was unprecedented: it exceeded the total number for that year in all the other 16 European Organization for Economic Cooperation and Development (OECD) countries (SOPEMI). The numbers of foreign entrants completely overwhelmed the reception and care facilities available in Germany.

At this time, public attitudes towards foreigners became severely strained and polarized and there was a steep increase in attacks on foreigners (Kanstroom, 1993: 156; Kuechler, 1996: 235). Analyses showed that hostility towards foreigners was motivated by very similar factors in east and west Germany (and indeed throughout Western Europe) relating to economic and social worries and a perception of relative deprivation. However, the *level* of anti-foreigner sentiment and a feeling of 'overcrowding' was significantly higher in the east, where the community was simultaneously experiencing profound economic dislocation following unification. Between 1990 and 1992, the index of manufacturing production in the former GDR fell by nearly 40 per cent; unemployment (including those registered on government schemes) rose to 37 per cent of the working population (Dyson, 1996: 205). Between 40 and 50 per cent of easterners expressed xenophobic sentiments compared with around 30 per cent of westerners (Kuechler, 1996). The east German community, already faced with the novelty of a multi-German identity,[2] was simultaneously confronted with the development of a multi-ethnic and multi-cultural society. The latent and overt xenophobia expressed in the eastern Länder can be seen as an indication of identity confusion in the face of globalizing cross-pressures.

European Union (EU) enlargement to the east

With unification, the eastern Länder of the former GDR were accepted into the EC as part of the enlarged territory of the FRG, bypassing the usual accession procedures to which other central and eastern European states have been subject (Spence, 1992). Privileged access to the EC was of undoubted economic advantage to the former GDR in its transition to a market economy and offers ongoing opportunities. The current prospect of EU enlargement to the east promises a pivotal position for the former GDR. Given its experience of economic and cultural inter-action with both the former socialist countries and (via the former FRG) with the West, the GDR-community has a unique position. It has the potential to develop as a communication centre for the existing EU member states and acceding central and eastern European member states and is in a prime position to pursue new market opportunities. On the other hand, the current Balkans conflict has prompted increasing concerns in Germany over questions of security, organized crime and a further wave of uncontrolled inward migration. The geographical position of the eastern Länder means that they are likely to bear the brunt of such developments. In addition, integration into the EC/EU has imposed a further layer of outside constraints on the development of the post-unification GDR-community, not all of which are welcomed. The prospective loss of the newly acquired Deutschmark to a common European currency came as a particular blow to the eastern German community; the Deutschmark had been employed by the West German Chancellor Kohl as a potent symbol of integration in mobilizing popular support in the GDR for German unification. In this way, for the GDR-community, accelerated EC/EU membership has mirrored the unification by transfer with the FRG. Both have cushioned the community from some pressures, particularly the extremes of economic hardship faced in other post-socialist countries. At the same time, they have exposed the GDR-community to uncertainty, upheaval and acceler-ated developments in areas which might be expected to impact on identity.

Identity in divided Germany

Commentators are divided over the question of whether the forty-year division between the Germanies effectively fostered two separate German identities, one 'eastern' and one 'western'. Two opposing cases can be argued (see, for example, Rose and Page, 1996): (i) that each of the Germanies developed separate identities; (ii) that one identity persisted, effectively defined in terms of the shared history of the Germans, which was upheld and further developed by the FRG as a 'reference culture' for the GDR. This debate is central both to the controversy surrounding the transfer paradigm and to understanding the full implications of that paradigm for identity in the former GDR. The view that each of the Germanies had developed separate identities questions the legitimacy of unification by transfer – at its most extreme, it represents this path to unification as 'colonization' or even 'Anschluss'. (The term Anschluss is highly emotive in German, because of its association with Hitler's illegal annexation of Austria.) The alternative view, that of a western repository of all-German identity, justifies unification by transfer as the rightful re-establishment of a 'natural' unity. This dichotomy was politicized and played out in the context of German–German relations in the postwar period, and is reflected in the internal intellectual discourse of the FRG.

East–west differentiation through 'state posturing'

As part of the postwar reinvention of the two Germanies, the wartime allied powers and successive postwar German political leaders had committed themselves to changing the inherited political culture of the German people. In the west, the aim had been to remove the authoritarian tendencies in the German culture which had been present since feudal times and to replace them with a commitment to democratic ideals. In the east, the political elites had aimed to realize a socialist society. In both Germanies, these goals were closely linked to a further state aim: that of restoring the territorial integrity and state sovereignty of divided Germany. As the two Germanies came to embody the ideological conflict of the Cold War, each envisaged a Germany reunified on terms acceptable to its own state values and those of its allies. In practice, the realization of a united Germany was closed to both German states through the structural constraints imposed by the Cold War international order. Instead, the state aim of reunification was pursued at the level of state propaganda, through mutual non-recognition, symbolic statements and policy gestures, and, particularly in the FRG, through jurisprudence (Schweigler, 1975: 21 fn8). These tactics were accompanied by verbally hostile and emotive exchanges between the Germanies. Through such 'state posturing' each German part-state justified its ideologically defined vision of a future Germany largely in terms of the perceived weaknesses of the other Germany. Through lack of opportunity for realisation, the policy priority of German reunification was to fade during the course of the Cold War years. Nevertheless, it is argued that the respective 'state myths' which evolved in the two Germanies on a future re-unified Germany helped to shape the political identity and political discourse of the FRG and GDR in such a way as to foster lasting social preconceptions, east and west, about the 'other side' (Hogwood, forthcoming).

Western German social preconceptions of eastern Germans came to be characterized by condescension, embarrassment and suspicion as to the moral integrity of the eastern community. They were formulated in the context of western perceptions of the past (notably the Nazi years), relations between the state and the individual (particularly the eastern 'passive' acceptance of the Stasi regime), and the economic community (the 'welfare' mentality of the easterners). As we shall see, the eastern social preconceptions of westerners comprised a deep sense of inferiority, envy of the social and economic freedoms of the west, resentment over the western blanket rejection of eastern values, and not a little helplessness. These preconceptions form the basis of social identity and social relations in united Germany. The Germans face an unprecedented experiment in the integration of two engineered and mutually opposed sets of cultural values, albeit with a shared historical heritage. Crucially, the German unification of 1990 was neither pursued nor perceived as a merger of equals; rather the west was tacitly acknowledged to have 'won' the struggle between the rival German cultures and ideologies. The social preconceptions noted above feed a shared perception of eastern Germans as 'second-class citizens' and the negative stereotypes of 'Ossi' (easterner) and 'Wessi' (westerner). Together, these factors suggest the potential for a lasting cultural divide between German communities in the new western and eastern Länder.

The elite-led state identity of the GDR (1949–1989) and the FRG as, 'reference culture'

The two German part-states of the postwar period each sought a distinct identity in fundamental opposition to one another, yet rooted in their common heritage. In the GDR (1949–89), efforts to promote an independent GDR identity were largely state-led and were explored sequentially, through a series of distinct priorities for identification. Anti-fascism was the 'dominant myth' of the GDR's legitimacy until the 1950s, when it was replaced by the 'cult of economic growth' (James, 1990: 175). This was supplemented from the 1980s by a new stress on the GDR as the inheritor of the German cultural tradition.

Both at the level of the state and at the popular level, aspirations in the GDR were in part constructed in reaction to the perceived success of the FRG in creating a successful economy and a legitimate state. Some – particularly western commentators – have argued that the GDR authorities' failure to create an independent East German identity was compounded by the fact that the FRG became the main source of identity for the East German people (for example, Hämäläinen, 1994; Thompson, 1996: 280). Hämäläinen asserts that East and West German intellectuals alike had consistently overestimated the strength of a separate East German identity and popular attachment to the GDR. He maintains not only that an 'all-German' identity developed around western values during the postwar period, but that it acted as one of the catalysts of the peaceful revolution of 1989 (1994: 59, 142). This shared sense of Germanness was demonstrated when the mass protests of late 1989 in the GDR changed their focus from demands for reform under the existing framework of the socialist state ('we are the people') to demands for unification ('we are one people'). He sees the victory of the centre-right grouping aligned with Kohl's CDU/CSU in the Volkskammer election of March 1990 as sufficient evidence of the failure of the GDR to establish a separate socialist identity amongst the East German people (Hämäläinen 1994: 144).

Social and attitudinal trends: differentiation and commonalities

Political sociologists have documented substantial differences in the fundamental values of eastern and western Germans which can be explained by the differential social, economic and political development of the two Germanies between 1949 and 1989. GDR society was defined by the individual's role in the workplace, strictly regulated by command structures. In contrast, FRG society was, by 1989, essentially a postmodern society where social life was defined outside the workplace, primarily in terms of 'leisure'. East Germans still display much lower levels of social trust than west Germans, finding it difficult to trust those outside their immediate family and circle of close friends. They struggle to cope with the conflict that is an inherent part of the competitive work and social environment of the west Germans. Martin and Silvia Greiffenhagen (1993) question whether a shared political culture can be founded on such diverse patterns of social values. Bauer-Kaase finds evidence of continuing social psychological tensions in the relationship between east and west Germans, popularized (and arguably exacerbated) in the media as the 'Ossi'/'Wessi' divide. Her findings show that only 6 per cent of east Germans and 14 per cent of west Germans viewed relations between the two groups as positive. 68 per cent of east Germans blamed the west Germans for the friction between 'Ossis' and 'Wessis' (Bauer-Kaase, 1993, cited in Rose and Page 1996: 5, 23). Research on personal goals and values offers a different perspective. Here are indications that both German societies have been undergoing a radical and remarkably similar process of change from the 1960s onwards; one characterized by a move away from a value-system centred on duty and obedience to one dominated by self-fulfilment. In particular, there are indications of much narrower differences between the values of the younger generations in east and west than there is between the older generations (Klages and Gensicke, 1993: 48–50, 53–5). This would seem to offer more hope of a future common identity, if not imminently.

Eastern identity: the events of 1989 and beyond

With the events of 1989, new forms of eastern identity began to take shape and to be openly expressed. From 'third way' socialism to the popular 'Ossi' identity (see below), the new forms of eastern identity have shared some key characteristics. All have been defined by two contexts which stand in a reciprocal relationship to one another. The first is the shared memory of life under the GDR, dominated by the state Socialist Unity Party (SED). The second is the memory and ongoing experience of the FRG as a reference culture. Two further shared features derive from this dual context. First, the new forms of eastern identity have been largely retrospective in nature, and also reactive rather than proactive. The third way socialism originating with the events of 1989 looked back to the ideals of the marxist revolutionaries for inspiration, comparing these with the failed promise of state socialism in the GDR. Post-unification forms of popular identity look back with some fondness on the 'rediscovered' positive attributes of life in the GDR. Finally, the new forms of eastern identity share a 'grassroots' quality. They express perceived or actual popular conflict with the postwar German regimes, east and west; they question German government values and actions. First and foremost, third way socialism voiced popular discontent with the unresponsive SED regime of the GDR. A secondary focus of the third way movement was the east Germans' perceived ideological conflict with the values of the FRG regime. Reflecting post-unification structural realities, those forms of eastern identity which have developed since 1989/1990 have largely voiced popular discontent with the all-German FRG regime and governments, but as a secondary focus have also reflect the shared experience of the constraints imposed by the former SED regime.

'Third way' socialism

In chronological terms, the first expression of a new, grassroots eastern identity was third way socialism. This was the incipient ideology of the protest and reform movement which shook the SED regime towards the end of 1989. (As such, third way socialism should not be confused with the 'politics of the middle way' currently espoused by the German SPD-Green government coalition and which has sometimes been compared to 'Blairism'.) Third way socialism was limited to a largely intellectual sector of society committed to the reinvention of socialism within the existing state framework of the GDR. It rejected the SED regime, which it saw as 'arrogant' and 'suffocated by incompetence' (Schlesinger, 1998: 100). It hoped instead to win reforms in the GDR which would bring about a 'true' socialist regime, more closely linked to the original communist principles which the GDR had patently failed to realize. As a movement, third way socialism was highly fragmented, and, initially at least, associated with intellectual misfits. Also, it was soon overtaken by the collapse of the GDR and unification through absorption into the FRG. Nevertheless, its legacy can be seen in various expressions of 'easternness' in united Germany. First, the concept of third way socialism remains as a live concern to an intellectual minority. Possibly more significantly, its priorities and characteristics continue to influence the development of the mass popular attitudes in the eastern Länder towards their own community and that of the wider Germany; attitudes which have begun to emerge since unification.

In his account of the emerging third way socialism in 1989, the East German radical Gunther de Bruyn (1990) refers to all of those characteristics noted above as central to new forms of eastern identity. He suggests that the GDR 'socialist' patriotism expressed by the reformers in 1989 was forged in the context of two sets of pressures: the rigid state socialism upheld by the SED and the complacent, inegalitarian FRG. He implies that third way socialism was reactive in nature in that it was forged through the experience of standing up against the state authorities during the events of 1989.

It seems that the activists of the opposition have developed a GDR patriotism that is stronger than the one hitherto prescribed from above. It is composed of pride in that which has been achieved through democratic protest, of insight into what is attainable in the Europe of today, of a vision of social justice and of defiance of the rich, paternalistically inclined relative in the West (to which one also owes thanks), and it doesn't take nationalist feelings seriously, but frequently suspects them of serving as a cover either for chauvinism or for the yearning for prosperity.

(de Bruyn, 1990, translated and reproduced in James and Stone, 1992: 136)

The east German 'identity of contrariness': reaction against western cultural hegemony

Much of the eastern identity now emerging at a popular level is elaborated with respect to specific characteristics of western culture, and is clearly a reaction against the western political, economic and cultural dominance of united Germany. This western dominance is exacerbated by the 'one Germany' myth which pervades the western political elites (Hogwood, forthcoming). It is reflected in the widespread elite assumption that easterners must accept western ways wholesale; they must be resocialized into a western mentality (Klages and Gensicke, 1993: 47). From a western perspective, then, the cultural learning process within united Germany is assumed to be unidirectional. The elites and public of the west do not believe they have anything to learn from the GDR cultural experience – if they so much as consider such a possibility. The east German retreat into a bitter, sulky 'identity of contrariness' (Trotzidentität, Jens Reich) can be seen as a reaction against this western cultural hegemony.

In his book on the problems of adjusting to the western German paradigm, the easterner Klaus Schlesinger's vitriolic comments offer a taste of the 'identity of contrariness'. Schlesinger (1998: 11–13) can't stand hearing the jumped-up monkeys on the talk-shows telling him how he coped with life in the GDR and why it wasn't worth it. He doesn't like the way they (the westerners) are tearing up and re-building half of the former East Berlin. The Alexanderplatz was certainly no grimmer than the Ernst-Reuter-Platz (in the former West Berlin) – so why don't they start over there? He describes the swarms of westerners buying up one plot of eastern land after another, who find it so quaint that there are still tree-lined alleys and storks nesting in the east. Don't they ever ask themselves why these beautiful birds steer clear of the free-est Germany there has ever been like the devil shuns holy water? He looks down on these people with wry condescension: they don't know what they're talking about, after all, and he finds their efforts at social climbing really rather sweet. Worse, for him, are the attitudes of his fellow-easterners who have 'converted' to the new western ways. He has nothing but contempt for people who give the impression they always knew that the former GDR was a complete waste of space, even while they were singing 'little white dove of peace' in the Young Pioneers. They're enough to make him bring up his coffee.

(N)Ostalgia (Ostalgie)

After the initial euphoria of German unification gave way to disillusionment in the GDR, east Germans began to identify 'positive' features of their lost socialist past – they were discovering a GDR identity in retrospect (*nachgeholte Identität*). Regrets for the lost security of life under the SED state have been dubbed 'Ostalgia' (Ostalgie), a play on words depicting a specifically 'eastern' nostalgia. Ostalgia acts as a focus both for the reinvention of the past in an attempt to salvage some collective dignity from unification on western terms, and the formulation of a collective identity for a self-aware community which does not identify fully with its western 'cousins'. Ostalgia is characterized by a somewhat masochistic nostalgia for the 'bad old days' (Merkl, 1995: 5). It is expressed in the social and cultural life of the east. For example, the 'Easty Girls' have become a popular cabaret act. They wear a Spice-Girl-style cut-off version of the Young Pioneer uniform and tour with an Erich Honecker lookalike, performing old Red revolution songs (*The Times Magazine* 15 March 1997). An Ostalgie market has sprung up to meet the social need to reminisce about the past. Tapes and CDs of the familiar socialist patriotic songs for children and young people are widely available. There are books, board games and 'trivial pursuit'-style games which reflect the Ostalgia theme, covering everything from sharp, satirical GDR jokes to the menus served up to visiting dignitaries on state occasions (Kaiser mail order <http://www.mokm.de>).

'Ossi' pride

Another specific expression of reactive popular identity can be found in the easterners' attempt to adapt the negative 'Ossi' stereotype to a positive focus for eastern identity. As presented in the media, the 'Ossi' and 'Wessi' stereotypes are those elaborated by the 'other side' and are essentially negative. The 'Ossi' is seen from the west as lazy, passive, lacking in initiative and drive, sly, secretive and having a scrounging 'welfare mentality'. The 'Wessi' is seen from the east as arrogant, pushy (a product of the 'elbow' society), humourless, selfish and greedy. (For characteristics of the 'Ossi'/'Wessi' stereotypes see, for example, Klages and Gensicke, 1993: 47.) Since unification, easterners have adapted their

'Ossi' tag to reflect those values perceived amongst themselves as both positive and characteristic of easterners. In contrast, west Germans tend to reject the 'Wessi' stereotype out of hand. As the dominant, self-referential culture, they have no need to take account of how they are viewed from the east, and therefore no need to elaborate a positive version of the 'Wessi' stereotype. Ironically, many of the features contributing to the positive or ideal-type of the 'Ossi' appear to be formulated with direct reference to perceived negative attributes of the cultural stereotype of the 'Wessi'. The positive ideal of the 'Ossi' is easy-going (compared to the pushy westerner); with a sharp sense of humour (unlike the westerner) honed through years of coping with life under the SED regime; and a strong sense of community (whereas westerners are selfish and greedy). This choice of attributes suggests that the emerging eastern identity is not primarily self-referential, but depends for its formulation on western standards and influences.

This is not to suggest that the western role model can provide a ready-made identity for easterners, negative or otherwise. The relationship of easterners to their western 'mentors' is a complex one. Easterners admire and aspire to many aspects of the western model. As Richter notes, one of the reasons for the failure of the reform movements to translate into mass parties capable of representing eastern interests within united Germany was their blanket rejection of western values. In particular, the reform movements' disdain for 'consumerism' and the West German 'elbow society' did not appeal to a GDR public who wanted a better material standard of living and whose standards were measured against the achievements of the FRG (Richter, 1994: 116–18). At the same time, the grudging expression of that admiration, the rather childish 'identity of contrariness', and the willing identification with their own positive version of the 'Ossi' stereotype, all reveal that easterners feel a need to pursue an identity separate from the western Germans.

Nowhere is this ambivalence more evident than in the eastern Germans' attitude towards consumerism. For eastern Germans, globalizing forces promoting materialist and postmodernist cultural developments throughout the postwar period had largely been mediated through the western German 'reference culture'. West Germany had been the eastern Germans' shop window to western values and developments, allowing a clear view, but without the chance for direct participation. Since unification, globalizing forces have had a far more direct influence on eastern Germans. Interestingly though, easterners continue to perceive globalizing forces through the traditional western German 'filter', and have reacted ambivalently to them. Staab (1997) describes how,

following unification, the sudden mass access to western-style consumption patterns in the former GDR was in pointed contrast to the
easterners' prior experience of limited supplies and suppressed consumer demands. On one hand, the easterners internalized consumerism
by approximating the levels of consumption found in the west. On the
other hand, they reacted by politicizing consumerism. Consequently,
patterns of consumption in the former GDR between 1989 and 1991
graphically demonstrate the extraordinary U-turn described in the
easterners' collective political identity during this period. In the
euphoria which followed unification, eastern consumers at first abandoned eastern products for western brands, irrespective of price or quality. Prompted by a combination of patriotism and consumer naivety,
such uncalculating behaviour attracted the unscrupulous, and the easterners were often exploited. Very soon, though, eastern Germans began
to assert their newly emerging, post-unification identity by changing
over to buying eastern goods in a way which reflected both 'Ostalgia'
and defiance against the western-led transformation of their lives.
Between December 1990 and December 1991, the proportion of eastern
households surveyed preferring eastern products over western had risen
from half to almost three-quarters. Easterners began to associate particular eastern products with romanticised past 'peaceful times' (*Friedens-
zeiten*), which had been more stable, secure and friendly than the new
turbulent times (Staab, 1997: 139–49). Valued for its apolitical associations with childhood and security, the eastern German character displayed at pedestrian crossings (the *Ampelmännchen*, the equivalent of
the British 'little green man') has been marketed in various guises as a
symbol of eastern identity (Duckenfield and Calhoun, 1997: 54–5, 67).
Market strategists have responded to the emergence of the ambivalent
eastern market culture by retaining the brand names of the socialist
period, but by changing the design, quality or presentation of their
products (Staab, 1997: 146).

Mapping the new eastern identity

At this stage of the consolidation of the new Germany, it is not possible
to arrive at a definitive conclusion as to whether the new eastern identity will prove to be merely transitional, or will become a lasting German
sub-culture. It is possible that this is a temporary phase of adjustment
to the wholesale westernization of the GDR polity in a very short space
of time. Alternatively, the east Germans might become entrenched as
a self-aware minority comparable to those found in the territorially

established western European countries, such as the Basques in Spain, or the Scots in the United Kingdom. A first attempt to map some of the characteristics and limitations of the new eastern identity suggests that, if current conditions prevail, an east–west cultural divide does have the potential to become entrenched.

First, the structurally entrenched minority position of the east Germans within united Germany, resulting from the 'transfer' paradigm of the unification process, suggests the maintenance of perceptions of east Germans as 'second-class citizens'. These structural realities are enhanced by a further pattern of 'attitudinal transfer' to unified Germany of a sense of western superiority, fostered during the Cold War years.

Turning to the nature and extent of the new eastern identity, many questions remain unanswerable to date. One feature is certain: the new eastern identity can be defined in territorial terms. It is territorially inclusive – all east Germans are 'in', irrespective of further structural or attitudinal divisions – and thereby exclusive, in that it admits no west Germans. Is the territory of the eastern Länder universally perceived from within as a self-contained territorial community, or is the perception of a separate eastern identity restricted to a particular sector of society? Some western commentators, particularly those of the centre-right, argue that 'Ostalgia' is a phenomenon which can be restricted to the 'losers' of unification and can therefore be expected to diminish as eastern society adjusts to western norms.

Is the new eastern identity stagnant, or does it show potential for development? Within its territorially defined framework, we have demonstrated the new eastern identity to be largely reactive and retrospective. Even the 'Ossi pride' element of eastern identity, which is linked to the current experience of life in post-unification Germany, is retrospective in that it is housed in cultural stereotypes which have their origin in the postwar structures of divided Germany. In itself, the backward-looking orientation of contemporary eastern identity need not imply the lack of potential for development. Indeed, contemporary European societies all depend to a certain extent on historical 'myths' which have transcended their original context to act as an integrative force for social and national identity (Hobsbawm and Ranger, 1983). Nevertheless, the fact that so much of the new eastern identity depends on the memory of shared experiences within the social structures of divided Germany, together with the convergence of social attitudes particularly amongst younger people in east and west, suggests that 'Ostalgic' myth-making might be limited to the postwar generations.

If, on the other hand, the structural marginalization of east German interests is exacerbated through continuing social and economic inequalities, the 'Ostalgic' impetus might pass on to the post-unification generation of east Germans, and form the basis of a lasting cultural myth.

The chances of such a development taking root depend in part on the successful political channelling of perceived separate eastern interests. Currently, only the Party of Democratic Socialism (PDS) appears capable of articulating (or, as some western commentators claim, constructing) and channelling specifically eastern interests within unified Germany. However, this potential is compromised by its strategic aims as a political party: it has ambitions to act not only as the mouthpiece of eastern interests, but also to represent a radical left alternative within the federal party system. The PDS has had difficulty in asserting this dual profile, and may in future be forced to choose between these aims, possibly at the expense of the party's ability effectively to channel regional interests (Krisch, 1996). At least in terms of popular support, the PDS can currently be considered an 'eastern' party. Both membership and electoral support derive almost entirely from the eastern Länder. The nature of this support would appear to substantiate the notion that 'Ostalgia' is a hallmark of the losers of unification, but also suggests that it has a wider *potential* applicability. The typical eastern PDS member is over 50 and a former SED member, and thereby typical of those favoured by the former GDR regime but left behind in the new Germany. At the same time, the typical PDS voter is younger (the strongest support for the party comes from those aged between 25 and 34) and in no sense a 'loser' in the new Germany. Falter and Klein (1994: 34) see the typical PDS supporter as a well-educated individual with a relatively positive view of the GDR; one who continues to hold some core values of socialism and who feels socially alienated from western German society and politics. They conclude that the typical PDS voter combines a mixture of 'ideology, nostalgia and protest' (cited in Krisch, 1996: 122–3). Given 'conducive' circumstances of continuing inequalities between the life chances of easterners and westerners, these findings suggest a potential source of political activism which might be mobilized by the PDS.

While, currently, easterners appear to be universally aware of their 'apartness' within unified Germany, it is unclear to what extent this is a transitional phenomenon, an expression of the social dislocation experienced with the rapid unification process. The convergence of personal aims and values amongst the young suggests that there is potential for inter-community integration in united Germany, but that this outcome is far from certain. The circumstances described above show considerable potential for the development of a lasting regional cleavage in German politics.[3] Factors which might promote the entrenchment of dislocation effects include the negation of community implicit in the stance adopted towards eastern interests by the dominant western elites. Refusing to recognize separate and conflicting regional interests within Germany, they subscribe instead to the state myth of 'one Germany'. The channelling of regional interests in the political system hinges on the PDS and the future resolution of its profile as a party of the 'left' and/or 'east'.

Notes

1 Scott Gissendanner (1996) gives a succinct account of the controversy surrounding the mode of unification in the German language literature.
2 Germany's archaic Citizenship Law (1913) distinguishes three categories of people: citizens, foreigners, and 'ethnic' or 'status' Germans. Ethnic Germans are people of German descent living outside the territorial boundaries of the FRG and holding the rights of citizenship in another country. In law, they are considered Germans and have automatic right of entry to and citizenship of the FRG (Kanstroom, 1993: 170–8). Prior to unification, east Germans entering the FRG comprised a subcategory of 'ethnic' German. In law, that category no longer exists, but it is argued here that there are in practice widespread perceptions of difference between west Germans and east Germans. In this way, there is currently a multi-German identity consisting of west Germans, east Germans and varieties of ethnic Germans, all of which can be represented as communities with distinct cultural values.
3 A regional cleavage, as defined by Lipset and Rokkan (1967), exists where: (i) society is characterized by lasting and fundamentally conflicting interests in different parts of the country; (ii) the different regional groups are conscious of their collective identity in regional terms; and (iii) regional identities are expressed organizationally: that is, by political parties which identify themselves primarily with these regional interests, rather than alternative affinities such as class or religious interests.

5
'You and Me Against the World': Christian Fundamentalists and White Poverty in the USA

Julie F. Scott

Introduction: fundamentalist religion and its revival

> The Fundamentalists who have emerged in the public arena...are a group with a distinct way of living and believing that sets them apart from both the modern secularized world and other Christians.
>
> (Ammerman, 1993: 3)

One of the most surprising trends in postwar religion, particularly in the West, has been the growth in fundamentalism in nearly all of the world religions, most notably in Islam and Christianity. The emergence of a revitalized and often radicalized fundamentalism as a key political and social force caught most sociologists of religion napping. As Ammerman (1993: 2), Marsden (1983: 150) and Marty and Appleby (1991: vii) all note, fundamentalism did not fit the overly neat secularization model which has dominated sociological analyses of religion for nearly a century. Theoretical approaches within the secularization thesis had promoted the view that institutional 'conventional' religion (Wolffe, 1993: 309–10) was increasingly marginalized from its traditional bases of political, social and moral authority. What religiosity remained among populations was 'privatized' and so idiosyncratic that it bore no 'social significance' (Wallis and Bruce, 1992; Wilson, 1966). Secularization, along with shifts toward modernization, rationalization, and societalization (see Wallis and Bruce, 1992), have all supposedly moved religion in this direction. Leading secularization theorists, such as Wilson (1966), did anticipate modest fundamentalist growth as a consequence of secularization: they suggested that the fundamentalist would seek refuge from the unbearable forces of modernity within a 'back to basics' meaning system. However, any upsurge in fundamentalism would be retreatist and regressive, not radical and revolutionary.

When Islamic fundamentalism created and energized popular revolutions across the Middle East from the 1950s onwards, political and social analysts were left with an inadequate sociological interpretative framework. The ultimate success of many of these movements demonstrated that these had not been merely retreatist nor reactionary. The politicization of Christian fundamentalists in the USA began in the late 1960s. It reached its peak in the 1980s, when Presidents Reagan and Bush were elected partly through the wealth and political clout of the fundamentalist right-wing coalitions (Ammerman, 1993; Johnson and Tamney, 1982; Hunter, 1988). By the late 1970s sociological interpretations of fundamentalism had to be, through necessity, revisited. The result has been a growth in studies of fundamentalism, particularly Islamic and Christian. One example is the five-volume Chicago Fundamentalism Project (Marty and Appleby, 1991–95). The Chicago Project was created with the explicit aim of placing the various types of fundamentalism(s) in their social, economic, cultural and political context(s) in order to present a more dynamic model of fundamentalism(s). Typical of most contemporary work on fundamentalism is a stress on such contextualizing analyses, in contrast to the overwhelmingly historical studies of the past (Wuthnow and Lawson, 1994: 18). If we begin to place fundamentalist activity back into its context we can locate within it powerful critiques of modernity and of the process of globalization. Indeed, rather than retreating from the modern, fundamentalists are actively engaging with it.

What is fundamentalism?

Fundamentalism, like so many labels used within the social sciences, is not without its problems. Those we label 'fundamentalist' typically reject the term (Ammerman, 1993). Some disciplines, most notably Theology and Sociology, disagree over exact definitions (Barr, 1977; Hunter, 1982). Many theorists reject the negative connotations of the word (Munson, 1995), while others stress the need to distinguish between different types of fundamentalism (Munson, 1995; Gupta, 1993). However, this chapter adopts the approach of Marty and Appleby (1991: viii) in viewing fundamentalism as a 'serviceable' and meaningful label to denote a wide variety of movements which do share what Marty and Appleby (1991: ix–xii) call 'family resemblances'. These criteria denote fundamentalism as the active and powerful meaning system that it is – thus breaking away from the overwhelmingly passive model of the fundamentalist utilized within the secularization thesis.

What any belief system ultimately does is to offer a framework for understanding and explaining the world, giving meaning to experience. Worldview is the word used to denote the 'comprehensive meaning systems', found in most religions, which locate experience within a unified system of explanation (Berger and Luckmann, 1966). The fundamentalist worldview has at its core agency and action. The two key components of this worldview are the belief that fundamentalists are 'chosen' by God and that there is a clear threat to the foundations of their worldview. These two elements mobilize fundamentalist communities against specific targets for specific reasons: they always know who they are fighting against and for what they are fighting. This struggle is given divine agency through their belief in being 'chosen': theirs is always a holy war. The final element of this worldview is community. Fundamentalism stresses community as a source of strength, an expression of solidarity and a resource for use. Each variety of fundamentalism has its own expressions of this worldview and unique aims. However, as will be discussed later the key elements of this worldview provide a resource for individuals in a variety of cultural contexts.

The Protestant fundamentalist worldview: a Missouri case study

Although we can view fundamentalists across the world as members of the same extended family, it is easier to view the fundamentalist worldview through the exploration of a specific 'variety'. This chapter focuses on Protestant fundamentalism in the USA and will be drawing on the author's own field research among a small community of apocalyptic Protestant fundamentalists: the God's Way[1] community. God's Way is located in the remote Ozarks region of Missouri. The Protestant fundamentalist worldview shares commonalties with other forms of fundamentalism, but also has some key differences. The worldview includes the following key elements (see Barr, 1977; Ammerman, 1993 for further details on Protestant fundamentalism):

- A sense of having a 'chosen' status. As has been previously noted, all fundamentalists believe themselves to be 'chosen' by God and this belief is at the core of their worldview. God 'calls' fundamentalists to him and maintains a special relationship with them. God's Way was founded by its original leader, Abraham Zion, following a series of divine revelations in which God 'called' Abraham to found the present-day community. Fundamentalists can always recount incidents where God has appeared to them or has sent a 'sign'. God's Way's history (they were founded in 1927) is filled with accounts of such messages and signs from God. The community's belief in its unique relationship with God informs and frames their daily lives and gives meaning and significance to every activity, however mundane. Being 'chosen' separates them from the rest of the world (with whom they are in opposition) whose members are termed the 'fallen'. 'Chosenness' justifies and gives shape to every other aspect of their worldview.

- Separation and opposition toward the rest of the world. Protestant groups distinguish between the 'true' believers and the rest of the world on the basis of 'chosen-ness'. God's Way viewed all non-members as 'fallen' – even those who belonged to other fundamentalist or evangelical churches in their area. This distinction between 'chosen' and 'fallen' leads most Protestant fundamentalist communities to maintain strong boundaries between themselves and the 'outside'. These boundaries can be physical (such as living in remote areas), social (only working/socializing/marrying/schooling and so on within the community) and/or mental (such as an insistence on home schooling, controlling media consumption within the community). Often these boundaries are expressed in terms of a purity/pollution dichotomy and that separation keeps them free from 'contamination' from the 'fallen'. Opposition to the outside world is partly maintained through God's Way's physical isolation from its neighbours. God's Way's infrequent trips away from the community's ranch were marked by specific cleansing rituals. Prayers were said on departure from and return to the ranch. Members would take numerous breaks during work away from the ranch to drink water from their own well, which they would bring with them in a flask. This was seen as a measure to maintain purity in a polluting environment. The members feared being away from the community for too long in case it made them less righteous.

This separation from the world also produces opposition to the world: the 'fallen' are by their lack of 'chosen-ness' not only physically polluting but also ideologically polluting. This leads Protestant fundamentalists to display high levels of discrimination against specific 'outsider' groups who are perceived to be threatening the values of their way of life. Discrimination is built-in to the fundamentalist worldview of 'chosen-ness' and separation from the world. This has been noted by McFarland (1989) and Kirkpatrick (1993) who found a correlation between fundamentalism and a general tendency to discriminate against non-fundamentalists which also involved specific targeting of groups (such as homosexuals) who directly threaten their belief system. God's Way view the outside world as the 'other' who have 'fallen'. However, they differentiated between specific groups. They were particularly anti-Semitic: they saw Jews as controlling and 'contaminating' government, finance and food supplies. They were anti-Catholic: they blamed the Catholic Church for editing and rewriting God's words (the Bible). Similarly, they blamed African-Americans for most contemporary social ills, such as drug abuse and sexual promiscuity.

- Living the religious life. Fundamentalists do not separate their religious beliefs from their everyday lives: faith is lived. This is due to their 'chosen' status. God's Way's members stressed the necessity of 'living correctly' because 'God is watching'. It was the responsibility of the 'chosen' to maintain a high standard in daily life. Such high standards involved everything from following the correct diet to conducting daily chores with a 'happy heart'. At the centre of living correctly is the maintenance of strong moral codes for living. God's Way, in common with most fundamentalists, prohibited premarital sex, contraception, swearing, and the use of tobacco, alcohol and coffee, among other things.

- Belief in the unerring nature of the Bible. The Bible is seen by Protestant fundamentalists to be the absolute true word of God. Groups, such as God's Way, use scripture to guide and plan their lives to an extreme degree (Ammerman, 1993).

- The inability to compromise in the face of opposition. A combination of believing themselves to be 'chosen' and the holding of the Bible to be the actual word of God means that Protestant fundamentalists afford no room for compromise in their views. For them the rest of the world is wrong and will be punished. God's Way's members typically refused to discuss religious matters as the act of debate assumed that there was something to be debated or questioned.

- Protestant Fundamentalists await the Second Coming of Christ. Protestant fundamentalists maintain a strong conviction that Christ will return to Earth either close to or after the year 2000. They are also typically apocalyptic, believing that this return will prompt the end of things on Earth as they are now. Scripture is interpreted to give clues to the end-time, as are a variety of 'signs'. God's Way, like other groups, keep a record of 'markers' of the approaching tribulation and use even the most mundane of events (such as a thunderstorm) as 'signs'. The members anticipate a Day of Judgement in which they will inherit the world while the 'fallen' shall die in a divine fire.

- Radical in sense of having an agenda for sociopolitical change. Fundamentalists always have a plan of action for change which is linked to a future time when their 'chosen' status will allow them to inherit the world. These activities are justified as 'right' because they are 'chosen' and their beliefs are 'true'. Plans for change are given clear shape by typically identifying the causes of current social ills. God's Way, being an apocalyptic group, await the end of time while going about their daily lives. They look for markers of the end, such as rising crime figures or reports of state corruption. God's Way, unlike other groups, show no desire to engage with the secular political arena and lobby for social reform, but they engage in small 'resistances', such as, only consuming food from their own land and refusing to be linked to local electricity and water networks. Less apocalyptic and isolated groups engage more directly with the secular through specific political lobbying and self-action, including founding home schools, self-help networks and so forth.

American Protestant fundamentalism, modernity and globalization

There are a number of good reasons for looking specifically at Protestant fundamentalism in the USA. Firstly, it is the most widely researched Christian variety. Secondly, it is the most politicized of the Christian fundamentalisms. Thirdly, Protestant fundamentalism historically originated and developed in the USA in response to the early consequences of modernization, a process which has become coterminous in recent decades with globalization. Lastly, there is already ample evidence that the effects of globalization are beginning to affect the lives of large sections of the American population. This is particularly noticeable when looking at rural populations in the USA which for so long have been shielded from urban problems but are now experiencing rising levels of poverty, unemployment and violent crime.

We can locate three key stages of Protestant fundamentalist development. Each stage coincides with and is linked to economic, political and cultural changes in the USA. These stages are: emergence during the early modernization period; growth in the postwar era; and consolidation in the period of globalization. More in-depth reviews of the history of Protestant fundamentalism in the USA can be found in Ahlstrom (1975), Dollar (1973), Marsden (1980) and Noll (1992).

Emergence

The seeds of Protestant fundamentalism were sown at the birth of the USA. The new nation was built upon the Enlightenment and modernist principles of its founders. This made the USA not only the first truly 'modern' nation but also one which would stand apart from the rest as 'special' (Parrington, 1964). The new republic was a white Protestant one demographically and in character for most of its first century: a 'Protestant empire' (Ahlstrom, 1975: I: 165). The American national polity's messianic view of itself as a 'chosen' country (Ahlstrom, 1975: I: 182; Bellah, 1967) formed part of this Protestant hegemony and white Protestants saw themselves as being doubly 'chosen' through their religion and their American identity: they were keepers of this national destiny. Today Protestant fundamentalist militias justify bomb attacks on government buildings through patriotic duty: their argument is that the state itself is failing the USA and so true patriots need to rise against it. Most mainstream fundamentalists hold similar if less militant sentiments (see McFarland, 1989; Kirkpatrick, 1993). However, no one denomination dominated this era due to a mobile immigrant population, freedom of religious expression and a statutory separation of religion and state. This afforded an environment for Protestantism to be eclectic and revivalist, evangelical and charismatic (Noll, 1992).

During the post-Civil War years the USA underwent a rapid process of modernization involving industrialization, urbanization and technological progress. At the same time there occurred mass immigration from Europe, bringing large numbers of people – mainly Catholics and Jews – from Eastern Europe and the Mediterranean. Modernization and this mass influx of immigrants began to dramatically alter the social and cultural environment of the USA. Protestant fundamentalism emerged at this time, developing from the evangelical, revivalist strand of Protestantism which had been growing steadily throughout the nineteenth century (Cole, 1931). By the 1880s a distinct coalition of conservative evangelical groups had formed. They initially rallied against Liberal Theology and particularly Biblical Criticism that challenged the infallibility of scripture. Liberal Theology had been the theological response to Darwinism and empiricism (Marsden, 1980; Noll, 1992). However, from a very early stage this movement also incorporated a stress on 'traditional' values and a desire to reassert a specific (read white,

Protestant) American identity in the face of emerging cultural and moral plurality. This emerging social critique can be indicated by the fact that early fundamentalism was exclusively based in the north eastern states, where social changes had had the most impact: the southern states and west had yet to be radically affected. The name fundamentalist was adopted from the series of pamphlets edited by A.C. Dixon between 1910 and 1915, entitled 'The Fundamentals' (Noll, 1992; Marsden, 1980). However, despite a series of moral and educational campaigns and some infamous courtroom battles over the teaching of evolution, the conservative coalitions failed to make much impact in the interwar years (Marsden, 1984). By the 1930s the lack of unity within the coalition and its insignificant public successes saw a move away from political action. In 1941 the shaky conservative coalition split into two sections, with evangelical and conservative members forming the National Association of Evangelicals while the fundamentalists formed the American Council of Churches (Marsden, 1984). This split was caused by irreconcilable differences in attitude towards the secular world, and by the emphasis on certain doctrinal tenets (Ammerman, 1993: 4–6). This early movement failed due to an overemphasis on theological matters, a lack of unity and clear political strategy, and it also failed to incorporate a wider political and social consensus.

Growth

Fundamentalists (and to a lesser extent evangelicals) became politicized during the 1960s and early 1970s. This move into the political arena was provoked by the key social changes of that period driven by a postwar consumer boom and a counter-cultural 'revolution'. Giddens (1991) characterizes this period as one of late modernity whereby society, driven by increased phenomena such as rationalization, societalization and pluralization (see Berger, 1967; Wallis and Bruce, 1992), embraces a consumer culture dominated by individualism. Lifestyle choices and concerns dominate within a consumer-led society and give rise to identity politics. Berger and Luckmann (1966) also emphasize the individualism of this era accounting for the postwar alteration in peoples' views of their social world and their relationship towards it through the process of privatization. Berger characterized this process as one in which individuals lose faith and trust in the state and public institutions, and instead they disengage from them. Worldviews become individualized and the individual seeks inner resources to negotiate society: meaning systems become highly idiosyncratic. This process can be negative giving rise to what Berger et al. (1973) characterize as the 'homeless' mind which exists in a seemingly perplexing world of cultural, social, and moral plurality: anything goes and everything seems to work (Berger et al., 1973; Foules, 1989).

If key structural changes created an environment for the growth of a new and more radical fundamentalism, it became politicized through specific sociocultural or 'lifestyle' issues (Johnson and Tamney, 1984). The early period of fundamentalism (pre-1950s) was centred around theological issues in the main. The postwar era saw fundamentalists entering the political arena when social reforms (prompted by rapid changes in postwar society) such as the Equal Rights Amendments (ERA), the legalization of abortion, increasing gay rights, and divorce reforms, began to be perceived as direct threats to the fundamentalist way of life. However, this does not fully explain the continued growth or energy of fundamentalists during this period or, indeed, later. Fundamentalists are notorious for their isolation and separation from the world and it would have been easier for them to retreat further from the world at this time. For example, God's Way community, like similar rural fundamentalist groups, seeks avoidance, where practicable, of the secular world and maintains strength and purpose through apocalypticism. Instead this growth in fundamentalism should be viewed as the beginning of a wide-ranging critique of social changes. Fundamentalism's opposition to the ERA or increased gay rights is not just about the fact that their worldview does not countenance such 'rights'. Fundamentalists of this period, through focusing on social (rather than political or economic) issues, can be seen as offering a critique for this shift toward social isolation and dislocation. Social and moral reforms such as abortion legalisation shifts moral obligations and rights from God and the collective to the individual (see Luker, 1984) – a trend fundamentalists see as dangerous both for belief but also for communal unity. Fundamentalism, with its emphasis on national identity, community, absolute morality, and coherence, provides a challenge to this social and mental 'homelessness' and also an alternative approach for living. This campaign to reassert 'traditional' values is also given agency through the fundamentalist belief in themselves as keepers of the 'soul' of America. God's Way community, like other fundamentalist groups, gauge the decline of the USA through increasing social reforms (like abortion, divorce and civil rights bills) which they see as promoting moral plurality and cultural heterogeneity.

By the 1970s what had been small localized lobbying groups had begun to form into larger coalitions of mutual interests and aims (Johnson and Tamney, 1984; Wald et al. 1989; Himmelstein, 1983).

Unlike the campaigns of the 1920s these groups were highly effective in utilizing modern media (particularly television) to promote their cause(s) (see Marty and Appleby, 1993a). They were also adept at fund raising and political lobbying (Johnson and Tamney, 1982; Liebman, 1983). Key groups included Jerry Falwell's 'Moral Majority', The Religious Roundtable, the American Coalition for Traditional Values, and the New Christian Right. Fundamentalists had used 'lifestyle' issues to create political lobbying groups which went beyond fundamentalist churches to embrace evangelicals and conservatives. Many of these coalitions had support from outside Protestantism striking a chord with conservative Catholics and Jews (Kellstedt et al., 1994; Tamney and Johnson, 1988).

Consolidation

The late 1970s can be seen as the period when globalization really began to accelerate. It is also the period of the greatest level of fundamentalist activity in politics, a time when America began to feel the effects of globalization in its own economic and political structures. Fundamentalists could be seen as among the first to challenge the validity of this global shift and its later hegemony.

Globalization is a contested term but it can be taken in its broadest sense to refer to the seemingly unstoppable and accelerating process whereby the world becomes increasingly interlinked and interdependent through convergence of its economic, cultural and political systems (Hall, 1992; Turner, 1991). This is facilitated by electronic media. The nation-state is subsumed within this network of global links and is to some extent controlled by supranational forces. Globalization is perceived to represent the advance of western (effectively American) 'culture' in a move towards a uniform global culture and polity. This shift toward uniformity and global decision-making results, increasingly, in the socio-economic and political marginalization of a large number of communities. However, this process can also give rise to greater cultural plurality and fusion, producing new identities at a local level (Albrow, 1996). This process of globalization has prompted wider fundamentalist activity on a number of fronts and fundamentalist reaction to globalization has been given a sense of urgency as its effects are interpreted against a millennialist framework. For example, God's Way were preoccupied with reading urban crime reports and accounts of urban decay which they read as 'signs' of the coming apocalypse. Similarly, other fundamentalist groups have taken the extension of the European Union and the signing of international trade agreements as apocalyptic portents (Boyer, 1992). Fundamentalists' critical discourse locates contemporary social malaise on two fronts, both increased by globalization: the domination of consumerism and increasing pluralization.

The effects of Reaganomics on the urban environment have been well documented, it left a legacy of urban poverty, crime, drug abuse, and infrastructural decline. However, less attention has been paid to rural depression in the 1980s, when federal aid to agriculture was severely reduced, leading to the continuing decline in mid-western communities. While global economics has brought increased prosperity to the west and east coasts the heartland of the south and mid-west have become increasingly isolated and marginalized. This has been exacerbated by changes in demographics and economic distribution which have led to the west and east coasts dominating politics – for example, President Clinton relied on the powerful west coast vote to be elected, rather than the traditional democratic southern vote. Globalization has created an ever-increasing divide between successful Americans who have prospered under new global trade and political agreements and increasingly marginalized populations who lack economic or political significance. Undoubtedly fundamentalism has grown during this period but we cannot see this as a retreatist step by disaffected individuals. Rather we should see it as an empowering one in which individuals seek out a critique of contemporary economics and politics which are driven by consumerist values. God's Way, for example, were only too aware of the fact that the local farmers who hired them as casual labour could cut wages when and if they liked. They did not blame the farmers, but were able to add this to their wider critique of central government. The community was also against using the local discount stores selling cheap imported food and clothing supplies that undermined American jobs. Fundamentalists are also critical of the cultural 'emptiness' promoted by consumerism which values cheapness over workmanship. God's Way would only buy American products as they deemed these to be of better quality, even if they were more expensive. The community also stressed the value of learning skills and of hard manual labour against automation and increased productivity. Fundamentalists in general see consumerism as promoting a cultural vacuum which helps to create social problems (Ammerman, 1993).

Fundamentalists oppose social pluralization that creates and privileges heterogeneity, culture fusion, moral plurality, and identity politics. This shift towards pluralization is interpreted as depriving many Americans of a political voice because political campaigns focus more and more on key interest groups and specific ethnic populations. The God's Way community was only too aware of its lack of political significance in the face of the powerful coastal vote, deciding after much deliberation that its members should vote in the 1992 presidential election. This was not because it would make a difference, but because it was their 'patriotic' duty. Fundamentalist campaigners also incorporated critiques of drug abuse, unemployment, crime, divorce rates, and other social issues, within their wider political discourses (see Ammerman, 1993; Johnson and Tamney, 1984; Wald, 1989; and Himmelstein, 1983). At the heart of this opposition to pluralization is a sense of fighting for America. Although fundamentalists criticize cheap imports, the creation of global trade agreements, and the expansion of organizations such as NATO and the EU, they are more interested and focused upon the state of America itself. Fundamentalists stress being 'true Americans' (Aho, 1990) and again offer a challenge to the state which they see as betraying the values of the USA's founders. Changes to the Constitution, such as gun reform or the ERA are not just seen as social reforms but challenges to the 'chosen' status of the nation. God's Way members referred to such social reforms as 'meddling' and viewed them as destructive to the mission of America.

While Presidents Reagan and Bush acknowledged the power of the Christian Right (including fundamentalists) and their support (financial and political) to their campaigns, many (Kivisto, 1994; Bruce, 1990; Smith, 1992) have criticized the overemphasis, placed by analysts, on the role of fundamentalist groups in electing and influencing both the Reagan and Bush administrations: they suggest that no key concessions were made to fundamentalists. However, it is possible to view the campaign as successful in two ways. Firstly, as Jerry Falwell has acknowledged, conservative consciousness has been raised (Ammerman, 1991). Conservatives, including fundamentalists, are more politicized and are now more adept at campaigning and lobbying. Secondly, key fundamentalist concerns surrounding the family and morality have been placed within the political discourse of mainstream American politics for the past twenty years: a reality that created certain problems for President Clinton. The failure to produce wide-reaching change can be explained partly through the overemphasis on one of two issues (say abortion or school prayer) rather than on a more sweeping political agenda. Fundamentalists did and do criticize economic policies, but they fail to do this in a coherent agenda, preferring to emphasize social and moral issues to their cost (Atwood, 1990). A lack of political success can also be attributed to the notorious in-fighting among fundamentalists (see Ammerman, 1990). Every fundamentalist group sees itself as uniquely 'chosen' as opposed to all other groups, therefore each group finds it hard to work together even towards a common goal. Protestant fundamentalism is now more inward looking and self-preoccupied: a review of webpages run by fundamentalists reveals a re-emphasis on specific issues relating to their own communities with advice on how to effect communal change rather than wider social change. This shift can be attributed partly to fundamentalists becoming more millennialist as we approached 2000 and partly due to the failure of the 1980s to provoke real political change. If we review fundamentalists' political activity of the 1980s, although it did tend to focus on key issues, campaigns also expressed a critique of the pluralism and consumerism of contemporary society. The blame for America's perceived decline was blamed upon such consumerist and pluralistic values. Thus, fundamentalism offers an explanation of social problems but also provides a solution.

Protestant fundamentalist population profile

Due to problems of definition, it is hard to fully chart the size and dimensions of contemporary Protestant fundamentalism in the USA. The Gallup data from the 1980s (Gallup 1981, 1983 and 1989) suggests that at least 40 per cent of Americans adhere to Biblical literalism and creationism. As these two traits are fundamentalist tenets it can be presumed that there is a large section of the American population who exhibit fundamentalist tendencies or sympathies. Fundamentalism has always been portrayed as white, blue-collar, rural and southern (see Hunter, 1983; Ammerman, 1993: 31). This stereotype has been promulgated for two reasons: firstly, it fits the 'fundamentalism as retreat from modernity' theorizing endemic within the secularization thesis and, secondly, statistical data has skewed the demographic profiles (Hunter, 1983). Thus, the large southern population of fundamentalists skews the picture toward the south and away from other regions which also have substantial fundamentalist populations. More careful reading of the data, shows that fundamentalism is found throughout the USA, albeit particularly strongly in the south, mid-west and the north-east. There is no definitive fundamentalist profile in the sense that each fundamentalist population reflects the demographics of the area in which it is located. The southern and mid-western populations are predominately rural, have lower levels of educational attainment and are blue-collar. Fundamentalists in these regions share the same profile. Likewise north-eastern fundamentalism is urban (particularly suburban), often college-educated, and middle-class, reflecting the wider population's profile. It is important to remember that the geographic and socio-economic dimensions of the various fundamentalist communities are closely tied to the aims and motivations of particular fundamentalists.

The dynamic nature of fundamentalism is also marked by its age and gender profiles. Fundamentalism recruits across the age ranges and equally between the genders (Ammerman, 1993: 25–39). This is markedly different from the trend in mainstream, conventional Protestant church populations which are female-dominated and ageing. The final important marker of American Protestant fundamentalism is its ethnic dimensions. It is overwhelmingly white. Since its inception fundamentalism has maintained a discourse of racial identity, with one of its aims being to challenge the perceived threat from non-Anglo-Saxon-Protestant communities (McFarland, 1989; Kirkpatrick, 1993). That fundamentalists tend to evince such high levels of prejudice toward specific communities is to be expected, given the oppositional quality of their worldview. We can see then that the fundamentalist population is a dynamic and constantly evolving one.

Fundamentalism as resistance

Fundamentalism has proven to be a successful source of resistance against the forces of globalization for many of those communities in the front line of sociocultural change. Islamic fundamentalism in the Middle East has allowed for the development of strong national identities in the face of external economic and political forces (see Arjomand, 1989; Ayubi, 1983; Turner, 1994). Christian fundamentalism has grown in eastern Europe since the fall of communism brought an uneven and unequal move towards capitalism. Fundamentalism is a worldview which has the potential to not only shelter individuals and communities buffeted by social change but also to empower those communities and give them a renewed sociopolitical agenda with which to resist those forces which threaten their way of life. Fundamentalism provides resistance in two ways: firstly, by offering converts a highly developed critique of contemporary social ills, and secondly, its worldview provides a number of ways to resist social malaise and cope with change.

Since its birth in the late nineteenth century fundamentalism has provided a challenge to modernization and an often effective critique of it. The fundamentalist worldview offers an explanation of what is going wrong in a specific society or even further afield.

Its strong explanatory mechanism offers, in a classic Weberian sense, a theodicy for suffering and misfortune (Gerth and Mills, 1991: 267–77). The individual can draw solace from this and can allow this discourse to express his/her own frustrations. However, what makes fundamentalism so potent is that it is not just about criticism but also offers the potential for communal and individual agency in the face of wider social change(s) through a powerful set of resistance strategies:

- The belief that socially isolated individuals can find a greater divine destiny and role for themselves is extremely empowering in itself. God's Way consist of only 35 people living on an Ozark in the middle of southern Missouri, yet their belief in their divine selection drives them onwards in the face of increasing poverty. The fervour of militant Islamic and Hindu fundamentalists, fuelled by their sense of divine 'calling', is well documented. The entire fundamentalist worldview and social orientation is driven and controlled by this sense of being 'chosen': it is the very essence of what makes them different and right.
- Separation – the separateness of fundamentalist communities can provide shelter for individuals who have felt damaged by the secular world; it can also increase their feeling of 'special-ness'.
- The oppositional quality of fundamentalism provides a sense of fighting back against something and it provides clear enemies. Fundamentalists actively engage in the process of 'othering' in which social ills are blamed on specific communities, however distant. God's Way, for example, blamed current political strife in the USA on the influence of Jews and homosexuals in Washington. They also attributed crime and drug abuse to African Americans. In a similar fashion, Islamic fundamentalists in the Middle East have 'othered' the West, particularly the USA, UK and France, and used the rhetoric of 'othering' to form the basis of an anti-western and pro-nationalist discourse (Turner, 1994). This has been particularly successful in the Iranian and Algerian revolutions.
- Fundamentalists are communal at their core and, as Ammerman (1993) outlines, use the collective to provide strength and support. Their communities might only consist of one church or may involve a wider national community (see Jewish fundamentalism in Israel) but they are seen as the lifeblood of an alternative worldview, giving solidarity, unity, strength in numbers, shared resources, and shared action.

- The millennialist quality of fundamentalism cannot be underestimated. The empowering and revolutionary nature of millennial movements has been well documented (see Cohn, 1957; Thompson, 1997) and is a key factor in Protestant fundamentalism.
- The emphasis on living correctly gives discipline and direction to individuals and can increase their sense of self-worth and purpose (see Kelly, 1977). Research on optimism and mental well-being has shown that fundamentalists always score high on psychological tests (Kroll et al., 1993). Such optimism makes them able to absorb setbacks (as does their sense of 'chosen-ness') and when added to their unwillingness to compromise makes them formidable opponents.

Such resistance strategies can be highly effective for communities feeling left behind by the rest of the world (see Marty and Appleby, 1993a and 1994). Fundamentalism offers a strong worldview providing clearly defined political and social critiques, coupled with solid organizational structures based on community.

Looking ahead

It is always hard to make accurate predictions about the future of fundamentalism, as earlier researchers found to their cost. However, some end points may be highlighted. National governments seem unable or unwilling to create barriers to globalization, whether on economic or cultural fronts. Indeed, the trend within international networks is for greater harmonization (as, for example, within the EU). Less economically or politically significant nations are particularly vulnerable to this lack of state-led resistance: for example, evangelical and fundamentalist churches have found fertile ground for converts and growth in the former Soviet Bloc nations as many of them have slipped into socio-economic decline. In Russia a new ultra-nationalist (and fundamentalist) wing is growing within the Russian Orthodox Church which stresses a return to the key tenets of belief and a strong Russian identity in opposition to the perceived excesses of westernization.

As globalization continues, communities around the world will endeavour to develop strategies of resistance and so fundamentalism will continue to be a potential resource for such resistance. Fundamentalism is here to stay as globalization's consequences begin to be felt more strongly. This is likely to manifest itself in a shift toward even more radical and militant measures, for example, the rise in militias among American Protestant fundamentalists in the rural mid-west. As the stakes, in terms of cultural and economic survival, get higher so more extreme actions must be expected and anticipated. The power and potency of fundamentalism should not be underestimated as a political and social force. As Marty and Appleby, directors of the Chicago Fundamentalism Project, note (1991: xii) 'the strange new world that is unfolding at the century's end' is producing 'new opportunities for fundamentalisms'.

Note

1   This is a pseudonym. All ethnographic materials from Julie F. Scott, 'Unfinished Sympathy: embodiment of faith in an American fundamentalist Christian Intentional Community' unpublished PhD thesis, University of Edinburgh, 1995).

Part II

Globalization: Opportunity and Creative Adaptation

6
Glocal Culture in the Thai Media: the Occidental 'Other' in TV Advertisements

Asawin Nedpogaeo

Introduction

Giddens (1998: 28) is surely correct when he observes that the theme of globalization was hardly mentioned ten years ago, yet now discussion of it is to be found everywhere, from political speeches to business manuals. However, the concept will be misunderstood, he warns, if we think of it solely in terms of economic interdependence and the mere existence of interconnections that are literally worldwide. Driven by a mixture of political and economic influences, globalization actually encompasses a much wider and more complex area since it is transforming the very social institutions in which people's lives are played out – even in the case of those living in the poorest regions. Furthermore, today's world of instantaneous electronic communication is very much responsible for the intensity and acceleration of globalization. By definition, globalization is the process by which the relatively separate areas of the globe come to intersect in a single imaginary 'space' (Hall, 1995: 190). However, this process is by no means fair and equal. In reality, different places, and different social groups within them, experience globalization in widely varying ways (Massey and Jess, 1995: 220). Globalization, then, is a process which, though it affects the whole globe, is in fact highly uneven in its impact. Some countries, cities and social groups are more actively engaged with its various processes than others and some people are more affected by it than others, whether adversely or in ways that lead to personal empowerment.

When thinking about identities it is important not to regard these as fixed, natural and timeless. As Hall suggests (1992: 296–7), such a view obscures the reality that all identities are contested, constructed and complex. A given national identity, for example, may appear to be unified but, as Hall (1992: 296–7) shows, this appearance is only possible because different forms of cultural power have been exercised in order to conceal deep internal divisions and differences. It follows that in reality national identities are really a product of differences that have been blended into one and, moreover, in this construction some elements will be excluded while others will experience inclusion. The same can be said about identities in general. In Hall's words, a fully unified, completed, secure and coherent identity is a fantasy. What these introductory comments clearly suggest is that neither globalization processes nor the making of identities can be free of the play of power relations. Both result in different levels and degrees of participation, inclusion and exclusion.

When we consider the relationship between globalization and changing identities, it is important to realize that the range of possibilities which can be anticipated is considerable. Some identities are eroded and/or eliminated because of their contact with global forces. Similarly, there may be a 'crisis of identity' as some observers have suggested, though in reality this is most likely only when a once-dominant identity becomes dislodged or threatened in its relations to others. As we saw in chapters 2 and 3, this has been very evident during the 1990s in the cases of Russia and Serbia. On the other hand, globalization may increase the range of cultural sources and resources available for identity construction. Here, therefore, it may lead to the strengthening of identities. Alternatively, it may encourage the production of hybrid identities, especially in the context of a post-traditional global society, where bounded societies and states are increasingly cut across by the circulation of other global cultural discourses (Barker, 1997: 191–2). In some cases, whole new identities could even be formed as a result of hybridization. Nevertheless, these more positive prospects concerning the impact of globalization upon identities should never allow us to forget that relations of power and hegemony located within every community, society and country are always central and intrinsic to all processes of identity construction.

Thailand and its identity construction

The formation of the self in the 'look' of the Other is central to the process of identity construction. In the case of Thailand, a national identity was first formed in the early twentieth century (Reynolds,

1998: 134). At several specific moments this 'Thainess' was made concrete and incorporated into state bureaucracy, its main features being disseminated through the media, the schools, and other institutions. Predictably, the possibility of creating a visible representation of Thainess was crucially linked to the existence of a range of additional images of nationhood pressing on Thailand from the outside. One such representation came from China which, in the 1910s, appeared as a harbinger of popular republicanism and so was profoundly threatening to the dynastic principle in Thailand at that time (Anderson, 1991: 101). Another emanated from Vietnam which during the 1970s came to symbolize a most inappropriate and undesirable otherness in the official Thai view (Thongchai 1994: 6). As the modern electronic media have became ever more available recently, it has become easier to find and to produce images and representations of Otherness. In relation to globalization, the Thai media landscape is said to be changing rapidly along with the speeding up of communications and their role in the globalization process. But as far as the construction of national identity is concerned, it seems that strong elements of continuity with Thai cultural elements drawn from the past remain highly influential. Thus, Thainess is based on a combination of traditional Thai culture and the selective appeal of foreign products and lifestyles. This mixture, however, involves a projection of Thainess that incorporates the West but does not give way to it, thereby avoiding the fear of foreign contamination and the need to erect barriers against what might otherwise be perceived as a dangerous external threat. The global – equivalent to the West in Thailand's case – is domesticated by and into the local. This is what I term glocal culture: the concept of localization of the global, or what Roland Robertson (1995: 25–44) calls glocalization.

From Orientalism to Occidentalism

It has been suggested that it is the modern electronic media, rather than academic or business discourses, which are primarily responsible for promulgating stereotypes and distributing images of the 'Other' (Moeran 1996: 79). If Orientalism is understood as a discourse of power whereby the Orient has been studied and comprehended according to its special, designated place in European/western experience as Said (1995: 1) suggests, it is by no means a phenomenon confined exclusively to Europe and the western world. In other words, Orientalism does not and will not stay at home. It has travelled and become part of the self-conceptualizing process employed by many peoples living outside Europe and the West. The Thai ruling elites, for example, witnessed first-hand how the European imperial powers ran their colonies in countries such as Burma, India and Malaya and how they dealt with the indigenous populations as 'the oriental Others' within their colonies. Moreover, the Thai elites adopted and employed a similar strategy with respect to the indigenous Thai and non-Thai populations who were viewed as 'internal' Others – the aliens within the gates. In this way European Orientalism was absorbed, adapted and re-implemented virtually unchanged by the local ruling elites. In other instances, for example, Japan, adopting Orientalism as a strategy has enabled a country to attain a new level of self-understanding through the re-evaluation or even re-invention of its own traditions which are almost always positive once transposed into these new roles. Here, of course, we are discussing another discourse which stems directly from Orientalism once the latter is in place, namely, Occidentalism. Similar to its counterpart, Occidentalism involves an essentializing simplification of the West (Carrier, 1995: 3). This discourse, too, is embedded in and dependent upon conceptions of power and the exercise of power. In this essay I examine Thai perceptions of that other complex mass, the West, and the ways in which it is rendered, recreated and represented in Thai advertising campaigns. This will be done by analysing three selected television advertisements recently broadcast in Thailand as the main focus of the study.

Some historical background

Thailand is one of the very few countries in Asia that escaped direct western colonialism. As a result, traditional values and culture, though at times altered, have remained in place without interruption. Similarly, the power structure within Thai society has evolved with no drastic changes to its internal order. This is quite unlike the situation prevailing in many countries where colonialism brought about the destruction of the traditional sociopolitical order. In the Thai case, on the contrary, it was the external or world order which had to be re-configured. As a result, there was a need for Thailand's own internal order to relativize itself in relation to this new global order. Traditionally, India was regarded as the centre of religious and cultural influence by the Thai elites, while China was at the top of the regional hierarchy of power and tribute (Thongchai, 1994). Both centres of the Thai world order, of course, were seriously humbled at various times during the nineteenth century as a result of intensive European imperialism. The British Imperial Army militarily overwhelmed India and also threatened China's autonomy. India was first administered by British Governor Generals in 1784 and finally in 1876 was governed by the Viceroy, the representative of Queen Victoria who then became Empress of India. China fought the Opium Wars with Britain during the period 1839–42 which led, first, to the Chinese leasing of Hong Kong, and,later, to its surrender to Britain in 1857 (Cunningham, 1991: 39–40). These two alarming events had a major impact on the Thai elites throughout those periods. Nevertheless, the decisive point at which the Thai elites decided to invent a new national identity and to strike out in a new direction occurred in 1826 when news of the Burmese defeat at the hands of the British reached Bangkok. Burma was Thailand's next-door neighbour.

Having been informed about the Burmese loss, the Thai elites under-standably sought a new policy direction. Indeed, the new pattern for the conduct of Thai relations with the West was set at this time. This pattern was symbolized by the conclusion of the Burney Treaty signed with Britain in June 1826 (Wyatt, 1984: 169). One of the significant conse-quences of this redirection was the emerging conception of the physical 'global'. Thongchai (1994: 29) reveals how the Thai (Siamese, as he prefers) view of the world has changed since the second quarter of the nineteenth century – when the Thai elites were introduced to western geographical knowledge and maps. Prior to this era, the Thai worldview was said to correspond to religious cosmology, not geographical reality. In one of its traditional maps used from the mid-fourteenth to mid-eighteenth centuries, the old Thai map only described countries as far as Japan in the east, to Sri Lanka, Arabia and what the map identified as 'Little Rome', *roam noi*, in the West (Thongchai, 1994: 29). The Thais had already known and encountered a number of Europeans by then; the Portuguese were the first to arrive as early as 1511. But the Thais had no idea where Europe was situated, let alone other parts of the world outside Asia. Little Rome, however, suggests the vague, but crucial start-ing point of Thai understanding of the far-away, Christian Europe. In summary, the collapse of its traditional worldview (1780–1850s) and the introduction of western maps, science and knowledge (1820–1830s), prompted the Thais, and the ruling elites in particular, to relativize themselves and reconceptualize the new material world, or the global, but to do so with the discourse of western power firmly attached to it.

Rendering westerners and the West

As mentioned earlier, Thailand has never been formally colonized. But many have suggested that while remaining free from external colonialism, the internal structure underwent a vast process of self-reform, variously described as 'Siamese colonialism' (Wyatt, 1984: 181), 'internal colonialism' (Hamilton, 1991: 373), and 'sponsored-modernization' (Cohen, 1991: 54). In this process of 'modernization by the king', the increasing availability of new and popular forms of narrative based on 'foreign' models and incorporating 'foreign' themes, paved the way for the circulation of new images of self and other, and laid the foundations for the cultural expressions of national identity (Hamilton, 1991: 345). To be sure, what was being described as 'foreign', in most cases, was identical with the 'West' – the new centre of Thai worldview. Hence, it is common to see Thai cultural identity being constructed by associating elements of the West, and sometimes explicitly featuring white westerners, or *farang*, in the Thai cultural discourse. Features of non-white foreigners, for example Chinese, Japanese, and Indian sometimes do exist. But the fact that all the above are generally perceived as Asians, thus closer to the Thais, meant that their representations carried less stark messages and had less impact, compared to the Occidental image imbued in *farang* presenters. This image also carries with it the broad conception of modernity. Thai people in general are said to 'admire Western creature comforts, technical know-how and consumer goods' (Wise, 1997: 21). As early as the 1860s, the Thai royal children in their preparation for the throne were introduced to an education that combined traditional Thai and modern Western elements (Wyatt, 1984: 190). Chulalongkorn, who later became king (1868–1910), was the chief object of the academic attentions of a British teacher, Anna Leonowens: the event that was made into a musical play and film known as *The King and I*. Chulalongkorn's son, Vajiravudh (king during the period 1910–25) who himself was educated in England, once wrote that 'Europeans are the owners of vast knowledge, goodness, beauty and development. They are of an excellent kind above all other human race... they are generous to us as if they are our father or perhaps even better' (Vajiravudh, date unknown: 44).

More recently, the Vietnam War (1960s–1970s) expanded the Thai Occidentalist/Orientalist discourses due to an intensive American presence in the country. It brought the outside world, the West, face to face with large segments of the population as never before. With this exposure came new ideas of social relationships which were later utilized as strategies for national identity construction by competing segments in Thai society. This trend continued when the tourism industry became the main source of national income in the 1980s and 1990s. This steady expansion of Thailand's foreign interaction has resulted in more possibilities for constructing Occidentalist discourses. As more and more discourses are being articulated, the opportunity also exists for these constructions to be made in a variety of both positive and negative ways.

Farang in Thai TV advertisements

Rather than covering a wide range of cultural products, in this discussion I have chosen to concentrate on television advertisements as the main focus of the study. When used in Thailand's advertisements, *farang*, the Thai description for European-ethnic foreigners, has in effect become socially constructed. This construction is by no means unique to Thailand. Indeed, it is rather typical in countries outside of the West for such images to be constructed. As Creighton (1995: 37) suggests in the case of Japan:

> The social construction of *gaijin* denies the individual uniqueness of Westerners, transforming all Caucasians into an essentialized category that reduces the complex variations among them. Just as Western orientalisms created self-occidentalisms through an implied contrast with a simplified West, Japanese renderings of *gaijin* are occidentalisms that stand opposed to Japanese orientalism about themselves.

By the same token, representations of *farang* in Thai advertisements create and highlight contrasting statements about the specialness of 'being Thai'. Of course, the representation of *farang* in Thai advertisements is not a new phenomenon. In fact, they have been used ever since the modern media were introduced into the country. However, the sharp difference is that past representations of *farang* appeared largely separate from the active domain where Thainess was being articulated (Kasian, 1995: 77). In other words, there were no direct links between the two unless these were unintentional. It is only recently in Thai advertisements that *farang* images have appeared in the Thai cultural context in such a way as to directly involve the straightforward articulation of Thainess. One point has to be made here; all of these advertisements are directed at the Thai public rather than Foreigners. For this reason, their function as depictions can provide insights concerning the representation and perpetuation of the 'Other' in the Thai society. More importantly, it is these very functions that are used by competing individuals and groups, in order to renegotiate and re-assert control over the politics of Thai identities.

1. Taming the Occident

The Petroleum Authority of Thailand (PTT) is the governmental state enterprise that has its own retailing petrol stations throughout the country. Since the beginning of the economic collapse in mid-1997, successive Thai governments have tried to create an atmosphere of nationalism in economic policy by persuading the general public to consume fewer imported goods and products from abroad. In the first half of 1999, PTT held the largest national market share of petrol retailing of any single company (27 per cent) while one other Thai-owned company, Bangchak, held another 8 per cent of the total market. The share of petrol retailing controlled collectively by the remaining foreign-owned companies, therefore, was nearly two-thirds. This economic context needs to be borne in mind in the discussion that follows.

As a state enterprise, PTT is obliged to implement the government's policies in its activities. In 1998, PTT broadcast a series of television advertisements for its petrol products. One of them featured an advertisement using a *farang* presenter in its story. In this particular television commercial, the female *farang* presenter is shown sitting in a car with the Thai male presenter. Seated with his partner in the immobile car, the man in the driving seat is starting to talk to the viewers. In his lively tone, here is what he tells the audience – in rather casual language:

Although I have a foreign wife, I'm not losing anything. Profit is circulated within the country. For petrol, I only get it from the Thai-owned station. Profit is circulated in our home land as well.

Here, the discussion accompanies the visual image of the man and the female *farang*. The viewers are informed that the two are actually husband and wife. While his *farang* wife says not a single word but only smiles, the man is assuring the viewers that it is all right to marry a foreigner. His assurance is supported by the next message expressed through body language: his hand is touching his wife's ballooned abdomen, indicating that she is presumably pregnant. In this sign system, his foreign wife denotes the essentialized European-ethnic foreigner, the white westerner; the connotation, in turn, is the West. Specifically, she has become the object of Thai idealization, in very much the same way the Japanese *gaijin* is considered as the bearer of style and beauty (Creighton, 1995: 143). In general, western women are perceived by Thais as enormous but pretty (Wise, 1997: 19). In this case, the attention is directed to the fact that she is the wife of the Thai man in the advertisement. Hence, she has family ties in this country making her *farang* but not completely an outsider. Furthermore, she is portrayed as pregnant. The family connection is in effect made closer and more emotional. The obvious implication is that their awaited baby will remain living in Thailand and this convinces the viewers that there is no loss but only gain in this intermarriage: the accommodation of western elements by Thais inside Thailand. Afterwards, the man moves on to his next message: advocating the PTT as Thai-refined oil. Here he employs the same logic as the one concerning his future baby. As long as things remain in Thai hands and in Thailand, there will never be loss but gain. The PTT oil uses the sign system of the Thai/Occidental-Other discourse, and the meaning generated from it, to convey its persuasive message. Symbolically in this advertisement, *farang* is used to bring potentially threatening Occident/the West/the global under control, rendering them pretty and polite, hence unthreatening. At the same time, this Occidentalism serves to reaffirm Thai centrality and its cultural identity. By portraying the obedient, silent but sweet *farang* wife of a Thai man, the outside West is controlled and made local. The global is localized: the 'glocal culture' is expressed and vindicated. Moreover, this discourse serves to affirm the position of those in Thai society who are able to 'tame', or at least negotiate fruitfully with, the Occident.

2. Occidentalizing Thai whisky: the Black Cat label

The tartan kilt, the Scottish Highland traditional dress, is perhaps one of the best-known ethnic costumes in the world (Chapman, 1995: 8). The kilt symbolizes the Scottish Highland regiments, British imperialism, Jacobite romanticism and Scotch whisky. The links made between Scotch whisky and Scottishness are a myth, just as pasta can be a con-notation of what Roland Barthes (1977: 33–5) calls 'Italianicity'. Barthes usefully showed how the Panzani advertisement can connote Italiani-city by denoting tomato, the pepper and the tricoloured hues (yellow, green, red) in posters. This Italianicity, Barthes suggests, is not Italy; it is 'the condensed essence of everything that could be Italian from spaghetti to painting'. Furthermore, it belongs to a certain genre of nationalities alongside Frenchicity, Germanicity or Spanishicity. In this chapter, rather than adopting the term Scottishicity in line with Barthes's examples, the term 'Scottishness' will be maintained. Similar to the Panzani advertisement, the Black Cat advertising campaign uses the same method to connote Scottishness to its Thai audience. It presumes that Thai viewers already possess and understand the cultural knowledge linking Scotch whisky and Scottishness. This is what Bathes means by 'ideology': a way of perceiving reality and society which assumes that some things are true while others are untrue. Given that the members of Thai society share this ideology – and the possible mythic meanings it carries – then there are possibilities for utilizing these with respect to the brand's messages.

In the advert, the *farang* male presenter is portrayed unmistakably as a Scotsman. He is wearing a tartan kilt and a black bearskin. He is also playing the bagpipes within a presumably Scottish scene consisting of a lake, mountain and castle. Moreover, the word 'Scotch' can be seen clearly on the bottle label right from the opening frame. Both visual and sound messages denote an immediate and unmistakable message, that this is a bottle of Scotch whisky. Once the frame stops zooming in, the viewers get the chance to have a good look at the *farang* presenter. At this moment, he starts speaking to the viewers in the Thai language. Certainly, this *farang* in the tartan kilt is supposed to represent the Other, but the Thai language used here is definitively a marker of Thainess.

> Speaking of Whisky, it has to come from Scotland. Because that's where Scotch Whisky originated, and which people generally prefer...But in these difficult economic times in Thailand today, as a whisky distiller, I'd like to suggest that Thais who like drinking foreign whisky, should turn to the Thai-brewed whisky instead. Black Cat – Black Thai, Cheers!

Here the presenter reconfirms the 'mythic meanings' by speaking about the pre-given notion of Scotch whisky and Scotland. The two are made to connect. The tartan kilt and the bagpipe denote Scottishness. The Scottishness in turn connotes Scotland that is famous for Scotch whisky. The messages connote good quality, originality and popularity. The presenter then claims that he is the whisky distiller, establishing himself as the professional practitioner to whose advice it is worth listening. In this time of Thailand's economic crisis, then, it is more sensible for the Thai viewers who like drinking Scotch to turn away from the imported ones, to the home-distilled brand: Black Cat. With him as the messenger and advocate, the Thai viewers can be sure of the Black Cat quality. It is up to the world standard since it is now guaranteed by the Scotsman himself.

It is important for the Thai-brand product such as Black Cat to feature the *farang* presenter in the tartan kilt in order to create a foreign image of its own product. In doing so, Black Cat can claim to have achieved the preconceived standard of Scotch whisky and Scottishness, but in a very Thai way. This TV advert finishes with the background melody, 'Auld Lang Syne', accompanying the narrator as he says: 'Realizing Thainess needs nobody to remind.' The melody has a double meaning in this context. 'Auld Lang Syne' is accepted, especially in the English-speaking world, as a typical Scottish song about friendship that is traditionally sung as clocks strike midnight on New Year's Eve. But for Thai people, the melody is more likely to be associated with the Thai song called *Samakkhi chumnum* (United gathering). This song is an example of foreign (western) influences that have been made 'Thai' for so long that its origin is virtually completely forgotten. In effect, the melody is thought of as 'Thai' and not as 'foreign'. Finally, after showing images of the Occidental Other, the advert affirms that being Thai is actually a self-realizing process which is so strong that it requires no outside confirmation or support. This twist serves to reassert the uniqueness and self-respect of Thai identity. The viewers are told to recognize it at all times. The Scottishness that culturally belongs to part of the West or the global is glocalized in this example so that Thainess can be imagined without having to be visually represented in the advert.

3. The Occident as imperialist threat

The last example concerns the television advertisement of a soap product branded 'Parrot'. In general, Parrot soap is perceived in Thailand as a good-value, home-made product. Like the previous two examples, Parrot soap adheres to the theme of 'Buy Thai' in the campaign initiated by the government. Its advertising campaign, however, turns to a rather more aggressive strategy compared to the PTT and Black Cat adverts. On the surface, this advert seems to imply an anti-colonialist message that is rather extraordinary since, as stressed earlier, Thailand was exempt from colonial rule. Nevertheless, it would be wrong to say that western, or more specifically European, colonialism has had no impact whatsoever on Thailand. Although many aspects of western culture are admired and incorporated, there are others that are not acceptable and are decisively rejected. Describing Thai beliefs about westerners, Naomi Wise (1997: 19) writes that for Thai people, 'regardless of their specific nationality, the (Western) men are seen as aggressive, "ugly Americans" who think that merely being Western and male makes them superior'. Certainly, this kind of rhetoric can be easily manipulated and readily exploited by any non-western country as part of a nationalist campaign. *Farang* character, then, can be made to represent Western imperialism in such a way as to create the idea that foreigness is threatening Thai values and society.

In 'The Romans in Films', Barthes (1993: 27–35) described how the label of Roman-ness can be represented by having all the characters wear 'fringes'. This hair on the forehead, according to Barthes, indicates a specific mixture of self-righteousness, virtue and conquest, all associated with the Ancient Roman Empire. For American audiences, the little Roman fringe typifies Roman-ness. It is this typification that is of interest here. In the Thai media, by the same token, white westerners whether they were from the British, French or the American Empires, could also be represented. In this Parrot soap ad, one particular *farang* character is created. He is a middle-aged man, well-dressed and formal in appearance. His top hat and tuxedo are symbols of good form: a costume that has gained high recognition since the British Victorian years of the nineteenth century (Briggs 1988: 266). Without any elaboration, one can initially assume that he represents a western-ness that could be European or American. As in previous cases, the presenter becomes an essentialized category: the Occidental Other. Effectively, it is this Occidentalism that stands opposed to Thai efforts to engage in re-Orientalizing itself.

In the scene, the *farang* character is present with a Thai family comprising father, mother and son. With his smiling face, the *farang* presenter starts speaking in Thai to the family. He instructs them to stand up, sit down, turn left, turn right and turn around. However, his cheerful voice and manner make the scene amusing rather than serious. The fact that he speaks in Thai allows the language to become a marker of Thainess just as in the Black Cat advert. The family, meanwhile, has followed all the instructions being given to them, although at one point the son does turn the wrong way. The son character, with his naivety and humour, is thus playing the 'young rebel' role vis-à-vis his own family, but more importantly in relation to the West. When the *farang* presenter tells the family to go and take a bath, the family again complies. But once they are told to use 'foreign soap' (imported), the mood suddenly changes. While both father and mother stand reluctantly, the son gracefully steps forward with a bar of Parrot soap in his hand. This patriotic act of the young son shocks the *farang* presenter so stunningly that he falls down and becomes unconscious. Meanwhile, the voice-over says 'Using a Thai product, nobody can boss you around'. This is reinforced by a caption which reads, 'Favour Thai, use Parrot soap'.

In the very last scene, the young son comes to the *farang* presenter and asks the question: 'Join us for a bath, Uncle?' From this depiction, it can be interpreted that although the West is acknowledged as more powerful (as indicated by formal dress and giving orders to the Thai family), western power is not entirely absolute. Thais (the family), despite being subordinates, have the right to stand up when national pride and integrity are at stake (being told to use foreign soap). Thus, western imperialism (represented by the *farang* presenter and foreign soap) is rejected, or defeated, rendering Thai identity and qualities as autonomous and outstanding. In this advert, the sign system, and its nationalist/anti-imperialist meanings, is entirely contained by Parrot soap. Yet, in addition, the presentation of the *farang* character as 'uncle' in the very last scene takes the meanings an important step further. On one hand, this identification clings to the humorous, casual theme of the advertisement and aims to be entertaining. Calling him uncle, the character becomes informal and more included. On the other, this uncle can be interpreted as 'Uncle Sam' or the United States of America, now the world's only superpower and often blamed for the way it performs its dominant role in the world. Here, the USA, having been defeated, is invited back to join the bath, implying the moral superiority of Thailand. Metaphorically, Parrot soap uses the 'David and Goliath theme' to portray Thailand's relationship with the West (America). By surviving the foreign threat, Thainess is effectively re-affirmed. Once again, the global is negotiated. In order for Thainess to be projected at the international level, glocalization has to be achieved. This glocalization in effect justifies the nationalist/patriotic discourse of Occidentalism, and thus helps to secure its own power in Thai society.

Conclusion

Representations of *farang* or white Westerners have reinforced the dichotomy of Them/Us in the construction of Thai identity. Ever since the second quarter of the nineteenth century, the construction of Thai identity has been largely based on its relation with the West and through western images and representations. The introduction, and later evolution of modern media have made such constructions much easier to realize. As one of the consequences of the globalization process, *farang* characters are used representatively to simplify the complex mass of the western world which, in most instances, can be identified as America and Europe. This strategy of Occidentalism is linked to glocal culture through the key role played by Thai media industries in localizing the global. The essentialised *farang*s are depicted either as admirable or deplorable. In either case, they represent otherness in Thai society;

they should be accommodated if admired, but would be rejected if deplored. Occidentalism in turn constitutes the re-Orientalism of Thainess: the positive evaluation and re-evaluation of Thai qualities. In addition, the economic crisis in the late 1990s has once again placed Thai identity in jeopardy because of the threat to the country's economic and political independence. By analysing three selected television advertisements we have seen how the West can be rendered so that it becomes not only accessible but can also be made to function as the Occidental Other in such a way as to permit the creation of Thainess. More importantly, those engaged in producing this discourse are, through that very process, given the opportunity to re-position themselves in this age of globalization so that their power and their control over other groups in Thai society are secure.

Acknowledgement

This research was conducted under a scholarship granted to the author by Thailand's Dhurakijpundit University. The author is especially grateful to Roza Tsagarousianou for comments on earlier versions of this chapter.

7
Globalization, Identity and 'Ireland'

G. Honor Fagan

Introduction

The recent upsurge of interest in the so-called 'Celtic Tiger' has produced some reflection on the greatly increased cultural confidence in the Ireland of the 1990s. There seems to be an implicit connection drawn between increased economic performance and greater cultural self-confidence. While this thesis is on the surface plausible, this chapter prefers to address the culture of the Celtic Tiger from the perspective of globalization. This chapter thus approaches the new 'Ireland' through an analysis of globalization and identity. The current international popularity of Irish music, dance, film and pubs has led some observers to detect a new Celtic cultural revival. This apparently contradicts the notion of cultural globalization as a new form of cultural imperialism that enfeebles national identity. Yet it is quite unclear what 'Ireland' is being spoken about in this new discursive terrain. Which Irish 'identity' is being (re)created in this new cauldron of globalization and hybridity in particular? We need to critically deconstruct what is meant by 'Irish identity'. The Irish example, in its hybridity (part European, part 'developing' and part postcolonial) and its liminality, provides an interesting case study. This chapter sets out to provide a more critical and self-critical perspective than that provided by those who see the cultural revival as mere superstructural reflection of the so-called Celtic Tiger, which views the transnational tourist spots as uncritically as does the casual European weekend visitor. Ireland's place in the world has changed in the last ten to 15 years, as has our sense of place. As a result of globalization, the way we analyse the world has also changed radically; for example, today the cultural is economic and the economic is cultural, although it does not work at the analytical level to totally collapse the two together. Globalization can only be understood by foregrounding the cultural because, as Jameson (1998) has argued recently, the relationship between culture and economics has fundamentally altered. The debate on the intersection of culture and economics to the debate on Ireland and globalization therefore needs to be related.

Why Ireland?

If you travel to Ireland by air, before you reach passport control at Dublin airport (an ambiguous site where there is difficulty distinguishing between the 'overseas' and the European Union (EU) traveller) you will see a large billboard. On it there is a 'leprechaun' – that eponymous figure of Irish 'folklore' – with a caption which reads: 'If you think this is an icon of traditional Ireland you are away with the fairies.' A small symbol in the corner indicates this is an advertisement for Icon, which cognoscenti will know as the marketing company for the ubiquitous 'Irish' cream liqueur Baileys. At first glance you might assume this is an ironic postmodern take on 'tradition' by one of the growing band of 'Irish' electronic and computer companies in the vanguard of Celtic Tiger myth-making. The image they (and much of the media) wish to portray is of a cool young entrepreneurial country buzzing with connectivity. Yet De Valera, with his 'hairshirt economics' and his sturdy youth 'dancing at the crossroads', happened just fifty years ago. It is this huge transformation, with all its gaps, contradictions and inconsistencies, which makes Ireland so interesting from the point of view of development theory (for an overview see Munck and Fagan, 1995). It is also, in its amalgam of the traditional, modern and 'postmodern', rich material for critical cultural studies. It is in that spirit that this chapter approaches the complex interactions of culture and globalization in that site in the global flows we call Ireland.

Though Ireland gained its independence from Britain in 1921 it was not until the Wall Street Crash of 1929 and the Great Depression of the 1930s that a consistent path of inward-oriented growth through industrialization began. While De Valera's notions of self-sufficiency may smack of romantic rightism, the late 1930s had laid the basis for industrialization in Ireland. De Valera achieved a conservative modernization in Ireland akin to the 'passive revolution' Antonio Gramsci spoke of for Italy. As Gramsci (1971: 109) put it, this is a case of 'molecular changes which in fact progressively modify the pre-existing composition of forces and hence became the matrix of new change'.

Thus De Valera, in this mixed conservative revolution, prepared the South of Ireland to enter the era of monopoly capitalism in spite of/or because of his dreams of a reactionary utopia. Protectionism began inevitably to give way to free trade. As T.K. Whittaker, a key figure in the post-1958 turn to the market, put it, 'there is really no choice for a country wishing to keep pace materially with the rest of Europe' (Whittaker, 1973: 415). Borrowing from abroad would finance the new policy.

Ireland joined the European Economic Community (EEC) in 1973 and the removal of protectionism was in full swing. As Denis O'Hearn (1998: 41–2) notes 'A country which had virtually clothed and shod itself in 1960 imported more than 71 per cent of its clothing in 1980'. The shift away from indigenous industry towards transnational investment operated across the board. It coincided with a period in which US transnational corporations (TNCs) were seeking profitable high-tech locations, particularly ones that would provide them with access to the European market. This outward-oriented growth (attraction of foreign investment and promotion of exports) did not immediately deliver the goods, but by the 1990s a new and more buoyant Irish economy was emerging. Officially, the boom began in mid-1994 when, in an obscure European investment assessment bulletin, the US investment bank Morgan Stanley asked, perhaps not too seriously, whether there was a 'Celtic Tiger' emerging to join the family of East Asian tiger economies. Of course, within a couple of years the much-vaunted East Asian tigers would look considerably more shaky.

The Irish boom may be real, but it has its limits: growth rates are half of those experienced in East Asia during the growth phase, and the question of sustainability is seriously in question given the limited base of the growth sector. Dependency on the whims of the transnational sector is even greater than in the 1970s, with the sector accounting for three-quarters of value-added in manufacturing by the mid-1990s. A handful of computer companies, such as the giant processor manufacturer Intel, literally hold the key to sustained growth rates. Ireland is less of a tiger than a leopard, however, being characterized by spots of development or, more accurately, growth. As with globalization, national economic growth has exacerbated the processes of social exclusion. Above all, cutting-edge technology coexists with traditional social relations. As Luke Gibbons put it a while back 'The IDA (Irish Development Association) image of Ireland as the silicon valley of Europe may not be so far removed after all from the valley of squinting windows' (1988: 218). The latter image of traditional rural Ireland is also a social reality today and is not just part of history.

Finally, getting back to y/our arrival at Dublin airport . . . If you were in Britain and wanted to visit Ireland you might telephone Ryanair, 'the cheap fares' airline. While you wait for the friendly operator you will listen to music you might recognize as coming from the hit 'Irish' show *Riverdance*. Billed as the sound of the new Ireland which still retains its traditional roots, it is really as much flamenco and Broadway as it is traditional Irish dancing (see O'Toole, 1998). From this postmodern pastiche and melange you might turn to thinking of Ryanair as a company. You will find it a model of the new 'hollowed-out' capitalist firm. Ryanair *is* its manager, Michael O'Leary, as it is its cheap but cheerful (actually aggressive) manner. It is, like Virgin Air and Easy Jet, its image. It also epitomizes the new, brash, confident capitalist class in Ireland in its recent handling of a baggage handlers' pay claim. Cheap fares mean poor wages. In a symbolic dispute Ryanair is trying to get the Irish state to give its business to them, in the spirit of free enterprise and 'Market rules OK', as against the more traditional 'modernist-statist' national carrier Aer Lingus. This story escapsulates many of the debates which are to follow.

Cultural revival?

Contemporary observers of the cultural scene in Ireland are impressed by its vitality. In her book *Ireland Today*, for example, Gemma Hussey refers to a 'new exuberance of self-expression which the country has never seen before' (1995: 470). She goes on to note the 'new Irish appetite for expression of its own identity' thwarted by the two 'big problems' of the 'the pressure of Anglo-American media' and the 'inexorable weakening of the Irish language' (1995: 471). The picture we get is one of a once-pristine and whole national identity reasserting itself on the world scene, challenged only by cultural imperialism and the decline of vernacular languages. Today Irish 'traditions' are doing well on the whole: 'Traditional music has been revived in its many forms, and enthrals tourists as much as Irish people, who are themselves, amazed at its richness' (Hussey, 1995: 484). Insularity is left behind as we join Europe and 'get in touch' with our traditions with a new self-confidence. Ireland has grown up, so to speak – we take our traditions with us but we are largely uncontaminated by unpleasant associations with the legacies of colonialism and an anti-imperialist position.

From more progressive political quarters we get a not dissimilar enthusiastic reception of Ireland's (Dublin's?) new cultural prominence. For Gerry Smyth (1997: 175), 'there appears to have been something resembling a pan-Celtic Revival in the years leading up to the millennium, the Irish element of which amounts to little less than another Cultural Renaissance'. Denis O'Hearn (1997: 117) refers in a similar vein to 'Ireland's cultural revival throughout the Western world [which] was evidenced in the popularity of the musical *Riverdance*...'. O'Hearn makes an explicit link between 'an apparently vibrant economy and a confident culture that, came to be known as the "Celtic Tiger"' (1997: 57). As with Gemma Hussey, the nation is not problematized and there is a simple acceptance of the new cultural identity industry practically untainted by any scepticism. Where the Left analysis differs from Gemma Hussey is in its implicit economism in which cultural transformations are simply 'read off' the economic revival, as a practically direct manifestation of the putative economic boom of the Southern Irish economy in the 1990s. Here economy determines culture. Missing from both problematics is the small matter of globalization, at least missing in the sense that the nation-state is seen as the only and obvious framework of analysis and political intervention.

Globalization: beyond the buzzword

The first wave of globalization theorizing tended to polarize into a 'for it' or 'against it' dichotomy, much as the debates around postmodernism have done. It is now possible to go 'beyond the buzzword' (Scholte, 1996), to develop a critical realist theory of globalization. Globalization should not be seen as the last grand narrative of the twentieth century. Moreover, it should be seen neither as a panacea nor as a demonizing force, as a certain Left discourse tends to do. It is neither unprecedented nor is it simply 'business as usual' in a world of autonomous nation-states. We could do worse than (provisionally) employ Daniel Drache's recent acute characterization of globalization as being one-third over-sold, one-third something we cannot understand because it is still unfolding, and one-third something radically new (Drache 1999: 7). Certainly, notions such as the 'death of the nation-state', the 'McDonaldization' of the world and the image of rampant, footloose and fancy-free TNCs roaming the globe are exaggerated. The information revolution, though, is real. In terms of globalization and culture we can perhaps discern ongoing changes that will radically alter the way we see and live in the world. As Held (1999: 327) assert 'There is no historical equivalent of the global reach and volume of cultural traffic through contemporary telecommunication, broadcasting and transport infra-structures'.

We already find it difficult to continue conceiving of the nation-state as a homogeneous cultural niche or cultural site. We see the develop-ment of genuine transnational cultures – for example, in the women's movement and environmentalism. Above all, we see the global cultural economy as characterized by flows. In Appadurai's (1990) influential formulation, these flows include ethnoscapes (the distribution of people), technoscapes (the distribution of technology), financescapes (the distribution of capital), mediascapes (the distribution of informat-ion) and ideascapes (the distribution of political ideas). When we look at the world in this way it is possible to understand why globalization has probably gone further at the cultural level. Indeed it is part of a broader 'culturalization' of social life. Globalization thus not only questions the nation-state script but also tends to increase the importance of subject-ivity and identity. Certainly identity formation cannot today be reduced to place (Ireland), but must be seen as a product of the complex set of flows identified by Appadurai (and others) and the networks of interact-ion which they generate.

We can perhaps start with Mlinar's analysis of territorial units as being in 'transition from *identity as an island* to *identity as a crossroad*' (Mlinar, 1992: 2). The nation-state can no longer (if it ever could) de-link from the global system. It is not an unproblematic, simple, homogeneous unit but a genuine crossroads where the global flow of peoples, foods and ideas intermingle and produce their hybrid cultural forms. This is the complex context-generative setting of culture in the era of global-ization. Culture, as creating the realm of meaning, cannot be reduced to 'national culture' – a term which hardly has any sense today. Nations have always been imagined communities (Anderson 1983) but today they are being re-imagined in the context of globalization. 'Ireland' is most clearly invented and re-invented, a place to be sure, but also a state of mind, an ideological construct. As John Waters (1998: 53) puts it: the state was founded, yes, in 1921 and then deconstructed and founded again in 1960 in accordance with the prefabricated history which had been constructed to make it thoroughly modern in every way. Cultural globalization is again transforming the context in which and the means through which Irish culture is being produced and reproduced.

The discourse of globalization has suffered a conceptual inflation in the 1990s, where everything and anything is described as globalization, but this does not mean that the effects of globalization are not real. Its economic, political, social and cultural effects are felt across the globe and a simple nation-state-centred optic or perspective is simply inadequate. Apart from the decline of the nation-state due to globalization perhaps the other most significant issue is the fundamentally altered relationship between culture and the economy today. As Jameson (1997: 67) alludes to it: 'Whoever says the production of culture says the production of everyday life – and without that, your economic system can scarcely continue to expand and implant itself'. To understand the 'Celtic Tiger' thus we need to go beyond a purely economic analysis to examine the cultural productivity of this model. The 'Celtic Tiger' is as much discursively constructed, as it is a product of Gross National Products (GNPs), Gross Domestic Products (GDPs) and Gini coefficients. For example, we could consider Paul Tansey's apparently unironic listing of Ireland's 'economic comparative advantages' in tourism: 'Ireland' is empty, old, green and accessible (Tansey, 1995: 199–200). These are hardly orthodox economic terms. To deconstruct these terms would take us right to the heart of the new imbrication of economics and culture in the era of globalization, which brings us back to Jameson's argument.

Globalization and culture

It is probably necessary to distinguish explicitly between the problematic of globalization and culture from an earlier one, 'cultural imperialism', with which it tends to be conflated. In his book on 'cultural imperialism' John Tomlinson has carried out a Marxist analysis which ends uneasily with the era of globalization, his open-ended conclusion being that 'Globalization may be distinguished from imperialism in that it is a far less coherent or culturally directed process' (Tomlinson, 1994: 175). The world has become more complex and cannot be reduced to bipolar oppositions. We cannot just see Americanization, standardization and 'McDonaldization' in the era of multipolar globalization. Local differences have not been done away with by the juggernaut of globalization; indeed, the new syncretism has brought them to the fore. Certainly global and local cultures cannot be taken as separate symbolic universes. Thus, something like the perceived Irish cultural boom of the 1990s cannot be analysed in local terms alone. The music of U2, for example, can only be understood in terms of the new relations between culture and globalization that have produced such 'glocal' musical processes. Their music is both local and global at one and the same time. The drive towards consumerism of an increasingly global-culture-based economy seems to be the order of the day. Local cultural strength is a source of power and gives competitive advantage in this economy.

With a hopefully permissible degree of simplification it is necessary to distinguish between a modernist, anti-modernist and postmodernist take on culture and globalization. For the modernist theorist, typical of US modernization theories of the early 1960s, modern culture will inexorably spread worldwide, transforming the world in its image. The world is a simple evolutionary place and the hierarchy of cultures is undisputed. For the anti-modernist (of the 'Jihad versus McWorld' posed conflict) this westernizing of the globe must be contested. Zia Sardar rejects what he sees as postmodernism's destabilizing of the notion of cultural authenticity and advocates instead a strategy of cultural auto-nomy: 'It means the ability and the power to make one's choices based on one's own culture and traditions' (Sardar, 1998: 283). Finally, the postmodernist view would emphasize cultural complexity in the post-colonial era of globalization. The failure of modernity cannot be viably (or democratically) contested by a traditional counter-modernism. The metanarrative of the Enlightenment tradition and its belief in universal progress can only be challenged by a postmodern account.

Let us now turn to Ireland as postcolonial. One of the key concepts to come out of the debates on postcolonialism is that of hybridity. Hybrid social formations and cultures show a juxtaposition and intermingling of premodern, modern and postmodern traits. Ireland, like Mexico or Brazil, can be seen as hybrid in this sense, also perhaps liminal given its position betwixt and between Europe and the developing world. In a suggestive analysis, based mainly on study of traditional crafts in Mex-ico, Nestor García Canclini (1995) concludes with some observations on the constructed and 'theatrical' nature of all tradition, including those of modernity. In a nice turn of phrase Canclini refers to how this anti-evolutionist 'postmodern' understanding of cultural politics 'refutes the original nature of traditions and the originality of innovations' (1995: 190). Culture has always been impure – it does not operate in a vacuum and is continuously being 'produced'. Contrasting with the dominant pessimistic views of globalization's impact on culture (in the cultural imperialism vein), Canclini takes a more open view of 'the eclectic contacts and borrowings enabled by globalization' as 'progressive and healthy' as Jameson (1998: 66) has recently put it. The new cultural products of 'Ireland' could not have found their niche in the world market if this was not the case. In fact, Ireland has captured a cultural advantage – global advantage follows from capture of local cultural strength in global society.

Globalization has redefined tradition: it is not just the distant past but also the 'tradition' of modernity. In this sense the 'Ireland' constructed in the 1920s is as 'invented' as the young European Ireland of today. For in the 1920s as Declan Kiberd (1995: 286) puts it: 'In theory, two kinds of freedom were available to the Irish: the return to a past, pre-colonial Gaelic identity... or the reconstruction of a national identity, beginning from the first principles all over again.' An appeal to 'trad-ition' or 'cultural authenticity' makes little sense when we realize how pragmatic an affair the construction of a national identity is. De Valera and the founders of the modern Irish state were in the business of constructing the 'right kind' of modernity for Ireland. This involved a pragmatic rather than a romantic vision with emphasis on 'right', where key catholic clergy and political leaders forged a modernity that would be appropriate to the Irish people as they saw it, which was then enshrined in our constitution. In today's (re)construction of Irish iden-tity, the reference points for this process are truly transnational. Whether it is the music of the Chieftains, the dance of *Riverdance* or the motifs of the new 'Irish film' we cannot understand these cultural expressions in purely national terms. They may even be constituted locally but it is with reference to a global market, local cultural keys turning in the global lock. These are hardly exclusive cultural identities and are fully part of the flows and counter-currents of globalization and cultural politics.

Culture and identity

What the above points us towards, or rather away from, is any essen-tialist notion of 'Irishness', which is fixed from time immemorial. Neither Irish culture nor identity can be seen self-contained, immutable or closed. A new state of flux, typical of postcolonialism and globaliza-tion opens up a new era of more fluid and uncertain construction of cultural identity. Declan Kiberd (1995: 653) argues that 'If the notion of "Ireland" seemed to some to have become problematic, that was only because the seamless garment once wrapped like a green flag around Cathleen Ni Houlihan had given way to a quilt of many patches and colours...'. Yet even this account seems to downplay the element of uncertainty and undecidability in the current situation. This is most manifest at the political level – where the future of the island is genu-inely uncertain at present – but also at the cultural level. It is hardly a comfortable quilt of cultural diversity that is being constructed where gender, ethnicity and religious conflicts become safely defused. Ireland's culture is currently showing its more ominous and threatening side. Current racism around the issue of immigration and refugees highlights some of the more worrying sides of the uncertainty we now face. This is hardly the optimistic scenario of Gemma Hussey for whom insularity has been replaced by 'the confidence of an outward-looking young generation' (1995: 484).

It is now accepted that globalization has unsettled traditional notions of identity. For some, there is a 'crisis of identity' as it becomes detached from national communities. Thus William Smyth, in relation to Ireland, declares that 'sureness of identity is a necessary defence against the forces of cultural standardisation' (1985: 14). Yet a discussion of 'who we are' need not lead to an essentializing form of identity formation. Nor, as we saw above, can cultural globalization be reduced to 'cultural standardisation'. The main point is that identity formation is necessarily incomplete and fluid, a contradictory and fragmented process not amenable to simple closure. In the wake of globalization, as Stuart Hall notes, 'the idea of culture as a set of autonomous, self-enclosed meaning systems and practices, begins to seem anachronistic' (Hall, 1995: 190) Nostalgia for a traditional organic Irish identity is not only anachronistic, but also impossible. Notions of what it means to be 'Irish' have always been contested, have always been fluid and have been constructed by cultural politics rather than given to us by God.

Richard Kearney's (1997: 101) dictum that 'For as long as Irish people think of themselves as Celtic Crusoes on a sequestered island, they ignore...the basic cultural truth that cultural creation comes from hybridisation, not purity, contamination not immunity, polyphony not monologue' is relevant here. Aside from a concept of 'truth' that sits ill with a poststructuralist theorist, this line of enquiry seems more fruitful than counterposing national 'authenticity' to cosmopolitan shallowness, uniformity and commercialization. Postcolonial Ireland has, arguably, been dominated by questions of cultural identity and the competing stories of who 'us' and the 'other' was. Today, the literary text is less likely to seek a single vision of a stable Irish society. For example, Roddy Doyle 'does not offer a snapshot of a stable society – a finished image of a finished reality. Rather, modern Irish society is shown to be in flux, a conclave of voices and visions...As an artist looking to engage with such a society is constrained to open meaning up rather than close it down' (Smyth, 1997: 67). The social scientist should, arguably, do the same.

By way of conclusion

Declan Kiberd once wrote that, 'If Ireland had never existed, the English would have invented it...' (1995: 9). This should put us in a reflexive frame of mind to understand the present cultural and political location of Ireland. In an analogy with the Leninist theory of Imperialism we could see 'Ireland' as a link in the chain (read network today) of globalization. 'Ireland' is something 'invented' by the new cultural globalization. *Riverdance* does not spring from the eternal wells of the Irish soul; rather, it is manufactured by the global cultural industry. It reflects all the hybridity, syncretism and even 'postmodernism' typical of globalization. It is not something authentically 'Irish' but, rather, a (re)invented tradition. Globalization has produced a 'world showcase of cultures' (Featherstone, 1995: 13) and in this stage 'Ireland' has achieved prominence. If this 'Ireland' – of *Riverdance*, of U2, of the global 'Irish pub', of Temple Bar – had not existed it would have had to have been invented by the new cultures of globalization.

Global cultural flows are not merely the product of flows between nation-states but are embedded in global scale processes, and it is misleading to think that this necessarily involves the weakening of national/local cultures, or entails global homogenization. Rather various diverse, rich and popular local cultures are resisting and feeding global culture. This is where Ireland should be placed today – rather than Irish 'culture' being weakened by global culture, or rather than resisting global culture, Irish culture is being produced at an amazing pace to feed the production of global culture. As social scientists we must urgently produce a political economy of the culture of 'Ireland' since we could argue that Ireland (more precisely, Dublin) is witnessing a culture-led regeneration and insertion into globalization on terms more favourable than could be expected from its economic importance in the global era.

8
Civil–Military Relations and Professional Military Identities After the Nation-State

Glen Segell

Introduction

In the 1980s and 1990s two developments challenged traditional military thinking: firstly, the end of the Cold War and its bipolar balance of power and secondly, the growing integration of the European Union (EU) states. Traditionally wars are ended and states are founded as a result of military activities, but not in these cases. Military minds have been further unsettled by a range of military conflicts that did not conform to the traditional pattern of nation-state versus nation-state. These included the conflicts in the Persian Gulf (1991) and Kosovo (1999), and the genocides in Rwanda and East Timor. For the military in the United Nations (UN) and North Atlantic Treaty Organization (NATO) forces involved in these conflicts, the obvious question was 'I am fighting but why am I not defending my country?' The very act of posing this question demands an examination of the nature of civil–military relations after the nation-state (Segell, 2000a: 189–201). Since the Treaty of Westphalia in 1648 armies have been national armies serving the civil authority in their nation-state. Following the end of the Cold War and under pressures from the forces of globalization, armies are having to rethink their identities as national forces. In an era in which nation-states and nationalism are no longer the primary motive for the use of armed forces, the subservience of armed forces to national civil control is being challenged. This chapter aims to unravel the debate on civil–military relations after the nation-state and to examine the globalization of the role of the armed forces.

Defining globalization and identity for civil–military relations

Civil–military relations may be defined as:

> ... a multiplicity of relationships between military men, institutions, and interests, on the one hand, and diverse and often conflicting nonmilitary men, institutions, and interests on the other... the relation between the armed forces as a whole and society as a whole...the relation between the leadership of the armed forces (the officer corps) as an elite group and other elite groups... and... the relation between the commanders of the armed forces and the top political leaders of society – it is the foundation of the management of the use of armed force and the armed forces.
>
> (Segell, 2000a: 1)

This definition means that civil–military relations are not confined to the national state, national security and nationalism. There is historical precedence for this because during both world wars British troops fought under the command of American generals (Huntington, 1957: 34) and had a dual identity as both British and Allied forces. Similarly, mercenary forces or even forces like the French Foreign Legion, have never really had an identity or civil–military relations defined by one state's (such as France's) nationalism and national identity (Janowitz, 1981: 97–9). Despite such dual identities military forces in western democracies have remained subservient to the elected national civil authority and have deep-rooted local identities grounded in class, regional, ethnic, national and religious realities. These identities have served as a basis for nationalism and national security within the nation-state. Civil–military relations, however, are not static and in particular the end of the Cold War has placed civil–military relations within new contexts. The process of regionalization, the EU and even more so the processes of globalization, all challenge sovereign state boundaries. National military forces are therefore increasingly encountering other cultures and experiencing transnational exchanges, that have resulted in the military expressing a need to redefine their identity and role.

NATO and rationalization, standardization and interoperationability (RSI)

In the European context this redefinition started with the RSI of policies, strategy and equipment which was a founding goal of NATO. RSI was introduced so that national contingents within NATO could fight as one unified force. The rationale was a practical one: economies of scale in production runs, sharing the burden of research and development to serve a common political goal and military strategy. The consequence was that a NATO member could not go to war against another member nor without the assistance of another NATO member. The first identifiable act setting this process in motion was the acquisition of titanium sponge by Britain, West Germany, and Italy from the USSR at the height of the Cold War. The sponge was needed for the variable geometry wings of the multi-role, collaborative Tornado project (Segell, 1998: 245).

The consequences of NATO's RSI were institutionalized in 1975 with the establishment of the Independent European Programme Group (IEPG) whose goal was to further NATO RSI solely among the European members and to reduce dependence upon American technology. Without knowing so at the time, the processes of global technology transfer had been set in motion. With industrial research and development convergence between civil and military technologies, this soon resulted in a global production line for military technologies in which individual nation-states became mere assembly lines. The ramifications of this were realized in the Gulf War when Germany, for constitutional reasons, was unable to provide the RAF with certain spare parts for the Tornado aircraft which had been jointly manufactured by Britain, Germany and Italy (Segell, 1997: 121). No nation-state in the year 2000 can claim to be self-sufficient in the manufacture of its military requirements, leaving both the civil and military authorities without full sovereignty in times of war. Similarly, there is no such thing as an independent defence industrial base within each nation-state. The military of each country are mutually dependent for weapons hence reducing the ability and capability for the independent use of force.

Transnational forces

The post-Cold War era has also seen the dvelopment of new transnational forces such as the combined French–German–Belgian EUROCORP (*International Herald Tribune*, 6 February 1998). EUROCORP has alternating French and German military leadership and is under the political-civil control of all three governments. EUROCORP soldiers therefore experience alternating and triangular civil–military relations. Surprisingly, perhaps, the need for EUROCORP member countries to participate in combined and joint task forces has been more readily acceptable to the military profession than to the elected political-civil bodies. Civil–military relations have thus become transnational in terms of civil control with no military reluctance nor resistance. The military have experienced a renaissance in their identity, with professionalism replacing patriotism and global values replacing national state security or national security concerns.

EUROCORP is just one example of a transnational military force under democratic transnational civil control. There is also a joint Danish–German–Polish Army that transcends even the European Union (*International Herald Tribune*, 24 February 1997). This army, which is essentially Prussian in its geography, combines the historic foes of the Danzig Corridor. Another such force is the Anglo-Dutch Amphibious force whose main role is to protect the North Sea oil rigs owned by multinational companies (MNCs) such as British Petroleum and Dutch Shell. This role has resulted in an identity crisis as many of the force's soldiers have openly questioned whether they should be in effect a mercenary force on commercial hire to two MNCs (*The Washington Post*, 11 February 1998). The role of the Amphibious forces contrasts with the Royal Navy's role during Imperial times, when their mission was to protect the sea routes and the United Kingdom.

These examples are just the tip of the iceberg. UN peace-making-keeping-enforcement troops have wondered if their civil authority is the UN Security Council or the USA. In neither case can they be considered to be fulfilling a role associated with the defence of a nation-state. Their identity has more to do with the consequences of globalization, such as concerns for humanitarian intervention through-out the globe. This is revealed also by the changing civil–military relations involved in humanitarian military operations in the former Yugoslavia. As a consequence of the processes of regionalization and globalization various military forces are being compelled by civil authorities to engage in transnational co-operation as peace-keepers rather than as warmongers. The national identities of the component forces are broken down by the UN assigning them acronyms that describe a force's role rather than their national origins. KFOR, for example, stands for the Kosovo Force, while UNIFIL stands for the UN Interim Force in Lebanon. Soldiers serving in these forces report that they develop a force identity based on the mission that transcends their national identities.

After the nation-state: unravelling the debates on civil–military relations

Once we accept the reality that the nation-state no longer holds the sole legitimate right to the use of military force then we can unravel the debate on civil–military relations after the nation-state. This debate will be examined under four headings. Firstly, 'The nation-state, nationalism and civil–military relations', which considers the impact of globalization and the end of the nation-state as the embodiment of singular nationalisms on civil–military relations. Secondly, the section 'Civil–military relations and identity' develops the identity thesis and role of the military in missions other than those in defence of a single nation-state. Then, 'National and Supranational Identity' examines the notion that individuals, be they soldiers or citizens, have more than one identity, by virtue of being, for example, an immigrant or by attachment to transnational symbols such as European passports. Finally, 'The Nation-State and Global Civil Society' extends the debate beyond symbolism and into the realm of belief systems. Each person, be they soldier or citizen, has both a local and a global existence. The most local being family and the most global being commonly held values associated with religion and human rights.

The nation-state, nationalism and civil–military relations

Even though the modern nation-state was born with the Treaty of Westphalia, it was only in the nineteenth and even more so in the twentieth century that Europeans and Americans began to talk much about national identity. This developed as a result of democratic principles – the right to vote and to be represented. For civil–military relations this was an identity relationship of citizen to soldier and of soldier to nation-state. The proliferation of sovereign states as a result of two world wars, the end of European empires and the Cold War, has led to an exmination of the implications of these developments for civil–military relations. Whereas once territorial disputes between nation-states were the cause of wars, it now appears that nation-states were part of the modernizing project in industrial societies (Agence France Presse International, 11 February 1998) and are no longer the sole actors in international relations. For example, the nation-states' forces participate in UN and NATO forces on humanitarian missions. Few if any nation-states can claim a homogeneous population with a unified national identity and hence a singular form of nationalism. Most if not all nation-states have heterogeneous populations with large percentages of first- and second-generation immigrant populations. These populations not only have dual allegiances but may also carry two passports. The role of the nation-state in international affairs is no longer to be based exclusively upon a national identity, nationalism and the patriotism of its military. Nation-states now have more universal aims and find themselves belonging to supranational entities such as the EU. At the same time their populations are caught up in a process of globalization involving international economic institutions, international media images and global values. Nation-states now serve the universal goals reflected in European political philosophy.

This creates a number of wider social or political consequences, both in the domestic context of the relations between soldier, citizen and state and in the international context of the use of military force in international affairs. In the latter context it questions the very notion that nation-states have the exclusive right to the legitimate use of armed force. In the former it questions the relation of the soldier, who is also a citizen, to that of the state. For the professional military or conscript armed forces this poses a dilemma. In a domestic context it is no longer possible to recruit or train solely for nationalistic purposes or missions. Joining the military must be seen to be a career for the defence of humanity; one's own nation-state is now to be seen as a core element of this humanity. In multinational operations the issue becomes apparent when soldiers question whether each national armed force is subservient to its own country's civil authority or to a supranational authority. This was a question for the various UN forces in Bosnia and NATO forces in Kosovo and Albania. This is not just a question for the military as it also has implications for democratically elected governments. Governments in the global media age can longer dispatch large and expensive military forces without a publicly justifiable cause. This has ramifications for civil–military relations on issues such as budget allocations and especially on the 'guns versus butter' issues of healthcare versus military spending. The allocation of taxpayers' money is a contentious issue in civil–military relations when the military are no longer serving the direct interests of the taxpayer. If taxpayers insist on funding only the nation-state's defence then humanitarian missions cannot be undertaken. Taxpayers need to adopt global values and a value system that supports humanitarian military operations.

Civil–military relations and identity

At this point we should give some further consideration to what exactly the widely used term 'identity' means. What exactly is a taxpayer's identity in a nation-state and what is that nation-state's identity in the international system? What we call a modern nation's 'identity' has at least a dual reference. On the one hand it refers to the major structuring institutions of the economy, polity and armed forces and on the other it concerns the 'way of life' in a more domestic and communal sense, practised by the dominant groups, including the armed forces. The armed forces are comprised of taxpaying citizens. A dogmatic socio-logical functionalism might argue that these ways of life must follow and respond to pressures from the economy and polity, but it is clear that in fact such ways of life have at least a relative independence. Similarly, while it is the case that modernization depends upon the autonomy of economic and cultural institutions from moral and communal control, in an established modern economy and polity, moral, social and cultural values may become liberated from the forces of the market place and take on a life of their own. This is equally true for civil–military relations as the military become independent from national civil control and transfer to transnational control by NATO, the EU and the UN for humanitarian and peace-keeping missions. Such missions have been successful – as in the case of Namibian independ-ence in 1989 – and complete failures – in the case of the UN Interim Force (UNIFIL) in Lebanon (1977–84).

UNIFIL involved around five national units, each assigned a different task. The Dutch in UNIFIL were the military police, the Canadians the logistic force and the Irish the patrol. It was only the high command structure that was of mixed nationality and no UN Security Council member was in UNIFIL. It was not surprising, therefore, that UNIFIL failed to achieve its objective. The lessons learnt from the Lebanese case were applied to the UN monitoring force deployed for the Namibian elections in 1988–89. This force was a completely mixed force with patrol and logistic units drawn from more than one national force. Hence, there was a feeling of unity at the soldiering level. The mission, rather than their individual nationality, formed the soldier's identity and all forces came under a single commander. Despite the military success of this force there was strong criticism. A debate ensued as to whether the UN 'Blue Berets' were in fact a new style of mercenary force. The soldiers were not defending their individual national interests; their collective budget and joint mission were approved through the United Nations, which is not a sovereign state. Moreover, their mission had no offensive military goals. This questioned the basic strategic notion taught in many military staff colleges that the best means to defend the nation-state is the aggressive projection of military power onto the enemy's territory. The consequences of this left many in the United Nations forces questioning not only their own identity but also the identity of the nation-state.

In fact all that is usually meant when we speak of the identity of the modern state is the way in which its members differentiate themselves and their own state from other states and their members. Of itself, this is a purely cognitive matter referring to the way in which entities are differentiated in the social world, but the term is also often taken to refer to an emotional attachment and a sense of belonging of a semi-sacred kind. The task here is to be clear as to the origins of such a sense of belonging in a modernizing nation-state. Hence if member states of EU and/or NATO share common goals then the military should not have an 'identity crisis' in serving the transnational civil authorities in collective security activities. The national and transnational civil authorities should share the same goal and hence the military of the individual nation-state will be serving its national interests by participating in collective military activities.

This is of significance for the identity of military forces when national-security interests reflect global values rather than nationalism. This was the case with NATO operations in Kosovo in 1999 – the 'national security' of peace in Europe was at stake. No NATO member state was fighting for nationalism, rather the political goal was humani-tarian intervention. The Serb force in Kosovo was not fighting in the defence of its own state nor for any cause based upon nationalism. It had a fundamental purpose determined by President Milosevic – namely, ethnic cleansing or genocide. The resident Kosovan population had a single purpose of individual survival which could collectively be interpreted as an ultimate goal of national sovereignty. Hence in Kosovo it is wrong to equate the individual soldier's identity with his citizenship of a nation-state. Despite this lack of nation-state or nationalistic iden-tity there were two ways in which all the military forces involved in Kosovo did have some sense of identity. Firstly, they were differentiated by their ways of life, cultures, religions and adherence to global values. Such a distinction is both invidious and desirable. It is invidious as it returns war in the Balkans to the period of Crusaders, with ethnic cleansing on one side and with religion as the *ius ad bellum*. It is desir-able as it brings to war collective humanitarian intervention, without the burden of European tribal-territorial nationalism that characterized the nineteenth and twentieth centuries on the other. This is neither a clash of states nor a clash of civilizations – it is the clash of global beliefs. In Kosovo there was a moral identification with global humanitarian beliefs and values that transcend state values for all the soldiers involved. The feeling of solidarity embodied in military comradeship was interlinked with religious beliefs on one side and humanitarian beliefs on the other. Such civil–military identities are also observed when a nation-state is absorbed into supranational or transnational entities such as the European Union. The soldier's emotional attachment, together with the defence of individual and separate national interests, produces a culture of resistance to solely national entities and to nationalism. Patriotism still exists but towards the separate military units such as to the regiment and to higher global values.

For civil–military relations this generates an upward move from national to supranational identity in security interests and a downward move from the nationalism of the nation-state to a military identity that transcends the nation-state. In effect the military becomes its own ethnic minority! – allegiance is to the military and not to the nation. Citizenship loyalty is to the military and global values and not to the state. Despite these changes of identity the civil authorities of each nation-state still retain control over its own military through such actions as budget allocation. Even this is diminishing with the growing transnational collaboration in weapon systems procurement.

National and supranational identity

As part of the debate, we now need to consider the question of supranational identity. In the United Kingdom, for example, the national identity comprises English, Scottish, Welsh and Irish dimensions. Immigrants tend to refer to themselves as British. Citizenship involves being a subject of Her Majesty the Queen who is the head of the sovereign state of the United Kingdom and Northern Ireland. In addition, passports and driving licences are issued as European Union documents on which each nation-state appears subordinate to that of the EU. It is therefore not surprising that identity is a question mark in many citizens' minds. The British military are instructed that their main mission is defence of the United Kingdom, yet also work within collective security organizations such as NATO and with global roles defined by the UN. There is also the added dimension of a single European Defence and Security Policy. Individual soldiers as well as the military planning agencies no longer provide a definitive answer to the question 'Are you fighting for Queen and Country?' (Sweetman, 1986: 38). The most likely answers stem from discussion in the EU of the possibility of a European identity transcending the nation-state identities. The military forces within the EU therefore seek to define themselves in contrast to extra-European entities and to emphasize the elements which the European states have in common. Civil–military relations have therefore evolved to the extent that military professionalism is the primary concern combined with a modicum of subordination to both the national and transnational political authorities. This is an interim stage in the evolving civil–military relations. A clearer chain of legitimacy and authority in civil–military control must evolve in supranational and transnational entities lest the military attempt to take control. It is likely that such an evolution of civil–military relations will clash with any multinational definition that the member states might themselves develop.

The problems for the military in defining their identity are compounded because European nation-states, and hence their military, are only just emerging from a millennium of tribalism manifest in different languages, cultures, religions, traditions and ethnic diversities. Despite combined military operations and the coalescence of economic activities, the EU still remains a union of traditional nation-states, all much affected by the ideology of nationalism. This has led to problems in dealing with ethnic minorities who are in reality citizens of other EU member states. As such they are only a minority in the state in which they currently reside but are not necessarily a minority in the sum total of EU populations.

The problem of nationalism and hence identity in Europe today, subject to the pressures of regionalization and globalization, is clearly a very complex one and has taken on new dimensions in the face of moves towards supranational union. The modern nation-states of Western Europe and America were based on the notion of citizenship. If one speaks of identity to refer only to the identity of citizenship, this does not of itself have any implications for emotional belonging. Emotional belonging is an essential ingredient for military esprit de corps and in civil–military relations for the subordination of the military to civil political control. Identity in the sense of emotional and moral belonging does, however, attach to the 'ways of life' of the members of the nation, or at least of the dominant group. Wars tend to reinforce this emotional and moral belonging. Whereas wars may have historically reinforced nationalism, wars today may reinforce global values. This can best be understood by looking at the concept of civil society in order to understand the evolution of civil–military relations from nationalism to globalism, that is to civil-society–military relations and not just civil–military relations.

Civil–military relations, the nation-state and global civil society

The notion of globalization is intertwined with the concept of civil society. The nation-state has required a set of institutional forms of governance maintaining an administrative monopoly over an economic, political, social and cultural territory with demarcated borders. Its rule is sanctioned by law. Democratic governments are unable to dominate their societies and individuals and groups have become increasingly vocal and active. Traditionally within nation-states it is possible to identify the arena in which the individual citizen participates in political and economic life – namely, in civil society. As part of the process of globalization a global civil society has evolved with its own beliefs and principles. The institutions of this global civil society include the church, education, trade unions and other organizations which act to a lesser or greater degree independently of the state (or states). Therefore, global civil society has been the arena of social and political protest particularly by human rights, animal rights, environmental, trade union and peace movements.

So, what are the implications of a global civil society for civil–military relations? The global civil society is spatially autonomous from the nation-state so it is characterized by the creation of new political spaces. These spaces are delineated by networks of defence–economic, defence–industrial, military–social and military–cultural relations. They are occupied by conscious military-related actors, in physically separated locations, who link together in networks for particular political and social purposes. In an increasingly interdependent world, in which issues have universal appeal and evoke universal moral stances, such movements have shifted away from the arena of national politics, towards the arena of global politics. Moreover issues such as human rights can only be effectively resolved globally, sometimes with the use of armed force, such as in East Timor. In these ways globalization creates a global civil society in which a global military and global civil society is better able to promote global values than national military–civil-society relations. It can achieve better results and have a greater influence than national civil societies. This has resulted in civil–military relations becoming civil-society–military relations.

For civil–military relations, when globalization questions the primacy of the nation-state in international relations, then civil society questions the primacy of civil-national-political control of a nation-state's military (Segell, 2000c). The major consequence of globalization for civil–military relations is the changing position of the nation-state within the international system. In an increasingly globalized world with a global civil society the nation-state can no longer remain autonomous. For civil–military relations this poses the question: 'What is the military role in a non-autonomous nation-state?' Once this question has been posed then the ensuing questions relate to the relations between the armed forces and society – namely, civil–military relations. This chapter has already given examples where the military are fighting within collaborative transnational and international organizations, without direct civil control from their own governments.

Global military forces and global civil society

The above reasoning may appear at first glance to be a gross simplification, but it does explain the success of the UN forces in the Persian Gulf (1991), NATO forces in Kosovo (1999) and also why there is a multinational force in East Timor. These examples show where military professionalism has transcended nationalism. Civil–military relations are no longer bounded by a nation-state's domestic politics. Civil–military relations are between the global civil society and the professional military forces. Politicians within nation-states have relinquished sole control and use of their military forces to global organizations, however reluctantly. The impact of globalization in such areas as economics, technology and culture is developing a multitude of global linkages breaking down the isolation and autonomy of the nation-state.

For the military we can observe this evolutionary process if we recollect that the Treaty of Westphalia was signed in the town of Munster which today is home to the headquarters of EUROCORP. The two Munsters, 350 years apart, bear similarities. The Treaty of Westphalia highlighted the reality that a nation-state could only been seen to exist when its government had an administrative reach throughout the territory over which it had sovereignty. Similarly, a transnational force can only be seen to have military jurisdiction globally through the concept of a global civil society – represented, for example, by UN declarations.

The evolutionary process of globalization and the development of a global civil society has led nation-states to recognize that they no longer have the sole legitimate use of armed force but rather that the community of nations have the legitimate use of armed force in support of global values. Nation-states no longer therefore have a monopoly control over their internal affairs, as it is now the role of the global civil society to defend global values such as human rights. The combined military forces of many nation-states may intervene and use armed force in another nation-state's domestic affairs to protect and promote the global values of civil society. Hence, nation-state armed forces have now become available to serve the interests of a global civil society. It follows that civil–military relations are no longer operating within individual states but between and amongst them. This has been institutionalized through collective security agreements such as the founding Charter of the UN and of the Brussels Pact establishing NATO.

Globalization and civil society

Civil-society–military relations also impact upon collaborative weapons procurement and collective security. It can be argued that the continued formation of international non-governmental organizations (INGOs), the growing power of MNCs and the ever-increasing influence of international regimes, each with their own agendas, beliefs and ideologies for technology development and use, provide the foundations of a global civil society for weapons procurement institutions. Here the important point for civil–military relations is that each organization has created a global arena, outside purely individual national interests, in which common values, aims, concerns and even ideologies are discussed and acted upon during the weapons procurement process. This global process impacts at the local level. For example, since the mid-1980s economic and political forces have required the contracting-out on a commercial basis of any activity undertaken by the military short of the use of force. Hence catering, base cleaning and even landmine clearing became commercial operations by private firms who had won the tender. These firms constitute a mainstay of civil-society–military relations as they are undertaking traditional military roles, without regard to national security, identity or nationalism.

A parting word on globalization and civil society must lead us to address the role of civil–military relations when the physical presence of a soldier is not required. This is especially pertinent because globalization has been in part promoted by communications networks. For civil–military relations such global interactions between and amongst civil society(ies) is manifest in the growing awareness of war waged on information infrastructures and on information itself. Historically, this has evolved out of the military activities of intelligence gathering and analysis, propaganda and even the mainstay of the Cold War – nuclear deterrence, or the perceptions of nation-state leaders of another nation-state's intents and capabilities, based on information or disinformation.

In all these military activities there is no need for an actual military presence nor is there a need for the use of armed force to achieve a tactical or strategic victory. Information flows freely and information is power. The consequences of such free flows of information are that they erode state controls and reduce the effectiveness of national governments by generating an informed civil society. This means that civil–military relations are no longer confined within the state – every soldier and citizen is an eye-witness to any war via media coverage. Defence management and the training of even a professional military force clearly has to be based on global values pertaining to beliefs in a civil society.

Conclusion

The military have already found a new role after the nation-state and nationalism: support of global values. As the nation-state moves away from nationalism, towards regionalization and globalization while adopting global values, then the military of each nation-state will no longer be subservient to a single national civil control but to the notion of 'A civil control'. In times of war this may be that of another similar regime in a collective security structure such as in a UN peace-keeping-making operation. Civil–military relations may also take on a structure akin to an institution based upon a former alliance structure, such as has been seen in NATO operations in Kosovo. In times of peace civil–military relations will move towards supporting civil society relations. Many former military activities will be undertaken by commercial or police entities. This conclusion can be clarified by the careful reflection that global civil society, manifest in the mutual dependence and the interdependence between nation-states, can no longer tolerate armed forces patrolling along borders that have long since ceased to exist for economic activities, when there is the unrestricted movement of workers and the free flow of information and technology.

The identity of the individual soldier and the military as a whole has also undergone a major shift due to globalization and civil society after the nation-state and nationalism. The individual soldier's phenomenal world is changing from a local defence of the nation-state to a global defence of global values. It is therefore plausible that structures to facilitate that change will come into being – namely, a global military society to supplement the global civil society. These changes will be evolutionary and may even take decades.

Finally, it must be noted that despite the thesis that civil–military relations can exist without the nation-state or nationalism, the nation-state still exists as a major entity in the international system because there still exists the desire to have territorial demarcation by and for ethnic groups or nations. With this desire comes the necessity of armed forces to protect that territorial demarcation. It is only when societies worldwide adopt global values that their daily life could best be served by a global civil society without state boundaries that nationalism and the nation-state will cease to exist. There will then be no need for an armed force to defend a territorial boundary; rather, it will be required to defend a civil society with global values. This will result in civil-society–military relations and not just civil–military relations but still within the scope of the definition presented at the start of this chapter.

9
On the Construction of Political Identity: Negotiations and Strategies Beyond the Nation–State

Darren J. O'Byrne

Political identity: some assumptions and preconceptions

One of the many consequences of processes of 'globalization' has been the *separation of nation and state*, and thus the *delinking of culture and politics* (on this, see Albrow and O'Byrne, 2000). Accordingly, citizenship, as a form of *political identity*, is separated from nationality. Citizenship can be understood as the negotiation, at the level of the individual, of the various strategies that are made available to the individual for political empowerment. It involves rights and duties, participation and membership, exclusion and inclusion, but these are all politically constructed concepts. This chapter considers how political identities are maintained under such conditions.

It is important to spell out at this point a possible point of controversy. Contrary to some popular contemporary thinking, identity is not empowering per se. Identities can *only* be empowering if they are politicized, and to be politicized they have to relate in a direct way to external power structures. These identities may begin as cultural, or gender, or other such identities. There seems to be no reason why all identities cannot be viewed as *potentially* empowering. However, so long as these identities remain free-floating, they remain depoliticized, and it is for this reason, perhaps, that much postmodern theorizing has lacked political 'direction'. To identify as a woman, for example, is a recognition of gender identity, and this identity connects the individual to a network of others who identify in a similar way. But so long as this identity remains in isolation, it is depoliticized. To identify as a woman is not in itself a political identity. To identify as a woman, however, and *to be aware of what this identity means in the context of a wider power structure which is patriarchal and sexist*, is by its very nature to recognize how one might politicize this identity to inspire practical action.

This is what is meant by the claim that political identity is *pragmatically* (we might say *linguistically*) socially constructed. The politicization lies in the very linkage between the inner sense of *identity* and the external set of social, economic, political and cultural conditions. Thus, the activist and self-professed 'world citizen' Garry Davis expresses his own sense of political identity in this way (that is, as a declaration of citizenship) because it allows him to relate directly to the conditions within which his various choices, as a social actor, are made (on this, see Davis, 1961). In his view (and mine), to declare oneself a 'citizen' is to empower oneself, but for that empowerment to have any real meaning, it must connect to real external conditions. Davis believes that any such declaration as 'I am a United States citizen' is actually meaningless, because the conditions which impact upon the individual's life are primarily *global*, and therefore to be meaningfully politicized, s/he must declare her- or himself to be a world citizen. It is not the purpose of this chapter to discuss this claim. This model is consciously followed in a quest to understand how citizenships are defined, and thus how political identities are developed and how *other identities might become politicized.*

Traditionally, political identity has been linked specifically to the nation-state. This is primarily because throughout modernity the nation-state has been the dominant form of political administration. We could say that it embodies a particular form of rationality which is territorial, and which seeks to bring the previously separate spheres of culture and politics together. The state, which represents the political dimension, does not have to be a nation as well. Similarly, the nation is a cultural construct that requires neither a form of political administration nor a geographically closed-off territory. The conflation of these two, which results in the nation-state, has not been problematic per se. Nation-states might, in theory, encompass any number of political centres (as in the case of federal countries such as the United States) and any number of cultural affiliations (the list of possible examples is endless). However, historically, cultural identification has provided the base of legitimation which has allowed for the political (and by extension the economic) sectors to flourish. Nation-states have required the support of the people, and in order to attain this have sought to ignore cultural pluralism and define the 'nation' in monocultural terms. Thus cultural identity has been suppressed by political identity, and this suppression is represented by the 'assimilationist' model of citizenship inclusion. Naturally, such an inclusion also requires an exclusion.

Conservative philosophies have sought to justify this process. They have argued on behalf of the 'essential' character of national identities. They have not questioned the nature of the relationship between the cultural nation and the political state (taking this instead for granted). Political identity and citizenship merge with cultural identity to form an allegedly essentialized identity which supports the unified nation-state model, and which duly excludes those who do not conform culturally to it. Furthermore, *political* allegiance is secured through this appeal to an almost tribal, apparently historically grounded, sense of shared cultural tradition.

Of course, the nation-state has never been the only source of political identity. Prior to, and throughout modernity, there has always been an alternative perspective that locates political identity and sovereignty (and thus the state itself) within the individual, or within humanity as a whole. How, then, does citizenship *as a form of political identity* come about? It does so, I would argue, as a socially constructed label which draws on, and between, a variety of experiences which exist at the level of the individual life world. Thus it predates any form of systemic colonization, such as that by the nation-state system. This point is important; political identity is not only socially constructed – it is *pragmatically socially constructed*. Furthermore, it is constructed across and between a variety of 'levels', each of which can be understood as an arena for social action. Such 'levels' do not operate in isolation from one another. Indeed, following Calhoun (1995) and Miller (1995), political identity is constructed through a variety of group affiliations and cultural categories, which include gender, religion, ethnicity and occupation – and *national* identity is itself constructed through such contested sources as language and territory.

Political identity under globalized conditions?

This chapter asks what strategies might exist to define political identity under contemporary conditions, conditions in which the nation-state is no longer the central social institution, and in which there is a separation of nation and state. Its purpose is to argue against 'essentialist' assumptions that presuppose a relationship between political identity and the nation-state. Its starting point is, to some degree, Giddens' (1991) assertion that in a late modernity characterized by increasing *reflexivity* the politicization of identity (an identity which is constructed, that is, through the various choices made available to the individual) takes place within the post-traditional, globalized realm of *life politics*.

Individuals make use of a variety of strategies in defining their own political identities. As Giddens suggests, each social actor 'not only "has", but *lives* a biography reflexively organised in terms of . . . information about possible ways of life' (Giddens, 1991: 14). Three interesting such strategies will be discussed in some depth. The first of these belongs to Alex Lifeson[1] who is in his early thirties, and single, and who currently works for Amnesty International, although his background is in the Arts. He has travelled extensively, and has lived abroad, and his community has essentially been a liberal one. Middle-class and well-educated, Lifeson openly identifies himself as a 'citizen of the world'. An earlier generation of sociologists might have looked upon him as the quintessential 'modern' world citizen: a bourgeois idealist espousing liberal beliefs in a common humanity. Yet Lifeson adopts an interesting strategy which allows him to identify with such a common humanity at a political level, whilst accepting an identification with his nation at a cultural level.

The second of these strategies principally concerns Al Brown. Al Brown appears in every respect to be a nationalist. Brought up in the decaying communities of the industrial north-east of England, he has little time for those 'idealists' who consider themselves citizens of the world. He appears to fit a stereotypical image of a northern, English male. Certainly, he is no longer 'working class', given that he is an accountant at a major London arts complex. We might at first see that his upbringing in a staunch 'traditional community' has shaped his cultural outlook, but we would be wrong. Just as the economic climate has changed, forcing cities such as Newcastle to either adapt or become wastelands, and forcing residents such as Al to move south and take up posts in the service sector, so have his views been shaped by forces and events which make any simplistic, reductionist account impossible.

Thirdly, we meet Ben Cunningham. For Ben, a thirty-four-year-old accountant from south London, cultural and political identifications are brought together under a single banner, which revolves primarily around the fact that Ben is black. We will see how Ben seeks to politicize his cultural identification with a global black community within the pragmatic context of a nation-state.

This is an *illustrative-purposive sample*. The intention is to draw from the experiences of these individuals examples of different strategies employed; they are to be used to *illustrate* the claim that political identity is socially constructed. The intention is not to suggest that these responses are 'typical'. Each of these responses represents a 'type', amongst surely many other types. Each person, with her or his unique biography, is able to advise us (as academics and researchers) on what categories are used, and we (as academics and researchers) should be able to draw from these life stories a better understanding of the practical implications of the theories which have been advanced.

The focus, then, is on these three distinct means of defining one's political identity. Lifeson's, it is argued, is essentially one of world citizenship, constructed and negotiated through a cultural identification with the nation-state. Brown's is a nation-state identity that is constructed and negotiated through reference to the local. Cunningham defines his identity in cultural, and more specifically black, terms, but empowers this *transnational* identity by political activity at the nation-state level. For each of the three, the *nation-state remains a site for action*. Then possible examples of a fourth such 'type', one which involves individuals constructing their sense of local identity through global affiliations and processes, will be offered.

World citizenship as a nation-state construction

Let us begin with how Alex Lifeson constructs his sense of political identity. Lifeson wants to identify *politically* with the world, but at the same time does so *culturally* with the nation-state. At first glance, he appears to fit many of the standard definitions which fit the 'modernist' label of world citizenship, and, accordingly, Lifeson sees no conflict in his 'dual' citizenship: *national*, at a practical level, and *world*, at what he calls a 'higher' level, defined by a sense of social responsibility towards the welfare of individuals worldwide.

Lifeson is, in his own words, a pragmatist. He identifies his loyalties very much in keeping with the specific conditions of the moment. His lifestyle enables him to do this. Indeed, his identification with 'the world' is primarily a political one. He identifies certain concerns as 'global' concerns and duly politicizes them:

> I think it comes down to the fact that I'm very aware that in different ways I face the same concerns as everyone else around the world. I can hardly describe myself as being poor, although I'm not wealthy, but I can identify with those kind of issues, being concerned about family and friends... That's a global issue... My concerns with education, be it for my family or myself, are equally valid for anyone,

anywhere in the globe. There might be different circumstances, but
there are the same concerns being raised, and that's where I identify
most strongly... with being a citizen of the world. My main concerns
are poverty and education.

Here, Lifeson is stressing the common concerns and interests faced
and held by all of us on this planet, as human beings. So it would appear
that his perspective draws on classical universalism. Like the universal-
ists of old, Lifeson has constructed his sense of world citizenship from
within the boundaries of a nation-state. More specifically, though, he
constructs it from within the boundaries of London, a global city.
Indeed, he professes to have a strong sense of British identity, albeit
restricted to certain areas and generalizations. He states that this affiliation emerges from his being accustomed to the social patterns and
culture associated with British identity. In his own words, it is a 'cultural
identification'.

Does Lifeson mean 'British' or 'English' here? While it is primarily at
this cultural level that Lifeson identifies with his nation, we should be
careful not to conflate 'cultural Englishness' with 'British national identity', as Miller (1995: 161–2) points out. Postwar changes, and, in particular, the decline of any sense of British 'superiority', have led some to:

> ... take refuge in what I shall call 'cultural Englishness'... the set of
> private characteristics and ways of doing things that are thought to
> be typically English: such things as drinking tea and patronising fish
> and chip shops, an enthusiasm for gardening, a love of the country-
> side, and so forth... There is nothing wrong with this cultural Eng-
> lishness, but it is not the same as British national identity... A
> national identity is a public phenomenon, not a private set of
> cultural values.
>
> (ibid.: 161)

So while he uses the term 'British', Lifeson's comments in fact reflect a
sense of 'cultural Englishness', and that this is indeed, as Miller is
suggesting, a reaction to postwar changes. At the same time, therefore,
it is the influence of global cultural diversity which allows him
to understand and to feel more a part of the world as a single place
(thus to some degree exhibiting the epistemological quality which is
central to Robertson's understanding of globality; see Robertson, 1992:
132). Indeed, when pressed, he confesses that he is unable to think of
any specific circumstances where his loyalty or identification to his

nation-state would take precedence over his identification with the world. So he clearly accepts that there has been a qualitative change in his worldview.

Alex Lifeson is one example of an individual with a particular kind of dual citizenship: nationalistic, in the cultural sense, and cosmopolitan, in a quasipolitical sense. However, Lifeson's construction of world citizenship is actually more complex than this simple duality might at first suggest, because it draws on a number of other factors. It seems significant that Lifeson works for a human rights organization, and thus actively operates within the realm of moral universalism. It is equally significant that he lives in London and appreciates its qualities. Lifeson is what we have elsewhere referred to as a 'cosmopolite' (Albrow et al., 1994: 25–7). For him, the locality is useful in so far as it allows him access to the multicultural diversity which he so enjoys. He thus seems to identify a direct link between the global (cultural diversity) and the local (as the immediate site of this diversity), bypassing the national. But as we have also seen, national citizenship continues to be important to him for a number of reasons. Some of them are still political. It is in this sense that he considers himself to be a pragmatist. He accepts that, by dwelling within the boundaries of a given nation-state, he must abide by the laws of that state. He must accept the legitimacy of the government, whether he approves of it or not. He pays tax and identifies with state-funded education and welfare programmes. But he would not fight for his country because, he explains, he is a pacifist. His sense of world citizenship and belonging thus outweighs any responsibilities he might have towards the defence of his country.

So, regardless of his identification with English culture, Alex Lifeson *is* a world citizen. Indeed, his political and educational priorities suggest that he is the quintessential modern world citizen. He is, it seems, the cosmopolitan modernist, the moral universalist who believes in a rather abstract commitment to a singular humanity. The acceleration of global change has, however, impacted upon Lifeson and world citizens like him. Just as globalization has allowed Lifeson to realize his otherwise nominalistic commitment to world citizenship (through his travel and his cultural interactions), so has it speeded up, in his view, the seemingly evolutionary process of global awareness which he advocates. He is now able to act in a pragmatic fashion upon the global stage, and to appreciate its diversity, as well as to identify with its commonality, without the need to surrender his faith in a humanistic, progressive, modern project.

National citizenship as a local construction

Al Brown appears in many respects to be the antithesis of Lifeson. Indeed, for Brown, the very idea of world citizenship is meaningless. Being a citizen, says Brown, means belonging to a place which has a corresponding 'Other':

> I mean, if there was a choice between being an Earth citizen and a Mars citizen, then I'd be an Earth citizen, but you can't actually be a world citizen because there's nowhere else to go! It [citizenship] means you belong somewhere. But if you belong to the world, then you don't actually belong anywhere, because everything's there, and nothing is outside it.

It is important for Al Brown to belong somewhere, and this is important in understanding his perspective. He is certainly not alone in understanding citizenship and belonging primarily in terms of an Other. This has been a common way of understanding belonging throughout time and space, and across the political spectrum. Arguing from the Right, David Marsland (1996) has also stated that if one belongs to the world, one belongs nowhere, and is thus lost and in search of a home. For Marsland, this is less to do with an *existential* need for belonging, than with an *essence* that he claims is found in the idea of the 'nation'. For Marsland, this is one of the main reasons why nationalism is so important for our understanding of the social condition. There are distinctive national identities and national characteristics of which, he argues, sociology has lost sight.

We might wish to connect this to the *linguistic* construction of political identity, and to the potential for turning that construction into political action, which, according to Garry Davis and others, *necessarily* leads to a politicized sense of the world, because it makes clear the external conditions which are otherwise undermined by nationalism. Indeed, the *chief political project of instrumental modernity has always been division*. By rationalizing his own reluctance to accept the *possibility* of world citizenship through recourse to the need for an Other, Brown appears to be perpetuating just this kind of project. However, we should not be too hard on Brown. While the creation of 'Otherness' is often considered to be divisive and negative, it is nevertheless found in all forms of allegedly progressive political philosophies throughout history. *Lifeson makes this distinction as well*, when he talks of 'English' traits. In many respects the two men are similar. The difference lies in the meaning they each give to citizenship. Whereas Lifeson understands it to be a form of political identity (in which case he can distinguish it from his cultural identity), Brown considers it to be about inclusion and membership (implying exclusion and non-membership). The reasons for this difference of opinion may be manifold. Clearly, it seems to restate the point that citizenship is a contested term, which has meant different things to different writers, often to suit specific conditions. One possible reason might be that Lifeson's sense of identity is constructed without a specific reference to a given place, or *locale*. Brown's, clearly, relies heavily upon such a sense of place. Is Al Brown the kind of man Marsland is appealing to in his defence of nationalism? On some levels, yes. For Brown, however, these questions of identity and belonging are all about levels, and these levels extend from the local, through the national, to, in the last instance, the global.

By local, Brown does not mean his immediate locality. He is forty-one, and has lived in London for some twenty years, but the Newcastle area is still home for him. He visits two or three times a year, and has strong positive feelings for the area. He recalls how, when he was living there, he spent nearly all his time in the area itself. He finally moved to look for work. This was in the early 1970s, which he concedes was a bad time economically for the area. If not for this, he accepts that he would probably still be there today. Indeed, his identification extends from this initial loyalty towards his local area. He is, he says, a 'Geordie' first and foremost. Before he left the area, he was a 'Geordie' and nothing else!

The move to London clearly tamed some of Al Brown's fierce localism, but it has left him in some kind of 'third space', or social limbo. Compared to people he knows back in the north-east, he describes himself as 'a cosmopolitan man of the world'. Compared to his current acquaintances, he feels he is just the opposite. It is significant though that, in describing himself in nationalistic terms, he concedes that he only came to identify as English once he moved to London. Brown is thus reminding us of a mistake we often make as academics: we are keen to invent 'degrees' and 'levels' without considering how those degrees and levels are relativized.[2] In Brown's case, this relativization is essential. He cannot define himself in absolute terms. While he readily accepts that he is no 'globalist', he is unsure of his own standing simply because he has experienced such varied environments. Nevertheless, he retains a perspective which stresses the most local as being the most identifiable, and therefore the most important. Thus, being English is more important to him than being British. Loyalty and identity depends upon the context. His affiliation would get *as local as possible*, and this explains his reluctance to consider world citizenship as an option, for not only is it as distant as possible from his precious local, but it also denies the existence of the Other; the opposition he mentions above. Significantly, Brown is not *opposed* to post-national identities; his nationalism is not grounded in *anti*-Otherness but in *pro*-localism.

Of course, this may be true, but studies have shown how an over-exposure to locality (particularly when reinforced by cultural codes which posit the local as preferable to the non-local) not only promotes localism by restricting globalism, but positively discourages such a wider worldview (see, for example, O'Byrne, 1997). Brown concedes that he recognizes the prevalence of a rabid localism (and intolerance) which he no longer identifies with. His views have changed, in a number of important ways. While he remains sympathetic to what happens in the north-east, he is less so than before, although he would be more interested in such news than any other kind. His attention, he states, has shifted towards matters that are of concern to England.

In this and other respects, Brown – who at first glance epitomizes the kind of nationalistic, localistic, 'little Englander' philosophy to which some right-wing commentators seek to appeal – is far from such a simple stereotype. His nationalism is not political, nor is it economic. He identifies with a culture that he considers to be specifically English. More than this, though, is his identification with his local level first and foremost. That he considers the most local to be necessarily the most significant for his own daily activities again reflects the kind of pragmatism he talks about. Even when he expresses concern over the 'threat' to English culture posed, for example, by the European Union, he locates these concerns within a pragmatism. In his own daily life, Brown finds it both easy and convenient to deal with such issues as are close at hand, and to identify himself accordingly. Yet his sense of the local no longer pertains to his physical location. Brown's localism is part of the cultural capital which forms his identity, and he has successfully maintained his relationship with it, despite being uprooted and disembedded. It is part of the *milieu* which he carries with him, de-linked from its *locale* (Durrschmidt, 1997). Brown, then, is part of the *white diaspora*, a group which, while being far from new, has been somewhat overlooked by academics and commentators. As with so many others who belong to this group, he identifies culturally with a region from which he has been forced, by circumstances beyond his control, to move.

Cultural identity/political action

For Brown, the nation-state represents both a cultural and a political entity that provides him with his sense of citizenship. For Lifeson, the nation-state remains the site for cultural identification. For Ben Cunningham, it means something different still. Ben Cunningham is a good example of what we might call a 'non-modern' citizen. This is in part due to the way he shifts and reconstructs his citizenship identity in accordance with different situations, and also because of the importance to him of the cultural components of such an identity, specifically ethnicity. Indeed, this is the first thing that he says when he is asked about his identity: he describes himself without hesitation as *black British*.

In qualifying this statement, Cunningham points to certain ambiguities, rooted in historical and geographical processes. The 'direct' influence on him is from the Caribbean, and, he claims, this would have led to him being labelled 'Afro-Caribbean' according to earlier census categories. Now, though, he insists on altering that definition to 'black British'. Here, Cunningham is juggling the various different meanings of his sources of identification – black, Afro-Caribbean, African, British. This black identity is essentially a cultural one: he concedes that he has a very strong cultural affiliation for a *global* black community, and emphasizes the importance of being aware of the history of such a community: a history which, through colonialism, slavery and migration, has long since abandoned the nation-statist presumptions which were at the heart of the modern project.

This is tempered, however, by a kind of pragmatism that reflects his political position within the nation-state. This is why he refers to himself as black British. Describing himself thus, he states, does not mean he is 'buying into' the history of Britain, or that he is proud of it. He recalls discussions among his peers in the 1970s, which focused on how identifying oneself as 'British' did indeed mean 'buying into' the history and the prejudices. He is now of the opinion that the nation-state into which he was born can have an altogether different use. Recognizing the underrepresentation of black people in powerful positions, Cunningham stresses the need to 'find other ways of defining what sense of power you have':

> I'm not in a powerful position, in terms of black people not generally having power, but nonetheless, if I don't call myself black British then inevitably it takes me out of that power setting, and says that I

don't have any power at all, and I never have power. So in a sense, it's saying, I am black British, so therefore I have a stake, so therefore I have a say, and I'm not going anywhere, that's it.

Although this experience is not unique to him – other studies (such as Eade, 1997) have shown similar reflections on personal and structural-cultural identity by members of the 'black community' – we should be careful not to generalize, because this evidence has always suggested that it is a combination of a shared sociocultural history (slavery, colonialism, migration, racism and so on) and a deeply personal quest for self-identity which generates such a philosophy. Cunningham is suggesting that on the whole a white British person is able to 'close off' her or his identity (by reducing it simply to 'Britishness'), without needing to consider the possible *consequences* of this for her or his position within the power structure. A black person is denied this luxury. While he concedes that all identities, including 'Englishness' or 'Britishness', are in fact hybrid, and socially constructed, he seeks to draw our attention to the extent to which inequalities persist in the process of identity construction. As an individual affected by this, he takes care to be aware of this power structure, and is equally careful to stake his claim and assert his 'Britishness', simply because these taken-for-granted identities would otherwise prevent him from doing so.

So, for Ben Cunningham, 'Britishness' means something radically different, but no less important than it does for Al Brown, or so many others. While he considers history to be important, he does not believe that it is necessary to 'buy into' all the historical baggage that accompanies such an identity. But for him, 'Britishness' is a personal affirmation of power, rather than an identification as such. It is thus a product of the colonial and postcolonial experiences of black people; the result of activities within the economic and political world-system which has brought about this nation-state affirmation (see Hall, 1992 and Gilroy, 1993). We can divorce it from neither Cunningham's own life history, nor from the history of the black community per se.

We have seen how 'nationals' such as Al Brown have made use of 'levels' of identification to describe their loyalties. In Brown's case, this began with the most local, and stretched outwards, so that Brown found it difficult at times to consider himself 'British'. Cunningham's story reminds us that there are other such degrees. Unlike both Lifeson and Brown, Cunningham's identity is formed not as much over *levels* as between various inter-cutting and free-floating *circles*. Like Lifeson, though, he happily accepts what he considers to be a 'dual nationality'.

He admits he would have failed the so- called 'Tebbit test', being an ardent follower of the West Indies cricket team, but this does not in any way dampen his enthusiasm for England's national football side. He tells of a friend who holds on to a vision of an ancestral homeland (India) which takes precedence over his birthplace (Kenya), and these are both more important than the place of residence (the United Kingdom). He puts this down to a shared – and unwritten – antagonism among the Commonwealth nations and their offspring towards the colonizing country. Cunningham does not operate according to these levels, and is even more pragmatic in terms of his identity construction than either Lifeson or Brown. So while Brown's is an internal rejection of Britishness, the critique described by Cunningham comes from the outside, looking in. *For both Al Brown and Ben Cunningham, an identification with some form of 'Britishness' exists solely for the sake of convenience.* Neither would regard it as an 'essential' quality, embedded in the nation-state.

Cunningham, however, rejects a simplistic view of his own loyalties. He says that his is a 'dual nationality' which 'shifts forwards and backwards' depending on circumstance. This rejection of simplistic accounts of cultural identity based on colonialism and homogeneity, in favour of a more complex, pluralistic and individualistic one, supports much of the 'postmodern' discourse over constructed identities.[3] He adheres less to an essentialist 'black identity' than to a fluid, contested and pragmatic one.

So, clearly, the idea of being British is important to Cunningham not because it represents a strong sense of citizenship identity, but because it empowers him to act within the political structure in a way that would serve his best interests. Being black has less to do with an essentialist notion of a black community than with a contested self-identity. Indeed, the very idea that such a community exists in the way that it is perceived appears, to Cunningham at least, to be a crude form of Orientalism. He describes how (white) people fail to understand the differences between West Indian cultures (such as between Jamaica, where his mother is from, and St Lucia, where his father came from). He adds that he does not feel he could move to the West Indies and 'fit in' or 'be a citizen'. This is part of what he calls the 'dislocating' aspect of his national identity, potentially free-floating if not for his identification as British, linked in many ways to the Jewish diaspora. The global black community is made up of multiple differences, *between nations*, *between cultures*, and these differences are significant.

Citizenship, for Cunningham, then, is very much about identity as well as empowerment. Cunningham has thus explained how, in the everyday course of his own daily life, he regularly *deconstructs and reconstructs* an identity that is dislocated, diasporic and 'free-floating'. But this is not just the case with 'black' identity. The same is true of 'Britishness' in general, which is more inclusive and multicultural than 'Englishness'. Beyond this, significantly but perhaps the subject of another essay, is his view of being European. He feels that a 'black European' identity is possible, because of the histories which accompany many of the European nations, which blends cultural identity and political action in a way which is more inclusive than 'black British' and more unified than the global 'black community'.

For Paul Gilroy (1993: 1) the attempt to be 'both European and black requires some specific forms of double consciousness'. Cunningham's 'dual nationalism' appears to be such an attempt. For Gilroy, however, this relationship (between identification with nation and identification with black culture) suggests a need for an understanding of the Atlantic as a unit of analysis in itself, so that we can better understand the complex history of black culture and politics, simply because this was the space of slavery (ibid.: 15). Ben Cunningham accepts this line of argument to a degree, but wants to move it beyond the realms of the Atlantic triangle. So he dismisses the suggestion that black British culture has emulated black American culture as a negative image of black culture in general. What he finds interesting, for example, about black musical culture in the contemporary age is that it is less to do with America than with the blending of sounds and images from around the world. These sounds and images are traditional images, which are not necessarily the products of colonialism and slavery. As Gilroy says, the recourse to black 'tradition' is important because, while modernity represents the history of slavery (and colonialism), tradition recalls dignity. The modern experience of slavery and colonialism brought about the western view of a homogeneous black culture. Recourse to traditional sounds and images rekindles the spirit of a heterogeneity among the black 'population' which stands as resistance to racist and social Darwinist labelling. The 'postmodern' experience plays homogeneity off against heterogeneity. It collects these diverse sounds and images from distinct and particularistic local cultures, and reconstitutes them into a distinctive black style, but based on difference rather than sameness. Cunningham adopts a similar model for political identity.

Local citizenship as a global construction

These strategies for the construction of political identity are by no means exclusive. As globalization seems to entail some parallel process of 'localization', so might we argue that the relationship between the local and the global, bypassing the level of the nation-state, is strengthened under globalized conditions. Localities thus possess wholly new meanings for residents influenced by globality. Imagine, perhaps, an activist, maybe a keen member of Friends of the Earth or Greenpeace, who takes seriously the famous 'local/global' slogan, and who duly identifies with and acts politically in her neighbourhood because of a sense of global awareness. Such an actor is, significantly, bypassing the nation-state and duly re-empowering local action. Thus a sense of local political identity is made possible through an appreciation of global processes.

There are other ways in which the global construction of local identity is identifiable. Philippa Hunter is what researchers have elsewhere dubbed a 'western elite enclave dweller' (Albrow et al., 1994: 27). For her, local community is defined according to the possibility of like-minded people gathered together in a fixed locality. However, this is made possible by the fact that wealthy Philippa and her friends enjoy social networks that span the globe. It is thus not multiculturalism or the separation of nation and state but time–space compression which she takes advantage of in constructing her local identity. In this respect she is remarkably similar to Naranjan Desai, a member of a south Asian family which is scattered all around the world (ibid.: 32). Naranjan keeps in regular contact with her relatives, but at the same time enjoys a healthy and active life in her community, Tooting, which shifts between the local and the global. For Naranjan, her sense of cultural identity as Indian is reinforced both by her global connections and her local activism. These are examples of individuals who act politically at the local level but who identify, either culturally, as in the case of Naranjan, or with regard to their social relationships, as with Philippa, globally. What is most interesting is that it is through their globalized identities that their local affiliations are constructed.

Summary

This chapter has outlined in detail three very broad and distinct strategies used by individuals to construct their sense of political identity, and gone on to suggest a fourth. These strategies were selected because the richness of information supplied by the informants made it possible to do so, but there is an infinite number of variations. Each of us has our own unique biography; thus each of us adopts a different strategy or set of strategies in the construction of our sense of identity.

In truth, it is not the very fact of, but rather the sheer range of, choices available to us as individual actors which is a feature of everyday life under globalized conditions. The construction of identity is a particular kind of social action which takes place within the context of external conditions. These conditions ('structures') do not determine this 'agency', but they do serve to frame the choices which are available to the actor within that context. It is necessary, therefore, to follow Giddens in connecting contemporary external conditions (those defined primarily by sweeping global changes) with increasing *reflexivity* at the level of agency. If modernity has always been about 'making choices' (the 'burden of modernity' being nothing less than the choice between 'right' and 'wrong'), then the sweeping nature of global transformations, and the inherent reflexivity of late modern life, make these choices more complex, more individualized. They move beyond the parameters set by earlier forms of political identity (those reliant primarily upon nation-state, class-based political systems), and towards what Giddens (1991: 214–17) has called 'life politics'. The construction of political identities today satisfies Giddens' features of life politics: political decision-making emerges from freedom of choice, and power as transformative capacity; self-actualization takes place within the context of global interdependence; and ethics are developed in accordance with how one should live in a 'post-traditional' order (Giddens, 1991: 215).

Political identity is *still* framed within the context of *available choices*. We should therefore be careful not to generalize. Extreme external conditions allow for more extreme types of political identity. However, even in those instances where there has been an extreme resurgence of national identity, we should remember that identities are formed often in *resistance* to extreme external conditions. Writers who have sought to defend national identity as primordial assume its centrality, and neglect the contested, socially constructed, and diverse nature of identity. Yet the emergence of a national identity of this kind, perhaps taking the form of an extreme nationalism, is a *political* rather than a *natural* achievement. National identity of this kind becomes strong when other sources of identity and identification are closed off.

Any suggestion that political identity is a primordial quality embedded within the context of the nation is challenged in some way by each of the three main subjects of this chapter. This is most clear in Cunningham's case, but equally true in Brown's and Lifeson's. Cunningham actively, consciously, deconstructs the presuppositions of identity, and appropriates national identity for solely political reasons. Brown operates in a similar fashion. He appropriates national identity in order to protect, and at times strengthen, his regional one. Both are members of their own diaspora, dislocated from any sense of the 'authentic' and transported into a complex web of interactions through which their identities gain substance. For each of these three, globality exists as a resource available to draw on. Both Lifeson and Cunningham draw on it in a limited way: Lifeson, who otherwise operates in keeping with moral universalism, does so in a way which moves him closer to dealing pragmatically and directly with the world in which he lives. Cunningham draws on the ideals of non-modern citizenship to re-empower himself *as sovereign*. Brown chooses, in a calculated way, not to subscribe to this overt globality, but, in doing so, he is *still* operating within the context of communicative action – albeit one in which the validity claim to truth is not satisfied. He rejects the world as a source of identity whilst recognizing its impact upon him in the wider sense. Brown is *not* the same as those 'localists' he encounters during his visits to his home-town. *His* anti-globalism is not the result of the transmission of localism as a form of cultural capital (as might be the case in many cultural communities and particularly in once-essentialized 'working-class communities' which might have stressed the virtues of loyalty to the local *as a defence of the class against the Other*: O'Byrne, 1997), but of a strategic restructuring of the linguistically-grounded act of definition itself.

Within *global* citizenship, such sources and opportunities as these are more apparent, and there to be re-opened. Multiculturalism and the appropriation of new communications technologies for the benefit of resurrecting a genuinely democratic public sphere are among the key components of such a citizenship. If *national* identity only assumed its role as a primary source of identification in and around the eighteenth and nineteenth centuries, through the emergence of centralized political change, geographical mobility, and mass communications which made the image of the 'nation' a visible one for people (Miller, 1995: 154), then we can identify, in the post-1945 era, similar transformations in political, social, cultural, economic and technological life that have made the image of the *globe* an equally accessible one. The steady decline of economic and political imperialism which fostered the notion of western 'superiority' in the postwar era has opened up a vacuum into which comes a range of alternative, previously repressed, sources of identification. Each citizen juggles these sources in such a way as to construct and reconstruct his or her sense of political identity – be it local, national, or global.

According to the biographies outlined in this chapter we can see that Lifeson draws on these sources in order to define himself as a world citizen without endangering his sense of national culture. Lifeson's identity has duly been defined as a *political* world citizenship constructed through a *cultural* identification with the nation. Brown utilizes the same resources for the reason of maintaining his local identity, even though he is no longer resident in that locale; indeed, possibly *because* of this, given that his everyday life takes place within the complexities of multiculturalism and global flows that operate within the global city. Accordingly, Brown's identity is a political citizenship at the nation-state level constructed through a *localized* form of cultural capital. Cunningham utilizes these resources, which are *historical* as well as *geographical*, to challenge any assumption of essence and to re-empower his own sense of self through this deconstruction and reconstruction. He thus strategically negotiates the relationship between a transnational cultural identity and a pragmatic identification with the nation- state as a site of *political* action. There are, of course, other possible options which are made possible (if not real) by the global conditions of late modernity. These are governed solely by the logics of our own biographies, and by the external conditions within which we live and within which the various choices made available to us are framed.

What is clear from these three cases is that political identity does not predate, but rather stems from, *cultural* identity. We are thus reminded that citizenships (local, national, global, et cetera) are forms of identity and identification which are both *constructed* and performed. By implication, the opportunities for the exercising of world citizenship in the contemporary age *do* exist, and are displayed through the (increasingly reflexive) actions and performances of individuals such as those mentioned in this chapter, which is, if nothing else, about *how people perform their citizenships*.

Acknowledgements

The author is grateful to Professor Martin Albrow and Dr John Eade for their continued support, and to Paul Kennedy and Catherine Danks for comments made on an earlier draft of this chapter.

Notes

1 The names of the respondents have been changed. All other biographical information is accurate.
2 There are many anthropological accounts of ethnicity, and in particular the 'relationist' approach, which avoid such essentialism (see Banks, 1996).
3 The link between nationalism and cultural identity, and the suggestion that ethnicity is more a political than a cultural construct, has been explored in detail in the work of Anthony Smith (1981).

Part III

Globalization: The Challenge of an Uncertain Future

10

The Immigration of Foreign Workers: a Mirror of Israel's Changing Identity

William Berthomière

Like so many people arriving from the Paris–Lod night-flight, I was patiently waiting in line 5 to give my tourist card to the border officer before taking a flight to Jerusalem. As a frequent visitor to Israel, I was used to queuing and drowsing in front of the counters. But this time, two events attracted my attention. Firstly, as we were dropped by the bus at the entrance to the terminal an unusual scene was occurring in a corner of the customs hall. A young police officer was insistently questioning a very elegant man holding an attaché case. So far, there was nothing really astonishing except the fact that the latter was wearing a lovely blue bubu braided with gold. A second, no less surprising event soon followed which helped me to recover from the languor of waiting. Despite the fact that the travellers seemed tired, I could feel a clamour of excitment growing behind me. Glancing quickly, I saw six or maybe seven young men of Asian origin queuing up. They were hastily threading their way towards the counters much to the growing annoyance of the 'patient ones', like me. Nevertheless, as the police officer saw the group, and as one of them raised an envelope, apparently containing a range of passports and documents, everything returned to tranquillity and order. They crossed the checkpoint and entered Israel. Very quickly, these two events which broke the monotony of my passage through customs, awoke me to the realization that a new phenomenon was affecting Israel: the immigration of foreign workers.

This new immigration requires analysis and detailed examination, just like any form of mobility. However, this particular example commands even greater interest because it operates in Israel, a country that until recently has only experienced one type of mobility: namely, the *aliyah*, the so-called Jewish immigration. Moreover, the questions generated by this new form of immigration go far beyond the inherent problems that arise in any country where migration has been commonplace. This is because this change is happening at a time when the Israeli ethnoscape (Appadurai, 1990: 296–7; Dieckhoff and Jaffrelot, 1998) – that is, the shifting, global flow of people engaged in constructing and conveying an imagined Israelity – is also undergoing modification; as not just external but also internal groups within Israel itself, especially the new-Zionists and the post-Zionists, among others, struggle to determine just what the precise nature of Israel's permanent and normal identity should be. Thus, in trying to understand Israel's current situation with respect to redefining its identity we need to analyse two sequences of changing events, which have recently intersected. On the one hand, there is the history of migratory movements into Israel since 1948, and the changes this has undergone. But on the other hand there is the issue raised by Israel's recent perception of itself in the 'function-mirror' (see Marié in Allah et al., 1977) provided by the Other – the presence for the first time of non-Jewish migrants from across the world bringing very different cultural values and lifestyles. Looking into the mirror provided by the Other and seeing a reflection of ourselves is very often like 'conversing with and about ourselves'. Indeed, as Marié (1977: 16) suggested in his analysis of migratory movements, 'Alterity brings to light the codification mechanisms and the self-regulations processes of our societies'.

Migration time: Israel time

The type of migration that Israel is facing today is changing the nature of its society. The recent immigration of foreign workers constitutes a third phase in the periodization of the migration history through which the nation has passed since its creation. In the course of this half a century of existence, there have been three fairly distinct periods of migratory inflow. First came the Kibboutz *galouyot* (the 'Gathering of exiles'), that symbolized the Zionist project and the rebirth of a Jewish nation in 'Eretz Israel', the Land of Israel. Then there was the period in which the Zionist project had to be redefined because of the declining rate of Jewish immigration into Israel. By the same token, however, this phase also provided the breathing space and the opportunity for Israel's sons and daughters from many countries to settle down, meet and come to understand one another for the first time. This was the period of self-reflection; the 'self-reflective time'. The final phase in its migratory history – the arrival of foreign workers – has generated a dual experience for Israeli citizens. For those with a secular orientation it has meant the opening up of society to global cultural flows whereas for those who retain an orthodox religious orientation it has meant 'exposure' to the potentially threatening world of the 'others'.

The *Aliyot* years: from the 'gathering time' to the 'self-reflective time'

Soon after the creation of the state, Israel began to welcome many thousands of Jewish migrants and to incorporate them into the idea of the Zionist project. As a consequence, the Jewish population doubled between 1948 and 1952. The first arrivals, the surviving Jewish communities from the *Shoah* and those originating from the Islamic territories, gave way in the 1960s to new immigrants from Romania and the Soviet Union. This period of the 'gathering time' for the exiles, however, did not last long because most members of the Jewish communities living in the developed countries were not normally interested in the *aliyah* (migration to Israel). For example, immigrants born in the USA, Canada, the United Kingdom and France constituted only 5.5 per cent of the total immigration registered in Israel between 1948 and 1996 (see Table 10.1). Certainly, the Six Day War gave an added, though temporary, impetus to the interest and involvement of important diasporas in the *aliyah*. Thus, in the period between 1965 and 1971 the numbers of immigrants arriving from South Africa, Argentina, Brazil, Canada, the USA and France amounted to 41 000, a threefold increase compared to the preceding period from 1961 to 1964 (12 000). Nevertheless, following this brief period the relationship between the Centre (Israel) and the Periphery (the members of the diaspora) returned to what it had been before as the rate of Jewish immigration declined once again. As immigration fell and the influx of new and external influences diminished, so Israel became more self-absorbed; as a nation it withdrew into itself.

The transition to the era of the 'self-reflective time' was not a smooth one. Israel's sociopolitical heritage was heavy with the baggage relating to the political ideology of the Founding Fathers of the state. This created considerable tensions both between Jews of Ashkenazim (west, central and east European) and Sepharadim (Iberian and North African) origins, that is between secular and religious Jews, and also between Vatikim (those established citizens who had been in Israel for some time) and Olim (new Jewish immigrants to Israel). In reality, this meeting between these various groups, which was meant to produce a 'fusion of the exiles' (*mizzoug galouyot*), led to the creation of a multicultural

Table 10.1 Israel's changing population, 1948–1996

	Period									
	1948–1960	1961	1961–1971	1972	1972–1982	1983	1983–1989	1990	1990–1996	1996
Jewish population (000)		1 981		2 752		3 412		3 946		4 637
Annual growth of Jewish population (%)	9.2		3		2.2		1.5		3.1	
Non-Jewish Population (000)		252		472		706		875		1 122
Annual growth of non-Jewish population (%)	3.6		4.5		3.7		3		4	

Source: Statistical Abstract of Israel 1997, (Bureau Central des Statistiques, Jerusalem).

society in which differences and tensions between the different Jewish communities became more and more obvious. Moreover, it became apparent that these problems were not merely ones of transition (Eisenstadt, 1986). This reshaping of Israeli society and its growing divisions were soon reflected in the system of political party allegiances and representation. In particular, these tensions concerning the nature of Israeli identity became clearly evident during – and were symbolized by – the 1977 elections when the sepharadim vote enabled the right-wing nationalist party, the Likud, to gain a majority. This revealed a desire on the part of many Israelis to move much closer towards the kind of society that the Founding Fathers had originally proposed

The Palestinian question further amplified and fuelled the deepening internal rupture within Israel society that was undermining national solidarity. Moreover, soon after the territorial conquests of 1967 and the encounter with the ' "Historical" Land of Israel', it became apparent that achieving a synthesis between 'People/Land/State' was going to be much more difficult to realize than originally assumed because of Zionism's messianic 'investments' in, and intentions with respect to, that project (Attias and Benbassa, 1998; Dieckhoff, 1993; and Leibowitz et al., 1995). Thus, the deep links between the national community and its history (the question of its internal borders) and its sense of cultural uniqueness as defined through its separateness and distinctiveness from the 'Others' (the issue concerning its external borders) – both so critical for Jewish identity – were to engulf Israel in a highly introspective struggle concerning what kind of society it should become (see Juteau, 1994).

By the end of the 1970s Israel had entered a new social era based on a very complex sociopolitical structure. The approach to immigration, as Storper Perez (1996) has argued, now shifted towards the idea that Israel should give priority to attaining a pluralist society rather than – or as a substitute for – pursuing an integrated one based on successful assimilation. As a consequence, Israeli society was increasingly viewed as consisting of a diverse range of culturally varied groups living together in a common yet rather unequal socio-economic framework. This 'new nation' had to be constructed as a mosaic and through the juxtaposition of successive layers of population and even though the Founding Fathers had yearned to create a unified national community out of the merging of Jewish cultures and historical backgrounds. However, it soon became apparent that these deep economic and social differences between Israel's social groups would obstruct any such process (Dieckhoff, 1998). It is this society, of social and economic division, that foreign workers encounter today. By the same token, it is precisely because

Israeli society is now widely perceived as having been weakened by these divisions, and continues to search for some kind of mutually acceptable equilibrium, that the new wave of immigrants is provoking so much interrogation and anxiety.

During the late 1980s a new influx of Jewish immigrants arrived (the *Aliyot*) from Ethiopia and from the former Soviet Union. Initially, these new migrants were greeted joyfully but very soon their legitimacy was being called into question and they were being regarded as responsible for the troubles within Israeli society. Such arguments were also tinged with racism and exclusionist sentiments. Despite their legitimate right to join Israel, since the Law of Return[1] clearly applied to them as well, these 'Others' (the Soviet and the Ethiopian migrants) seemed to undermine and endanger the creation of an Israeli identity even more. Thus, it was widely feared that their presence was delaying the 'production of Israelity' (Berthomière, 1998). It was inevitable, therefore, that the arriving of foreign workers would add to the cultural diversity which was already disturbing Israeli society.

The immigration of foreign workers – 'the time of a world perspective'

The whole question of Israel's identity, and the need to redefine it, was brought very much to the fore once again when it opened its borders to foreign workers thereby exposing the country to a new set of socio-cultural influences. It is probable, moreover, that the unresolved issue of the Israeli–Palestinian conflict added to the general uncertainty created by this new social change. The modifications to Israel's social fabric resulting from the non-Jewish presence have become clearly perceptible. Firstly, the foreign workers have taken the place of the Palestinians on whom Israel formally depended for much of its non-Jewish workforce. Secondly, whereas the early batches of foreign workers who are legally entitled to enter for the purposes of work mostly arrived from eastern Europe and south Asia, more recently they have been flocking to Israel from dozens of countries and many regions across the world.

Towards a new socio-professional environment

Since the 1967 victory, the Israeli socio-professional environment has been organized around an economic space in which the Palestinian population largely filled the gaps in the labour force arising from the slowdown in the rate of Jewish migration and population increase. Israeli businessmen mainly faced labour shortages in the building trade and in agriculture and so these were the sectors especially dependent upon

Palestinian workers. During the 1970s and 1980s, the patterns and trends in employment increasingly reflected those in the economy as a whole and its different needs. Thus, an economic system arose in which the Jewish population took the skilled jobs, leaving the non-valorized ones – or the difficult, dangerous and dirty work – to the Palestinians. This system endured because it enabled many firms to keep their wage costs down. Meanwhile, in social terms there were apparently few obstacles preventing employers from underpaying their less-skilled Palestinian workers because most were resident in the West Bank and Gaza and so did not have to bear the cost of life in Israel (Borowski and Yanay, 1997).

However, from the end of 1987, the 'Intifada' became a reality and this has redrawn the socio-professional landscape and forced a change in the labour situation which been established for two decades. Israel's economic structure became trapped by a double spiral of decline which oscillated between the stresses, strains and costs provoked by the Palestinian revolt, on one side, and Israeli repression on the other. Slowly, it declined. In particular, the closure of the Occupied territories (the West Bank and the Gaza Strip) increasingly prevented Palestinian labour from entering the once-active economic regions. Consequently, Israeli entrepreneurs had to look for their labour elsewhere.

Spontaneously, and probably through an 'historical reflex', both business entrepreneurs and the government built their hope on the new *olim*, arriving from the former Soviet Union. Unfortunately, because the Jews from the former Soviet Union enjoyed one of the highest levels of education within the diaspora, it was impossible to replace Palestinian workers with soviet workers (Bartram, 1998). During the 1980s, some temporary permits allowing the entry of foreign workers were granted to employers in a few specialized industries to help them overcome the shortfall in labour supply. As in the case of most other southern European countries, such permits were mainly given to people of Asian origin especially those from the Philippines. However, from the beginning of 1990 and faced with this growing incompatibility between supply and demand, Israeli employers increased their pressure on the government, demanding that the country be opened up in order to permit the temporary immigration of foreign labour on a much larger scale. Between January and March 1991, 9500 permissions were granted (from 12 500 applications) and by the end of that year nearly 15 000 further permits had been granted, mostly to temporary agricultural workers (Borowski and Yanay, 1997).

From this date, the resort to foreign labour gradually became an established fact. Despite the Oslo Agreement of 1993, terrorist attacks

continued to increase with the result that the flow of Palestinian workers into Israel decreased even further. Between 1989 and 1996, the
number of work permits allocated to Palestinians from the West Bank
and from Gaza declined from 105 000 (6.7 per cent of the employed
people in Israel) to 19 000 (0.9 per cent), whereas those granted to non-
Palestinian workers increased from 3400 (0.2 per cent) to 103 000 (5 per
cent) (Bartram, 1998). As can be seen from Table 10.3, by the beginning
of 1998, the number of legal foreign workers registered at the Institute of
National Insurance had reached approximately 80 000 persons. In addition, Table 10.2 shows that among the many nationalities of foreign
workers in Israel, the Romanians and the Thais constitute the largest
contingents. The first have mainly been employed in order to replace
Palestinian workers who formerly worked in the building industry while
the second have mostly filled the gap left by departing Palestinians in
agriculture. Overall, it seems clear from the data in Tables 10.2 and 10.3
that by 1998 these changes in the social character of its economy had
embedded Israel firmly into the 'world system'.

Israel and globalization

Any observer of migration patterns in Israel today needs to be aware
that it is no longer sufficient to concentrate solely or even mainly on
analysing the flows of Jewish migrants. Whereas the young Israeli
State was essentially rooted in an 'extra- internationalism' – a relational
system based solely on the Jewish community and structured around a
territorial centrality in which the periphery was synonymous with the
diaspora – much more recently Israel has become engulfed by globalization. The new migration movement that Israel is facing, is, in fact,

Table 10.2   Foreign workers entering Israel with work permits by
main countries of origin

Country of origin	1995	1997
Romania	28 400	24 394
Thailand	12 600	7 108
Philippines	3 700	4 461
Turkey	3 200	4 500
Former Soviet Union	1 500	3 626
China	1 400	n.a.
Bulgaria	1 300	n.a.

Source: CBS, Jerusalem.
n.a. – not available.

Table 10.3 The employment of foreign workers by economic sector

Economic sector	*1998* (000s)
Construction	29.2
Agriculture	19.8
'Business services'[a]	13.2
Accommodation services and restaurants	4
Health, welfare and social work	3.7
Manufacturing	2.1
Other	5.5

Source: data from the National Insurance Institute.
Note: a. mostly subcontracted to the construction sector, but also cleaning, temporary work, etc.

comparable to the general dynamics of the migratory reconfigurations that have been in operation throughout the past ten years in Europe. The history of south–north mobility saw Mediterranean countries such as Spain, Italy and Greece progressively changing their roles: from the role of being a transit country, of being a migratory springboard for Europe, to one of being a land welcoming inward flows. This reversal was caused by two changes: Firstly, the earlier avenues for traditional immigration into countries such as France, Germany, and mainly Belgium, were closed and, secondly, the implementation of the Schengen Agreement has reinforced this process.

It appears, therefore, that the recomposition of European immigration patterns, associated with the building of 'fortress Europe', and the relocation of the centre of gravity for south–north mobility flows towards the Mediterranean countries, have combined to transform Israel into a new immigration space offering huge potentialities. The presence of illegal workers in Israel further testifies to this evolution. Thus, for the year 1996, the Statistics Central Department estimated that a further 80 000 people, illegally present in Israel and mostly from the developing countries, could be added to the 80 000 legal workers. In 1995, a preliminary estimation revealed that out of the 114 000 'visa overstayers', around 47 000 were from the more prosperous countries of the Third World while the remainder were from the poorest and least successful countries (see Table 10.4). The presence among these foreign migrants of people of African (Ghanaians and mainly Nigerians) and South American nationalities (Colombians and Peruvians) strongly confirms Israel's entrance into the international migratory system.

Table 10.4 'Visa overstayers' in Israel from Third World countries in 1997 (estimated numbers)

				Estimations				
FSU	*Poland*	*Romania*	*Colombia*	*Brazil*	*Jordan*	*Philippines*	*Argentina*	*Thailand*
10 200	3 200	2 800	2 500	1 900	1 500	1 300	1 200	1 100
Nigeria	*Turkey*	*Greece*	*Ethiopia*	*Portugal*	*Mexico*	*Bulgaria*	*India*	*Ghana*
1 100	1 100	900	900	800	800	700	600	500

Source: Central Bureau of Statistics, Press release, 1997.
Note:
FSU: former Soviet Union.

Probably because of its relative lack of experience in coping with the presence of large numbers of foreign residents, Israel seems to be finding it rather difficult to adjust to this new situation. In addition, the opening of Israel to these migratory networks marks the country's exposure to the cultures of the world's economically peripheral nations. Even though Israel is far from losing its own identity, it will have to learn to accommodate – however reluctantly – the cultural identities of the newcomers. Even if the need to adapt to these new influences does not present insuperable problems from the perspective of most citizens, this is not the same for the government. Thus, as Bigo (1996 and 1998) has argued, the government appears to operate with a north European conception of 'strangers' in that it regards the mere presence of difference as something which not only threatens national identity but which may also conspire to subvert internal security. However, the problem also goes beyond such issues as the supposed threat to national security. For Israeli society as a whole, the presence of these foreign workers over a long period of time is compelling its citizens to reconsider what they understand by and expect from a 'normalized' society and social life.

The perception of the 'Other' and understanding the self

The self-questioning stimulated by the growing presence of foreign labour in Israel is reinforcing other events and factors which are also bringing the issue of Israel's national identity to centre stage – for example, the controversy and debate over the evolution of the Peace Process. Consequently, it is worth considering in more detail. Israel authorized its entrepreneurs to undertake research in order to discover the role played by foreign labour in the economy and to ascertain the extent of the problems created by their presence. This seems to indicate that the country has begun to recognize the need to assume some responsibility for the decision to encourage large-scale foreign migrations. Following a long period of negotiations, in which the associations established in order to mobilize the defence of foreign workers – especially Kav La'Oved – played a crucial role, the social situation of these migrants seems to be improving. A recent publication in the newspaper *Ha'aretz*, entitled 'Foreign workers have rights too' (Porat, 1998), symbolizes the degree to which the rights of foreign workers have won recognition and even so their rights are still not awarded sufficient respect and many migrants continue to experience ill treatment just as in most states which depend on immigrant labour.

The Israeli government has also not been exempt from mistreating immigrants and turning a blind eye to inequities, as the following cases demonstrate. Recently, and following the arrest of a Thai worker for suspected murder, the minister of Employment (Eli Yishai) declared that 'the entrance of foreign workers has had a fatal effect on Israeli society' (quoted in Gorenberg, 1998). A similar example was revealed by the refusal to issue foreign workers with chemical protection kits in the event of Iraqi air attacks on Israel (Hayoun, 1998). There is some evidence that Israeli society is beginning to react to these and other illustrations of discrimination against foreign workers and is becoming aware of the social problems created by such treatment (Gorenberg, 1998). Nevertheless, the attempt by some foreign workers to alter their status as temporary employees and to achieve permanent residency rights is perceived by many citizens as a threat. In 1998, a headline in the Israeli press focused attention on this particular issue with a highly provocative title: 'Don't fall in love with a foreign worker' (Shohat, 1998).

The intensity of the social debate that has developed around the issue of foreign workers shows that Israel is becoming 'a country similar to the others'. Its tendency to attract foreign migrants who are searching for a way of improving their life chances is also not unrelated to the tendency on the part of many observers to promote Israel as an economic 'success story'. According to the OECD, with a gross domestic product (GDP) per capita of $12 737 in 1990, Israel was well ahead of all the other countries categorized as belonging to the south Mediterranean group/Maghreb group. The equivalent figure for the second country in this group, Turkey, was $6038.

The presence of foreign workers has brought with it essential questions about human rights and how to achieve social integration. The Israeli State has taken a central role in relation to these issues but the debates also reach beyond those interrogations. Thus, although the presence of the 'Other' has been regarded as an indication on the part of some citizens that the country is now on a path to normalization, others are convinced that it can only lead to the dissolution of the state's Jewish identity. For the latter, therefore, the priority is to avoid normalization. Indeed, the arrival and presence of foreign workers and, above all, the possibility of their eventual settlement in the country, has widened still further and focused attention on the deep split which exists between the neo-Zionists the post-Zionists. As Ram (1998: 223) has suggested, the neo-Zionist position 'represents a retreat to a sense of identity, a nationalist, racist and anti-democratic trend that tries to heighten the barriers around its national Israeli identity'. Such leanings are partly explicable in terms of the violence associated with the Israeli–Arab conflict and the lack of integration in the economy. Even though the issue of whether the immigrants will eventually be allowed to settle permanently or not is far from being resolved, their very presence means that they continue to offer a mirror in which Israeli identity is reflected and questioned. Indeed, for these new-Zionists, this presence brings globalization into the heart of the country's affairs and accentuates their desire to preserve the original and 'traditional' uniqueness of Israeli identity at all costs (see Dieckhoff and Jaffrelot, 1998). On the other hand, Ram (1998: 223) defines the post-Zionist position as expressing a 'libertarian trend which aims at reducing the barriers to national identity and of integrating the "Other"'. What we see here, then, is the further deepening of the profound schism lying at the centre of Israeli society between two populations each trying to aquire and assert their own identities. One strongly favours a Jewish state while the other seeks to establish a democratic, post-Zionist state (Ram, 1998: 230).

Locked into this debate between either a Jewish state or a state for the Jews, Israeli society finds itself today at a crossroads. Formerly, these two trends were combined within the homogeneous ideology of the labour movement. Yet, today, the terms in which the narrative of nationalism has been reconfigured means that the perpetuation of national unity appears more and more in doubt. The key questions today are whether Israel's citizens retain the capacity and the wish to continue living together as members of one state and how it may be possible to sustain the management of a society 'in which one part of the population is on the Internet, and the other one is on the Torah' (Dieckhoff, 1998: 20).

Adopting a longer time perspective, it is possible to envisage a society where the foreign workers have been allowed to become permanent settlers, but clearly this will require the political ascendancy of the adherents of the post-Zionist party. The reformulation of nationalism along such lines would then mean that the situation in Israel resembled that found in Catalonia in Spain, where nationalist sentiments – boosted by a high rate of immigration – were nevertheless channelled towards the creation of a coherent and recognized identity without leading to conflict or separatism. There is also the opposite hypothesis, where the neo-Zionists succeed in defining the character of Israel's future national identity – though this possibility is probably decreasing all the time. Here, there is a preference for returning to the previous situation where Palestinian labour is employed once again. It is doubtful, however, whether this would succeed in calming the current agitation surrounding Israeli identity – especially given the continuing presence of the foreign workers. In any case, such a return to earlier practices seems difficult to realize. In part, this is because the closure of the Occupied territories has reduced the social bonds – tenuous but nevertheless real – which formally united Israeli employers and the Palestinian workers. But, in addition, the Palestinian elite considers this rupture as a necessary part of the process required in order to wean Palestinians from their former, albeit reluctant, dependence on Israel.

Any attempt to draw conclusions from this analysis is inevitably fraught with risks. Clearly, much more empirical research on the changing nature of Israeli society needs to be undertaken by social scientists. In conceptual terms, however, we could say that the country is in the throes of coming to terms with how local identity can and must be rewritten given Israel's confrontation with globalizing forces. One of the quotations selected by Levinas for his work, *Humanism de L'Autre Homme* (1972: 95), seems especially pertinent here and perhaps symbolizes Israel's current dilemma: 'If I don't answer for me, who will? But if I answer only for me, am I still being myself?' (Talmud de Babylone – traité Aboth 6a)

Acknowledgement

I would like to thak Dr Ari Paltiel for his assistance and also Carole Fautrez for help with the English translation of this chapter.

Note

1   The Law of Return (1950) stipulates that any Jew has a right to immigrate to Israel. The 1979 amendment to this Law extended this right to family members of any Jew (see Anteby, 1998).

11
Identities, Truth and Reconciliation in South Africa: Some International Concerns

Elizabeth Stanley

This chapter examines a range of human rights concerns raised by issues relating to truth, reconciliation and identities in a global context. After covering the Truth and Reconciliation Commission (TRC) in South Africa in some depth, this chapter analyses the TRC in order to illustrate the argument that globalization and identities are central to debates on transitional democracies, but relates the ideas and dilemmas raised into a broader field. Indeed, most of the issues highlighted about the use of truth-finding, and its consequences for identities, have a direct bearing on debates about globalization, migration and the movement of peoples, inter- and intra-state violence, social justice issues, human rights and critical theory. In this chapter 'identities' are framed by how individuals or collective groups perceive, and make sense of their own individuality, based on how they make sense of their 'selves', how they make sense of others and, of course, their reaction to how they are perceived by others.

The global context

Globalization has now become 'a crucial theme as well as a key analytical concept' (Kayatekin and Ruccio, 1998: 76). Perhaps the most important question for any scholar involved in human rights work is: What are the links between human rights, truth, justice, reconciliation and globalization? In responding to this broad question, this chapter aims to examine issues of 'dealing with the past' in South Africa, focusing on a discussion of how the TRC, in particular, has impacted on individual and group identifications. The term globalization, as

Bauman (1998: 59) points out, frequently refers to those 'unintended and unanticipated' effects of the new world order rather than to those global 'initiatives' undertaken by transnational companies, financial corporations, powerful states and legal bodies designed to universalize order-making and markets. Without doubt, this articulation of globalization as promoting free and indeterminate possibilities 'camouflages the organization of power' within the global order (Silbey, 1997: 233).

Within a human rights discourse, this globalization thesis is borne out in the growing interconnectedness of truth, justice and reconciliatory mechanisms. Academically, there is the emergence of a burgeoning literature that focuses on a comparative analysis of human rights work, truth commissions, and international justice (Boraine et al., 1994; Hayner, 1994; Hamber, 1998). This is led by human rights organizations such as Amnesty and Human Rights Watch that operate on an international level. Alongside this, there has been a move to establish international legal mechanisms to deal with human rights and war crimes violators. This has recently accelerated with the establishment of an International Criminal Court agreed by the Treaty of Rome, on 17 July 1998. Clearly, if this court proves effective, the potential for extending the rule of law on a global scale is enormous (Human Rights Watch, 1998). Finally, we can see that events and processes undertaken in one country are 'stimulating' events and processes in others, as structures that are based on accessing truth and promoting reconciliation are developed at a global level (McGrew, 1992). The structure of the South African TRC, for example, developed from an awareness of the activities of other transitional states particularly within Latin America and Eastern Europe. As Kader Asmal (in Boraine et al., 1994: viii) identifies, 'we learnt a great deal from foreigners who cared about their countries'. In addition, the South African experience has already begun to inform the ways in which other countries undergoing transition, such as Northern Ireland and Sierra Leone, attempt to deal with their past.

For anyone interested in rights issues, these transnational projects seem to be positive steps in attempts to control and deal with horrific acts such as torture, disappearances and war crimes across the world. As new attempts to deal with such concerns become evident, the interest shown by the international community on academic, political, legal and individual levels also increases. Without doubt, this has been the case with regards to South Africa where the transition to democracy has been closely scrutinized across the world.

The South African context

The repression suffered by the masses of South Africa is well documented as is the struggle against apartheid (Monama, 1996). From the separation policies that led up to the first National Party (NP) victory in 1948, to the ensuing major apartheid legislation, the segregation and regulation of indigenous groups for economic ends was clear (Johns and Davis, 1991). Under apartheid, the black people of South Africa suffered violent racial oppression, subjugation, economic deprivation, detention, arrests, the banning of political parties, torture, massacre and balkanization into the notorious Bantustans. This treatment, led by the NP, began to face both national and international resistance, with the international media providing an alternative source of communication for the nationally banned resistance parties (Thomas, 1997). From the 1970s to Nelson Mandela's release in 1990 under the direction of the newly elected president F. W. de Klerk, the maintenance of apartheid represented a microcosm of social injustice within a global arena.

In South Africa throughout the twentieth century, almost all identities were legislated. These national identities were generally static, adhered to, resisted and enforced; yet, they were clear and the definitions represented a certain element of consensus. At his inauguration in 1994, President Nelson Mandela commented that South African identity could be seen as a 'rainbow nation at peace with itself and the world'. Together with a clear recognition of South Africa's place in a global arena, the traditionally defined identities were upheld, with the (naïve) optimism of groups living harmoniously, side by side. Post apartheid, these identities became open to negotiation, as there was no agreed upon reality or single discourse to which South Africans could refer. As Beinart (1994: 4) states, South Africa today is 'precisely and fully in the process of inventing illusions'. With the transition to democracy, South Africa set about to find a new truth.

The Truth and Reconciliation Commission (TRC) was the principal means of establishing an agreed reality of South Africa's violent past. Established shortly after Mandela's succession to power, under the Promotion of National Unity and Reconciliation Act of 1995, the South African TRC constitutes the most ambitious attempt, so far, to deal with crimes of a past regime through a concept of truth. The importance of identities was clear from the outset as the TRC was obliged to uncover who did what, when and to whom. The TRC had an investigative unit and three principal, functionally defined committees. The first committee recorded human rights violations that took place between 1 March 1960 and 5 December 1993, the second focused on granting amnesties to individuals who fully recounted political acts and the third focused on Reparations and Rehabilitation by establishing the fate and whereabouts of victims and recommending reparatory measures.

Headed by Archbishop Desmond Tutu, the Commission was initially staffed by 17 individuals, chosen from a selection of almost 500 nominations. The TRC Final Report (1998) shows that consideration was given to 'ensure the broadest possible representation in terms of skills, culture, language, faith and gender'. From the outset, however, the Commission was vilified by political parties, such as the National Party (NP) and the Inkatha Freedom Party (IFP) and the media, particularly *Rapport* and *Die Burger*, as being biased towards the African National Congress (ANC) (Muller, 1997). As a result, these parties did not actively participate in the Commission process. In addition to feelings of being excluded from the Commission's infrastructure, some NP and IFP members have also been determined not to undermine their own positive identities. These individuals do not want to be nationally represented as 'perpetrators' nor do they want to claim responsibility for violations. As such, their stories remain untold. This means that a comprehensive history based in collective memories and stories is looking quite remote. What will this mean for South Africa in the future? The TRC has published its Final Report heralded as *the* version of events, yet there are sections of the SA population who are underrepresented. Here, the truth about the past will be framed by victims' stories and this will obviously lose some of the diversity of experiences under apartheid.

However, the Commission has still been successful in accessing diverse stories – over 21 000 statements from victims and over 9000 applications for amnesty have been heard. From this point alone, it is clear that the TRC has listened to and acknowledged many individual stories and much pain. It is difficult to believe that most of these stories and memories would have been publicly acknowledged without this process. Without doubt, the TRC has offered a chance to 'reduce the number of lies being circulated unchallenged' in public, official discourse (Ignatieff, 1996). Importantly, it has allowed survivors to frame their own experiences in their own language. When it is remembered that many victims have never been listened to before, that many have been systematically dehumanized and demonized as political tools, it becomes evident how important this process can be in reaffirming the importance of individual identities. It confers on people the right and ability to believe that what happened to them, as individuals, actually matters. For this reason, many have wanted the truth to be acknowledged, however painful (Monama, 1996).

Such has been the number of stories and memories brought to the Commission that the past can no longer be denied. Many have been amazed by the sheer intensity and amount of violations brought to light. In an interview with the author (February 1998), Yasmin Sooka, a TRC Commissioner, stated that there have been different levels of self-deception, from those saying that they did not know these things were happening at all to those that say 'these things were kept away from us'. A lot of people did not realize the scale of violence, even those that worked within the anti-apartheid movement have an acute sense of shock that it was so gross, they were unaware of the extent to which the violence had grown and the depths it had reached. An indication of the brutality of the latter part of the resistance from 1990 to 1994, is that the Commission recorded 5695 killings, yet the TRC Report (2 (7), 1998: 7–15) estimates that 14 000 South Africans died in politically related incidents between mid-1990 and April 1994. The extent of torture, severe ill treatment and abduction is, similarly, incomprehensibly vast. Given a narrow mandate, the Commission did not specifically focus on the wider acts of violence that affected swathes of the population. As the TRC Final Report (1 (2) 1998: 45–6) makes clear, 'for at least 3.5 million black South Africans apartheid meant collective expulsions, forced migration, bulldozing, gutting or seizure of homes, the mandatory carrying of passes, forced removals into rural ghettos and increased poverty and desperation'. Violence was a part of everyday life.

Myth and identity in South Africa

Much of recent South African life has been based on ideological myths – for example, the idea that white settlers were the civilized and advanced population, who should therefore dutifully assume the economic and political burden of upholding a decent nation. There were also carefully placed claims that hit-squad activities, undertaken by white security-police officers, were actually cases of 'black-on-black' violence, 'suggesting to the world that barbaric natives were predictably going for each other's throats as the necessary constraints of white overlordship were relaxed. The truth . . . was somewhat different' (Asmal et al., 1997: 102). There are many other examples and like all good myths, these have exaggerated, dramatized and reinterpreted life in South Africa. Moreover, they have been believed – and to an extent they still are. Of course, these myths have also been disputed, which is one of the reasons why apartheid was fiercely challenged and resisted. They are hard to dispel, however, and remain especially powerful in the construction and reconstruction of identities.

Within South Africa identities have been tightly demarcated (Connolly, 1991) as the government based its legislation and policies on strict categorizations of ethnic identities. The politics of difference, under apartheid, was based on the principle of 'naming races'. The Population Classification Act of 1952, for example, listed Whites (Blankes), Blacks (Swartes), Indians (Indiers) and Coloureds (Kleurlinge) as 'self-evident, autonomous populations' (Beinart, 1994: 144). Other legislation, such as the Pass Laws, repealed in 1986, were one method of ensuring that these legally constructed identities were adhered to and, when necessary, enforced. Yet, it can also be seen that, with the transition to a democratic South Africa, identities are also historically contingent. As Connolly (1991: 203) notes, identities are 'particular, constructed and relational' and South Africa, as a transitional state, is no exception in these struggles over individual/collective identifications and representations.

One could argue that the state is the 'pivotal embodiment of collective identity' in that identities and their associated ideologies can be politically managed (Archard, 1995). This is clearly evident in South Africa where myths created 'common enemies', thereby bolstering a 'politics of exclusion'. Indeed, the ruling white population upheld the ideological construction of apartheid through the very maintenance and management of negative representations of black populations at both the national and the international levels. This management of identities relates directly to the key concern of 'truth' in that, historically, the truth of events in South Africa was made *for* the people not *by* the people. Evidently, the official truth of events in South Africa stood outside the actual reality experienced by most of the population. Undisputably, the victims of the apartheid-fuelled discrimination and violence already knew the truth. They lived and suffered under apartheid – they already know what happened. Similarly, white and black perpetrators of violence already know what they did, so what becomes important here is acknowledgement. Thus, the TRC aimed to provide a collective acknowledgement of individual memories of events, of individualized and complex truths. Articulating memories, that is recalling to mind individual facts or experiences, has been all important in unearthing a truth that is not solely owned by those who wield power.

Telling stories about the past, legitimizing individual experience, has led to a reassessment of individual and group representations. For instance, the TRC Report has pulled apart many stereotypes. So, the Afrikaner, Johan Smit, claimed that his eight-year-old son, who was killed by an ANC bomb, had died 'in the cause of the oppressed people' (HRV Submission, 29 April 1996). His attempt to 'see things from the other side', within a personally highly distressing situation, falls outside the expected Afrikaans' response to violence from apartheid resisters (Beresford, 1998). Further, at a Human Rights Violation Hearing in Port Elizabeth, the ANC activist MP, Cikizwa Ivy Gcina, gave testimony on her detention in 1985. She praised her prison warder, Irene Crouse, saying 'She made me take the medicine and massaged me. Then after that I could at least try and sleep.' As a result Irene, within her state-institution role, was described as having 'risen above the system' (TRC Final Report 5 (9), 1998: 66–9). Finally, Winnie Mandela, the 'mother of the nation' and a clear representative of the apartheid struggle around the world, was stated to have been involved in cases of murder and severe ill treatment against her own people.

Unexpectedly, the traditional simple classification of individuals as either 'victims' or 'perpetrators' is demonstrated to be irrelevant in the lived experiences of many individuals. Individual identities may not sit so easily with the identities that individuals are assigned by virtue of their defined group or national status; individuals do not always act in stereotypical fashion. So, whilst the truth for some people has been an important step, offering a means to satisfy the victim's desire for justice and to give the perpetrators an opportunity for personal cleansing; there are victims who do not fit neatly into the assigned, restorative role of 'forgiver' and who, instead, want punitive action taken against their aggressors. For example, the family of Steve Biko, who died in police custody in 1977, argued vehemently against indemnity and many South Africans could hardly blame them. With no improvement in life and a loved one murdered, why should they forgive? Furthermore, why should we expect such people to forgive and be reconciled (Rolston, 1999)?, particularly as perpetrators frequently do not demonstrate repentance. These newly emergent identities have had powerful reper-cussions within South Africa and have also impacted on how we, around the world, continue to make sense of apartheid and ensuing attempts for reconciliation.

Confused and confusing identities

Within South Africa, and within most countries that have suffered gross human rights violations, the distinction between who is a 'victim' and who is a 'perpetrator' becomes increasingly blurred. Those traditionally viewed as victims are also perpetrators and those traditonally viewed as perpetrators may also be victims. Gross human rights violations were committed by ANC members, the 'victims' of the apartheid system. Eugene de Kock, an ex-security-police officer jailed for over 200 years for his part in killing and torture, views himself as a victim of police service policies; he was just doing his job, following the terms of 'due obedience'. On this level, and between these two extremes, it becomes difficult for an individual to identify him/herself as a 'victim' or a 'perpetrator'. This particularly so when one considers that all the white population benefited from the apartheid era to some extent, even those who did not directly support apartheid. How then can distinctions be made between the 'victims' and 'perpetrators'? How may these increasingly blurred distinctions be brought into focus? Within the TRC context, detailed attempts have been made to carve out a moral high ground between the resisters and enforcers of apartheid. This has been undertaken to make distinctions between the kinds of violence that were undertaken. Thus, it has been argued that the resisters were fighting a moral cause, that the main objective of the ANC was to promote democracy, and that in 1973, the UN had identified apartheid, in itself, as a 'crime against humanity' (Asmal et al., 1997).

Such issues have caused problems for the Commission because certain groups, such as the NP, believe that the TRC's moral agendas have been used to cover up ANC atrocities. Furthermore, that it has been used as a propaganda tool in order to muddy the water so that ANC activists do not have to bear their burden of responsibility for their human rights violations (Myburgh, 1996). In this way the ANC's collective identity as 'victim' can be upheld. This reasoning also provides a way for NP members to avoid guilt, shame and responsibility for their own actions. To a certain extent, these criticisms have had an impact on the ANC, borne out by their attempt to delay the publication of the TRC Report in late October 1998. Thabo Mbeki, the newly elected president of South Africa, categorized the Report's balanced criticism of the ANCs own violations as 'wrong and misguided' (Woollacott, 1998). He felt that the ANC were too heavily blamed for their part in atrocities, regardless of their moral high ground. In this sense, the Report upset all myths – even those about groups who are popularly deemed to be 'victims'.

At a recent conference in Belfast (Incore, 1998), Marie Smyth, a worker on the Cost of the Troubles Study in Northern Ireland, indicated that it is possible to talk about hierarchies of pain and responsibility within transitional countries. Smyth based this claim on the following arguments: some individuals, families and communities have suffered more than others, without complicity in the events and atrocities; some individuals, families and communities have harmed and killed more than others through choice-based action; and, some people have more power to change things than others. With reference to the third point – that some people have more power to change things – it could also be argued that some people have more power to leave things as they are. Thus, the everyday reality of relations between 'victims' and 'perpetrators' has not changed in South Africa (Pilger, 1998b). Thus, the beatings, torture, disappearances undertaken by the security personnel and police have continued (*Newsnight*, 19 April 1999, *BBC* 2). Meanwhile, the judiciary that upheld apartheid is still intact with little future prospects for change (Dyzenhaus, 1998). In addition, apartheid's economic base has hardly changed; apart from a number of black figureheads in large businesses, the economy continues as before. When across the world, wine drinkers raised a sigh of relief when they felt able to buy South African produce, the white vineyard owners rubbed their hands with glee. Certainly, for these people, profits are up. Perhaps more importantly, their economic power base is now legitimized by the ANC government.

Furthermore, on an anecdotal level, it would appear that those black workers who have achieved promotion above the previous glass ceiling are quite happy, in the main, to go along with the deal. Walking around supermarkets in Johannesburg, one becomes accustomed to seeing black maids pushing a trolley behind an affluent white woman. Now, one can see the same black maids following the affluent black women. Here, Godobo-Madikizela (1996) argues that there is a 'silent quest' to change identity in that successful blacks are primarily concerned with becoming individually accepted by whites. Identities, then, are transient, they are ever-changing – they are open to interpretation and reinterpretation. They are also framed by economic power and development.

Embracing identities

'A penny for your thoughts' is a phrase we often use to coax some one to open up, to say what is on their mind. In South Africa, this idea has taken on a new meaning to the extent that a political economy of truth has emerged. Individuals who come before the Commission have an interest in being categorized. For a person to be labelled or identified as a 'victim' means a chance of receiving reparation assistance – which could be in the form of money, an educational scholarship and/or improved housing. This 'victim' identity provides an important legal status (Ewick and Silbey, 1998) because it may lead to substantial benefits, particularly for those living in rural areas where basic services are lacking. Yet, the TRC is also said to have antagonized communities by naming some residents as victims and not others. This has posed conflictual problems for those living side by side, who may see themselves as having gone through similar experiences.

On the other hand, for an individual to be labelled as a 'perpetrator' means that they can, through the amnesty process, be relieved of any future prosecution for their actions. A carrot-and-stick approach was adopted by the TRC to encourage people to come forward and tell their stories; if they gave full disclosure and the acts are deemed to be political in nature, a direct amnesty was given. If the story did not fit these guidelines or a perpetrator (who is indicted by a victim) did not come forward, then the case is directed towards prosecution. Here, it becomes clear that there is a struggle between power and resistance in formulating identities. Some individuals want to be named either as a victim or a perpetrator and, of course, some do not want to be named at all. This is the case for perpetrators, but it also applies to victims, such as women who were the victims of sexual violence.

Sidelining identities: gender and the TRC

It has been noted that the TRC has failed to listen to women's stories. There have been three sessions dedicated to women and yet many stories have gone unheard. This is not to say that women have not come forward as they have. *Truthtalk* (1998), the official newsletter of the TRC, estimates that 53 per cent of statements made to the Commission were by women, but that these were often about important male partners or relatives, rather than about themselves. In this sense, women have been cast as secondary victims (Goldblatt and Meintjes, 1996). This is the result of a number of factors. Firstly, the narrow mandate given by the TRC on acts of 'killing, abduction, torture and severe ill-treatment' has meant that women's experiences have been overlooked, even though many women had entirely different experiences of the apartheid regime in South Africa. If a husband disappeared, it would be the woman who walked from hospital to hospital, often covering hundreds of miles in the search. These specific experiences, together with the fact that women 'bore the brunt of oppression' – such as forced removals, low wages, pass arrests, lack of education, limited fresh water, and so on – is not represented in the TRC mandate (Goldblatt and Meintjes, 1996;

Hamber and Kibble, 1999: 10). Secondly, women who have been subject to atrocities have often stated that although the TRC was much more informal than the court system process it was still intimidating. This is especially so if violations against them were of a sexual nature. The small number of hearings directed towards women has been insufficient in cases where sensitivity is paramount. This sidelining of women's stories evidently raises questions about how complete this truth-gathering process can be. Furthermore, it brings into question how we, as outsiders, view South African history and who we identify as the chief victims, given that our own views of victims' sufferings are based on this distorted 'official' truth of events.

Shaping identities

Characteristically, the more powerful organizations, groups and individuals are faring better in this battle for positive identification. South African politicians and business personnel are only too aware of the need to consolidate a positive identity to maintain their status at the national and global levels. Hence individuals such as Winnie Mandela, Chief Buthelezi and F. W. de Klerk have all, with the help of expensive legal representation, managed to retain their power and status within South Africa. Their involvement in the maintenance and brutalities of apartheid is 'overlooked' within the national need for political stability. These positive representations have also, to a greater or lesser extent, been accepted internationally. Where adverse representations have been demonstrated, the actions of Commissioners, from articulating support for the individual, undertaking symbolic acts of comradeship to emphasizing the need for reconciliation, have neutralized their negative impact.

Similarly, through the TRC, other groups have maintained a clear control over their perceived national identities. Whilst the victims of apartheid, such as the militarized young people (highlighted below), are cast as the new villains of democratic South Africa, big businesses, such as Armscor the apartheid armaments producer, 'rose from the depths of moral culpability to the elevated status of "national asset". Armaments which once repressed pro-democracy activists in South Africa are now being exported to Indonesia where they are used against activists in East Timor' (Nattrass, 1999: 390). The TRC, operating within a state that is committed to development within a global economy, posed no real challenge to these self-altered identities.

It is clear that collective identities are more positively reconstructed, altered and defined when the individual or group maintains a position of power. Unfortunately, the TRC seems to have accepted these defined, national identities. Consequently, individuals working within the media, business or judiciary, who may have upheld the apartheid state, have not had to outline their individual responsibility. In a sense, these individuals have benefited from a 'structural immunity' that submerges individual identities into a broader national identity. Of course, some individuals have acknowledged individual responsibility here, but they are few and far between. This is, perhaps, where individual and national identities connect. Whilst certain sections of the population come to terms with their individual part in apartheid, those involved within state organizations are individually 'silenced' to underpin social cohesiveness, in line with the need to participate in the global economy. Within this realm of power it is useful to use Brecher and Costello's (1994) globalization thesis, to distinguish between 'identities from above' – that is those controlled nationally by powerful groups, including those provided by the TRC, to demonstrate a cohesive framework – and 'identities from below' – that is those more complex identities that are demonstrated through individual statements.

Who listens? Formulating identities post-TRC

In other instances, however, the TRC has attempted to outline the structural conditions that fuelled apartheid. Yet, even where the Commission has been careful in its representation of groups, the social knowledge of those groups may remain negative. For example, in the Special Hearings on Children and Youth, explanations of current violence, on public and private levels, were explored. These hearings highlighted the histories of resistance-military wing members, aged between 11 and 21, whose main purpose was to 'protect' those areas that had become targets for state repression. These youngsters, operating throughout the 1980s and 1990s, were highly trained in the use of weaponry and explosives; they were also frequently subject to harrowing acts of torture, sexual assaults and beatings, in police attempts to extract confessions. Today, many are unable to function in 'normal' society. They have no other skills as their childhood opportunities of education and training were traded for armed struggle. As the TRC Report states, 'there was no preparation for the consequences of such actions' (TRC Final Report 4 (9), 1998: 12).

These individuals 'born in the eye of the storm' (ibid.) are frequently demonized as the principal perpetrators of violence in South Africa. The new label on Johannesburg, as the most dangerous city in the world, with individuals risking car-jacking and sexual violence, is frequently blamed

on these black 'ex-victims' of apartheid, whilst the new victims are identified to be the white population. This would appear to be a cruel twist of
fate because the current violence would be better understood within the
historical context established by the TRC. In this sense, the TRC has made
a real contribution to the understanding of present-day South Africa but,
given that the new victims are those who retain the power (within the
media, the economy and the judiciary), this contextualization of violence is neutralized across the world (Cohen, 1993).

Aside from crime, another key concern in the new South Africa has
been the issue of relocation, with ongoing tensions around land law and
the incredibly slow return of peoples to their 'homeland'. Here, it can be
seen that identities are strongly felt in the need to move back, from
shanty towns, to a perceived 'rightful place'. One instance could be seen
in the summer of 1998 when 3000 people relocated themselves to an
area in Cape Town that they named 'Freedom City', daring the country's
largest ANC Council to evict them. This was reported in *The Guardian*
(5 May 1998: 12), along with a picture of one of the makeshift houses
erected on the site. The picture was highly illustrative – it showed a
young boy, outside his new home, with a placard that read 'It's Mine
Forever'. It would seem that individual and group representations may
be closely linked to claimed land rights. As Pile and Keith (1997) argue,
the politics of identity is finely linked to a politics of place. Predictably,
this determined focus on space has also been taken up by more powerful
groups. Fergal Keane (1996) has documented attempts made by multinational corporations (MNCs) to take over the squatter camp land occupied by blacks around Johannesburg. Space has become all-important in
the protection and expansion of economic interests. From the need
to expand on to squatter land, to the establishment of middle-class
'confined towns' guarded by private security, the maintenance of apartheid is upheld on every corner. Where does this leave the majority of
South Africans?

Kader Asmal, who helped to set up the Commission, has said that
South Africa is going through three reform processes simultaneously:
democratization, deracialization and development (Asmal et al., 1997).
Further, as far as development is concerned, white groups have to be
aware that this has to be more than the perception of opening the golf
club up to new members (Steel, 1997). Instead, development has to be
as basic as providing electricity, digging wells and the relocation of
individuals. There has been some success here with the ANC erecting
750 000 new homes for the poor and three million homes have been
provided with electricity and running water (McGreal, 1999). South

Africa remains in economic turmoil; it still has an outstanding multi-billion-dollar loan and is confronted by the neoliberal demands of the International Monetary Fund (IMF). Thus, apartheid is legitimized on national and global terms. As John Pilger clarifies (1998a: 18) 'apartheid has not died, it continues by other means . . . the servants are still serving, the squatters are still squatting (and being evicted by white-led police) and the majority are still waiting – while the "madams" and the "baases" experience no real change in life'.

Conclusions: international concerns

South Africa has demonstrated that a country can face the past; it has demonstrated the capacity to partly reconstitute the past in line with how victims experienced that lived reality. It would be difficult to deny that this reconstitution within a global spotlight has gained far more exposure and analysis than any of the twenty other Truth Commissions around the world (Hamber and Kibble, 1999). Arguably, the TRC has been a closely reported attempt to challenge global history and promote societal cohesiveness. The South African politicians and activists, who skilfully used the international media in the apartheid era, have recognized this potential; and although the TRC has gained its legitimacy from being uniquely grounded in South African history, it has also been globally 'wise'. The Commission will, undoubtedly, remain an important reference point for how we all deal with the past.

There have been struggles, however, and although the TRC also looks to the future in making its recommendations, it cannot control current national events. In the eyes of the world, South Africa remains a country of conflict . . . albeit civil and economic as opposed to political conflict. Clearly, it cannot be overlooked that the TRC has been woven into the political, economic and social structures that have independently begun to formulate new 'post-apartheid' truths and representations. From this viewpoint, (collective) identities have not moved on, rather their change has been heavily resisted by those who hold power. Memories may have brought cases of individual reconciliation and framed individual identity but, collectively, nothing much has changed. Even though the TRC report is nearly one million words long and demonstrates a wealth of human experience and historical accountability, it cannot dissolve years of conflict and power struggles on its own, overnight.

In approaching an analysis of identities, truth and reconciliation on local levels, a focus on individuals is imperative and yet a recognition of the social, political, economic and cultural environment and processes in which individuals are located has to be taken. In essence, any analyses have to be placed in a broader global framework as the attempt by South Africa to deal with the past extends beyond the legal and campaigning framework and into the realms of the global economy and humanitarian aid. Even though there has been international support for the TRC, financial assistance has been minimal. Further, both the IMF and the World Bank demand 'efforts at both democratization' and an appearance of adhering to the 'rule of law as conditions for financial aid' (Silbey, 1997: 221). It would appear that this places South Africa in a position that continues to serve the conditions of apartheid through neocolonialism. Whilst the primary financial powers 'plot' morality and uphold structural divisions, the organization of global power remains hidden. For South Africa, trapped within the cogs of a western-framed global economy, reconciliation through financial equality remains a remote possibility. This may be an obvious point, yet arguably it is one that is inadequately explored within human rights analysis.

Moreover, these experiences within South Africa throw considerable light on other conflictual situations. This South African example is important on a global level because it emphasizes the real struggles that are fought over representations and identities. Identities have been shown to be transitory and fragmentary; they can be imposed on certain individuals, embraced by some and manipulated by others. All these identities have been framed by power and resistance, they have also been framed by the determining contexts of neocolonialism, patriarchy and capitalism. In addition, they are complex as they move beyond the stereotypes. Consequently, they are incredibly important not just for the individuals themselves but for all of us, as their representation forms the basis upon which we make sense of the world, evaluate the apartheid era, decide what we accept as truth, how far we go in our demands for justice and how we view current events in South Africa. This argument could be applied to any number of conflicts in the world, from Kosovo to Sierra Leone to Rwanda. Everywhere, the issues relating to the importance of acknowledging identities and truth in a bid for reconciliation are similar. Although human rights are increasingly interconnected, it is evident that one size does not fit all. When gross human rights violations have occurred, it is imperative that they are dealt with in a contextual way, in an individualized way. To recognize that individual stories, and their ensuing acknowledgement, are important is arguably the first step to reconciliation.

12
Globalization and National Identity Rituals in Brazil and the USA: the Politics of Pleasure Versus the Politics of Protest

Lauren Langman

Introduction

Today, among the actors and forces which would foster particular identities stand powerful multinational corporations (MNCs). Their profits and legitimacy depend on consumer-based identities. Promises of the 'goods' life sustain the hegemony of the MNCs or at least secure tacit acceptance of the new global system. Much like religious or patriotic identities in the past, consumption-based identities and activities sustain capital's hegemony by locating the person in an identity-granting community and by mediating the articulations of selfhood through commodified goods and/or experiences. The globalized 'culture industries' have colonized desire now articulated through consumption-based identities. Here, various goods, fashions, lifestyles and cultural tastes provide the person with fantasied identities, meanings and gratifying experiences in 'shopping mall selfhood' (Langman, 1992). Consumption fosters a migration of subjectivity from the alienating, constraining and often dehumanizing worlds of everyday life to the more gratifying and desirable dream worlds of leisure and lifestyle.

The ludic carnival culture of the Middle Ages provided a liminal time and a site of resistance while valorizing the vulgar, the obscene and the erotic. The legacies of that repressed culture came to the New World along with imperialism and the quest for colonies. Several centuries later these cultural legacies have resurfaced in the form of contemporary cultural rituals better known as the carnival of Brazil and the superbowl of the United States. Both provide unique, meaningful, gratifying identities to their celebrants, even if only in fantasy. But these rituals also offer insights about globalization and identity. Thus, for the most part, globalized carnivalesque identities sustain capital's domination by fostering the migration of subjectivity from concerns with political economy to sites of privatized hedonism – especially erotic or violent imageries. In this way, and as in the past, the potential for mass opposition to the hegemon of global capital is neutralized. Yet there is also another possibility. Before globalization destroys the emancipatory promise of the Enlightenment through ludic carnivals of reactionary violence, the same electronic channels of information flows used by MNCs have engendered a new generation of cyberactivists who lead counter-hegemonic movements (Castells, 1997).

Globalization

The restructuring of political economy

In recent decades there has been an unprecedented transformation of national capitalisms. Technologically advanced, computer-based forms of post-Fordist, flexible production and electronic communication joined to produce goods more cheaply and to make profitable investment possible anywhere in the world. With new technologies of computerization, digitalization and communication, corporations have become uncoupled from their nations of origin so restructuring the international political economy. Not only did capitalist enterprises shift to global markets, but there have been a number of investments, mergers and consolidations of older 'national' companies into globally organized MNCs with investors, offices and plants dispersed throughout the world. Manufacturing moved from developed nations to less developed nations with lower wages and few restrictions on pollution. New flows of information and capital transformed the nature of trade and commerce, much of which became increasingly based on the production of sign values expressed in consumer goods, cultural forms, tourism and so on. Moreover, in this new political economy the 'culture industries' of the USA have taken the lion's share of the world's movies, television programming and popular culture, and thus exercise a disproportionate influence over popular consciousness.

The MNCs have become an autonomous political economic force with their own systems of regulation through organizations such as the International Monetary Fund (IMF), World Bank and the World Trade Organization (WTO). Investment decisions are made on the basis of short-term profits and often based on the technological logic of computer models. Everywhere, the logic of globalized capital has impacted on government policy leading to reduced investment in social welfare and the disempowerment of local resistance, despite social concerns and support for the welfare state (Teeple, 1995).

Consumer society and its culture industries

By the end of the nineteenth century there was a proliferation of consumer goods, shopping arcades and department stores. However, given citizen reluctance to indulge in consumption, it became necessary to initiate cultural changes to transform consciousness. Advertising joined with psychology to promise desirable images and identities through consumption (Ewen, 1976). By the 1920s, the foundations of consumer society were in place. With the postwar recoveries of the USA, Western Europe and Japan, consumer society revived along with the spread of television. Luxury goods such as cars became commonplace while a vast range of goods and appliances appeared. The arcades that heralded the emergence of consumer society had become massive shopping malls, dream worlds of consumption. The now valorized identities became a moment of colonized desire realized in commodified forms of signification while amusement became the goal of the 'goods' life (Langman, 1992). As globalization provided ever more goods and services, consumerism became the basis for its hegemony, notwithstanding that many workers could not buy the products they made for world markets (Sklair, 1995).

At the same time, and with greater leisure time and discretionary income at the beginning of the century, cultural consumption became an integral moment of consumer society. People began to read dime novels, attend amusement parks, listen to recorded music and radio and frequent movies. Capitalist 'culture industries' produced a commodified mass culture that degraded tastes through a vulgar and mundane escapism. This mystified class domination and affirmed the status quo. Domination was not so much through submission to reactionary political leadership as through the erosion of a critical, emancipatory consciousness in favour of authoritarianism, conformism and one-dimensional thought (Marcuse, 1964). Other writers, informed by Althusser and Gramsci, have suggested that media-based hegemony was based less on obedience than on willing assent to the dominant class's views of reality subtly encoded in the media. Audiences' incorporation into media based subcultures of music, film or television further served to sustain class relations. Television played a central role in consumerism and the rise of amusement society. It provides an endless stream of spectacles, extravagant images and events that appeal to the emotions rather than logic or reason (De Bord, 1970). It also furnishes desirable identities, relationships and experiences and affirms the system by promising a better life through consumption. In short, the culture industries provide a wide range of commodified fantastic identities and gratifications that secured the hegemony of global capital.

Glocalization

Globalization, as Robertson (1992) has noted, does not mean universal homogeneity despite the proliferation of McDonald's or the size of *Baywatch* audiences. Notwithstanding the universalizing aspects of globalized capital, and the widespread distribution of its mass-mediated popular culture, specific social meanings and expressions of identities remain situated within local sites, each with its own social formations and historical legacies. Indeed, one consequence of globalization has been the valorization and celebrations of localized identities as a resistance to globalization and the demise of cultural variations.

Carnivalization of the world

The carnival, a popular celebration of festive rituals and practices, emerged in feudal Europe as a moment of peasant folk culture (Bakhtin, 1968). The ludic culture of the carnival was a time and place of inversion and resistance that granted peasants more pleasurable moments apart from degradation and toil. All that was otherwise forbidden and constrained was celebrated in frenzied form. There was a suspension of the usual codes of morality with indulgence in wine, song, dance and sex. Carnival was a time of licence and abandon that valorized the vulgar, the erotic, the obscene, the lower body, excreta and the grotesque. Typical patterns of hierarchy, deference and demeanour were ignored, indeed repudiated in favour of that which was proscribed. Boundaries were violated. Thus, carnivals and fairs offered times and places of popular resistance where deviance and reversals of norms could be sanctioned and official elite culture could be repudiated. The sacrosanct elites of Church and State were typically parodied, mocked, hectored and ridiculed.

This transgression of moral boundaries was alluring to ordinary people for many reasons (Stallybrass and White, 1986). To parody or to mock authority gave individuals a sense of power and integrated them into a community of resistance. Whether one engaged in serious drinking, casual sex or mocking the bishop or king, carnival allowed subalterns to find alternative communities, dignified identities, recognition, empowerment and meanings apart from everyday life and the dominant norms and structures of elite power.

According to Turner (1969), as an organization of constraint, a social structure dialectically fosters alternative realms apart from the typicality of the quotidian. There is a bifurcation of reality into the normative structure and a liminal anti-structure. The liminal stands apart from the usual as illness stands in opposition to the typicality of health. Liminal realms are times and sites of freedom, agency empowerment, equality, licence and spontaneity. The liminal realm may also be the site for resistance struggles and where norms are flouted and acts or feelings are expressed that are normally forbidden or taboo. Carnival thus created a liminal culture of the ludic that granted feudal peasants pleasurable moments of indulgence and resistance if only for fleeting moments in marginal, interstitial or even imaginary sites of otherwise prohibited gratification. By episodically granting pleasurable identities, carnival stabilized the feudal order.

Capitalism required the domination of rational action over affectivity – in Weber's terms – or the domination of ego over id in Freudian terms or the flourishing of civility and manners charted by Elias. As capitalism grew, the carnivals and fairs waned. The culture of emotional (sexual) restraint associated with the Protestant ethic became dominant. When capitalism moved into its consumer phase, however, it became necessary to temper the restraints upon indulgence necessary in the early stages of capitalism. Thus carnival returned, albeit as commodity. To gain audiences for commercials, popular culture has slowly but surely lowered standards of taste to recapture the sensual appeal and resistance of carnival. The boundaries of high journalism and the tabloids have become blurred and television programing is increasingly grotesque and vulgar. Finally the costumes, lyrics and performances of some musical subcultures, especially heavy metal, punk and industrial rock are ever more grotesque. The mass-produced and -mediated commodified forms of carnivalization as liminal sites of dream and inversion, of resistance and submerged identities realized, is now an essential feature of globalized consumerism.

Cyberfeudalism

Globalization has produced unprecedented wealth both for established corporations that have become global and for new classes of entrepreneurs in computer-related fields, software, e-commerce, the leisure industries, financial investments and so on. But this vast new wealth is ever more unequally distributed. The wealth and incomes of the new managerial and entrepreneurial classes have skyrocketed while most workers have lost ground. A few hundred billionaires enjoy as much wealth as almost half the world's population. I have termed this system 'cyberfeudalism' (Langman, 1998a). Much like the Middle Ages, a small minority of cyberlords who control information rather than land, rule while the masses – the cyberserfs, closely resembling impoverished medieval peasants – are kept enthralled by mass-mediated spectacles and carnivals of consumption but remain indifferent to critiques of inequality or political mobilization.

At the same time, globalization has perpetuated the dehumanization typical of rational organizations and the inequalities of work experience, between the powerless, alienated majority and the technical/managerial elites, which have always existed under capitalist industrialization. Thus, the armies of technicians, semi-skilled workers and service workers who clean hotels and offices, staff retail stores or fast food outlets or who provide the ever-increasing security services, have expanded. The exploited wage labourers described by Engels and Marx can still be found in Third World sweatshops. The failure of capitalism to provide decent incomes or meaningful and gratifying identities, that integrate the person into a community and that permit recognition, dignity and the expression of agency, creates the spaces for carnivals. However, ephemeral and fantastic are the meanings and gratifications which they promise, they nevertheless remain attractive. Even the dysfunctions of capital operate so as to secure its profits and domination.

Identity, hegemony and desire

In this section I discuss three important aspects of identity: their historical and psychological roots, their contested nature and links to hegemonic power structures and their association with bodily desires. Identities have psychological roots linked to history. Insofar as identities include value orientations that are internalized as essential aspects of character, identities that emerged under one set of material conditions may endure for generations, mediated through the superego even when conditions change (Horkheimer, 1972). More specifically, identification is an unconscious process in which the child identifies not just with parents but with their superegos. Thus, the values of earlier generations may be unconsciously transmitted and persist despite major structural changes. These archaic psychological dispositions may foster characterologically based 'elective affinities' for certain cultural practices. The legacies of the English Protestant colonizers of North America disposed social actors towards football while the Easter traditions of Portuguese settlers, melded with those of African slaves and indigenous tribes of Brazil, generated an orientation towards carnival. Puritanism prefigured a uniquely self-disciplined asceticism and an aggressive cultural character. The Catholics of southern Europe were far more likely to indulge the spirits of the flesh and the vine. These historical legacies have mediated the effects of globalization.

Secondly, identities are intertwined with issues of power, justice and equality. Contestations between classes or movements over valorized or denigrated identities have always occurred. Gramsci suggested that the ability of the Church to construct the identities of subaltern classes sustained its power as well as that of the economic elites. It did this by naturalizing the arbitrariness of historical events and by disguising elite interests while representing both as the common good, thereby fostering willing assent to structures of domination. With industrialization and possibilities for proletarian mobilizations against capital, nationalist ideologies flourished and 'citizenship' was created in order to unite classes into 'peoples' who would realize their cultural interests while simultaneously securing the political and economic interests of dominant elites.

More recently, the compression of space, time and distance associated with globalization has markedly impacted on peoples' lives and on the nature of identities (Giddens, 1992). Moreover, contested identities have continued to be an integral part of what Castells (1997) has termed the 'network society'. Thus, he has suggested that some identities, typically religious or nationalistic ones, continue to serve to legitimate a society, its class structure and/or particular leaders. An example here would be the ludic identities of the carnival. Here, structures of domination impose identities that legitimate those structures. Even forms of cultural resistance, emerging from the bottom, may become co-opted by the 'culture industries'. Various musical styles such as rock and roll, heavy metal, reggae, or gangsta, subcultures of resistance identities, displace discontent from structural arrangements and/or political challenges to the liminal culture of the carnival. Just as the articulation of cultural resistance against the values of the dominant elites served to stabilize the feudal system, so too, mass-mediated carnivalization operates in much the same way today.

Yet Castells (1997) has also argued that under the conditions of globalization identities of resistance may also emerge – either in the attempt to reverse social change and perhaps return society to a pristine state or in order to direct it to more progressive forms. Some progressive resistances would create new projects of identity and patterns of social interaction. Feminism is the most important of such movements but others are emerging as I will suggest later.

Thirdly, identities are not simply cognitive or rational choices. Freudian theory has affirmed the importance of embodiment as the basis of desire, unconscious emotions, behavior, consciousness and reflexive selfhood. Although we might critique Freud's ideas about sex and aggressive drives as determinants of individual motivation, he nonetheless secured a bodily basis for emotions, feelings and selfhood. Moreover, the ability of hegemonic discourses to colonize embodiness qua sexual or aggressive articulations has long been understood by elites. Marcuse (1955) suggested counter-hegemonic possibilities.

Affects become socialized into emotions. Depending on the codes of the group, these, in turn, may become experienced or expressed as feelings (Hochschild, 1983). People become socialized to seek or to avoid certain emotions and/or experiences. Perhaps the most important emotions that individuals actively seek are the following: community and attachments to others; social recognition and dignity; and a degree of agency and empowerment (Langman, 1998a). These are not necessarily independent. For example, the denial or loss of respect and dignity can foster shame and humiliation and this, in turn, may trigger rage, anger and violence in the attempt to ameliorate a loss of self-esteem (Fromm, 1941; Scheff, 1994; Langman, 1998b). Individual selfhood becomes articulated in various identities or subcultural scripts that provide some emotional satisfactions. Thus, certain cultural rituals that join people together mark the intersection of collective identity and embodiness, selfhood and desire. Carnival and superbowl are just such spectacles of the body that celebrate distinct, indeed sacralized cultural identities whilst providing celebrants with gratifying experiences. Much like collective religious rituals, they unify the participants and evoke and/or express identities and emotions often denied while simultaneously serving hegemonic functions.

Brazil does carnival

Carnival comes to the New World

Brazil was colonized by Portuguese Catholics seeking fortunes for their king and themselves. Early explorers described Brazil as a sexual paradise, an erotic Eden where native people and later slaves were without modesty or restraint (da Matta, 1991; Parker, 1991). There was 'no sin south of the equator'. Brazil's myth of origin begins with the plantation owner's big house set apart from the slave quarters. Among other cruelties, slavery meant that patriarchal lust led to the carnal indulgence of ravished slaves. But this history became a mythic tale of a warm intimacy of master and slave that produced a mixed race of Brazilians in a peaceful, harmonious multiracial society (Freye, 1986). The free and open sexuality of the male owners and subaltern women, and the seclusion and control of elite women in the house, were telling aspects of the myths and realities of Brazil's origins.

In the 1830s carnival was imported from Venice by colonial elites to make Brazil more 'modern' and European. Carnival was transformed and became the major ritual celebrating the unique history and montage of Brazilian identity. Carnival is now largely a public festival of the poor from the shanty towns teeming with the unemployed. Alternatively, the urban poor work in low-waged jobs. Sometimes jobs are connected to globalization – for example, work in hotels and restaurants – or people may be employed as domestic servants for the elites or they may be members of the poorly paid industrial proletariat. (Brazil has the greatest inequality in Latin America.) Carnival celebrates the social history and traditions of these poor citizens as opposed to the official history celebrated by elites in state, festivals such as Independence Day. Carnival is produced by the people without elite ownership.

Carnal carnival, inversion and resistance

Carnival is a vast public spectacle with millions of celebrants. Boundaries between participants (performers) and spectators tend to be quite blurred. For the poor and the outcasts, there are a myriad of street festivals with informal musical groups and spontaneous celebrations, aided and abetted by large quantities of *cache* (sugar cane liquor). Carnival, as an inversion of what is typical, is a festival of the night and not the day. The poor claim the streets, plazas and public spaces of the affluent where they can inhabit alternative realms apart from the squalour and hardship of their actual lives. For a few moments they can be kings and queens ruling over kingdoms of fantasy. Explosions of revelry burst and barriers fall as huge crowds gather to drink, dance, sing, shout, prank, flirt and sometimes even make love (Linger, 1992). As against the 'normal' world of work, carnival offers merrymaking and play (*brincar* and *brincadiera*, meaning to play yet with sexual overtones). To the hierarchy of gender there is an equality of desire as females can initiate eroticism as equals. Carnival repudiates the everyday life of the home, work, job and Church; the dominated worlds of order and restraint. (da Matta, 1991). To the norms of restraint, indulgence is the rule. Anything goes and sexual indulgence is one of the central moments of carnival. In the liminal anti-structures of ironic inversion and sensual indulgence, a good time is had by all.

During carnival, spouses criticize each other and everyone criticizes the government. The *entrudo*, an aggressive provocation, becomes a ritualized form of empowerment in which subordinates gain symbolic equality by throwing such things as corn starch, water, confetti or mud on another. Carnival is a time of *desabafar* (catharsis) casting out what is held below, allowing restrained feelings and passions to be released. Carnival is also a time of *briga*, loosely an invitation or readiness to fight to save or defend honour. *Desabafar* and *briga* can be seen as socially tolerated expressions of aggression.

The elaborate dress, masks and costumes – erotic, profane, satirical, grotesque, the good, bad and ugly as essential moments of carnival – are rooted in the archaic depths of the unconscious which momentarily find expression. 'Carnival costumes help to create a world of mediation, encounter and moral compensation. Thus they produce a social field that is cosmopolitan and universal, that is supremely, polysemic' (da Matta, 1991). To experience luxury and fantasy the poor dress like kings and queens. Although the costumes are expensive they provide fantasied splendour. Beings, roles and categories that are typically separated are brought together: the thief and cop, prostitute and lady of the house, transvestite and he-man, all dance together. Cross-dressing is widespread. Men dress as women, women as men and drag queens can be public and flaunt their sexuality. The costumes, especially of women and drag queens, often combine whimsy with eroticism. Whether erotic, grotesque or absurd, the party clothes or elaborate costumes are moments of inversion or reversal of what are usually separate domains.

The patriarchal legacy of the colonial era intersected with race and gender systems to create a sharp duality between men and women. The master had several slave mistresses/concubines, his passive wife/mother was the eternal virgin. Carnival, however, creates a ludic anti-structure of equality that empowers women through erotic agency in a society that is typically patriarchal and repressive. Female modesty and reserve typical of everyday life in the home wane as women wear highly revealing clothing – and often little of that. Yet, they are rarely approached aggressively; the otherwise macho men appear timid. (While carnival is licentious, it does not give licence to assault.) Exhibitionism and desire become 'normal' as carnival aesthetic valorizes female sensuality and sexuality through scanty, erotic dress and often exposed breasts. Such inversions empower women by repudiating male standards and thus celebrate the permissible collective eros of carnival (Parker, 1991). Moreover, as women take charge of their sexuality, they express the other side of the virgin. The whore takes centre stage in the streets, the parades and the ballrooms. Anonymous and indeed egalitarian sexuality is also part and parcel of the festival. The streets and beaches become meeting grounds for all kinds of lovers, straight and gay, black and white, rich and poor. Liaisons can occur between strangers who wear masks – and often little more.

Carnival identities and desire fulfilled

A life of constant deprivation is the reality for most carnival celebrants. But carnival is a dreamlike fantasy realm where what is otherwise denied becomes abundant and frustrated desires are fulfilled in realms of experience apart from the typical. Carnival, as a release from the not so hidden injuries of class and gender, gives license to expel the frustrations of subaltern being and identity. Carnival values life over death, joy over sadness, wealth over poverty. It provides moments of community and dignity little found in the quotidian of the impoverished and degraded. Here the janitor may be a great dancer, the maid a talented singer and the factory worker a songwriter-musician. Brazilians leave aside their hierarchical, repressive society to live more freely and individually.

It is in the context of carnival that we can now understand sexuality and aggression, not as Freudian motives, but realms of valorized bodily-based selfhood that grant agency and recognition in fantasied microspheres of empowerment. Carnival repairs the self and provides agency and honour to those who otherwise lack these resources. The 'return of the repressed' in fantastic form tells the truth of intertwined social, sexual and political domination.

> Carnival does not really provide freedom, but dreams and simulations of what freedom might look like. For a few days, there are few cares. Carnival is a necessary sham, an exercise in denial not only of mortality, but of the whole hurt and sadness bound up with living as a human being with other human beings, one's needs and desires are never fully satisfied. That it is a sham does not nullify Carnival's psychological utility, to the contrary, Carnival proposes that one had better know how to delude onself. It prescribes a self-conscious expulsion of burdens as a generalized antidote to fear and suffering.
>
> (Linger, 1992: 79)

Carnival serves to maintain the structures of inequality that have been a part of Brazil from its earliest days as a colony to its present position as the eighth largest industrial power in the now globalized world. Given the structuring of everyday life and the inequalities of wealth and gender, carnival is an intrinsic part of Brazil.

Carnival and globalization

Carnival, as a localized identity in a globalized world, as a ritualized expression of a unique national culture and identity, stands as resistance to homogenization. Compared to Brazil, few other countries experience such extreme social stratification, yet perhaps nowhere else is the atmosphere so laden with erotic allure, licence and toleration. But as a celebration of exotic license, carnival has itself become a part of the globalization its participants would rather resist since it has become essential in the competition to attract global tourists. With the growth of international tourism and carnival websites, flights and hotel space are sold out months ahead of time. Even as Brazil's carnival provides psychic compensation to the Brazilian poor, it brings millions of dollars of revenue to the rich. But as carnival has become located in the global market, so it has also been increasingly commodified; infiltrated by commercialization. Many of the songs are now based on popular music borrowed from the 'culture industry' rather than the spontaneous productions of the people. The themes and floats of the parade often attempt to imitate Hollywood's versions of spectacle.

Perhaps the ultimate 'inversion' of carnival is that a local festival of and by the Brazilian poor has become a favourite destination for the privileged. They flock to Brazil in order to join those very celebrants who typically drive their cabs, clean their rooms and serve/prepare their food. In this way, the commodification of carnival reproduces the social conditions that require carnival. Moreover, perhaps this is the way of the future; as capitalism enters its globalized stage, and inequality grows, so too does, carnivalization. Brazil's carnival thus demonstrates how ludic indulgence and liminal inversions can serve to sustain growing inequalities in a globalized world.

From American football to superbowl

Durkheim's analysis of totemic religion suggested that a dispersed people would annually gather together to sustain their solidarity and affirm their identities in dramatic ritual. Sports, in general, foster a 'common' identity. Football celebrates a general allegiance to an

American identity and superbowl has become the supreme performance of that identity. Superbowl – like carnival as a ludic festival – celebrates in fantastic form, a distinct cultural identity that maintains national 'uniqueness' in a globalized age. But as carnival celebrates an egalitarian Eros, football is a simulation of phallic aggression and male combat. Superbowl, football's penultimate celebratory ritual, seeks to valorize and affirm in spectacular forms American culture and its mythical heroes who enact its exemplary identity performances. Thus, like carnival, it is rooted in a distinct historical tradition and can be seen as a way of performing localized identities and of celebrating resistance to a globalized age. But whereas carnival is compensatory, superbowl is a celebratory simulation of a now globalized corporate capitalism.

Sport in consumer capitalist societies is an economic enterprise and an ideological mirror of this system. By the late 1960s, with the rapid postwar growth of college-educated, managerial, professional classes, football overtook baseball in popularity. With television broadcasting, football's audience expanded even more rapidly as it was increasingly watched by viewers who were not college-educated. Football became a big business and superbowl was created as the spectacular culmination of the football season. It is now the most widely celebrated event in American popular culture surpassing the World Series, Academy Awards or Miss America contests. It has the largest television audience in the world; over 120 million Americans watch it and almost a billion others watch it in 60 countries. This most popular spectator event is celebrated in bars and homes where the 'superbowl party' of beer, pretzels and pizza has become the primary ritual of the annual football season. Superbowl has become a site where the MNCs as sponsors and advertisers celebrate a distinctly American identity and acknowledge the disproportionate power of the USA over the global market, especially the latter's 'culture industries'.

From backward colony to industrial behemoth

While celebrations of male violence to control territory go back to prehistory, the dispositions towards football as a violent contest of male teams seeking territorial power and control were foretold in the earliest moments of American culture (Langman, 1992; Wilkinson, 1984). Football was rooted in earlier European traditions. Certain Mardi Gras festivals used oval leather balls that represented eggs. Early colonists played some sort of team game using an inflated pig bladder for a ball. While its roots include English soccer and rugby, football became a highly unique American sport rooted in the aggressive aspects of the American character as embedded in Puritan sensibility and a hostile environment. It has also obtained a more explicit urban tempo (Cummings, 1972: 104). A crucial moment of early Puritanism was the increasing economic power of the male qua economic actor as opposed to the clan, family or guild. Protestantism reflected the world of masculine asceticism that displaced female emotion. The legacy of that heritage has been a valorization of masculine violence and the elevation to mythic status of warrior heroes who enact in symbolic form the aggressive, competitive nature of corporate life.

Industrialization severed the connection between work and self-realization and economic independence. Consequently, people have increasingly turned to sport for a sense of self and identity (Cummings, 1972). Corporate careers appeared 'less masculine' than entrepreneurship, soldiering or frontier life. At the same time, the numbers of elite women going to college increased. A great fear among elite males was growing effeminacy. Football began as an expression of violence in a game that would both mirror economic life and dramatize an aggressive masculinity 'appropriate' for elite college students. Football emerged when the national elites were attempting to forge an inclusive national identity that would valorize masculine aggression following a bloody civil war. The problem for these elites was how to valorize a distinctly masculine American identity and the phallic aggression of war demanded by corporate capital, without risking the attendant death and destruction. At the same time, it was believed that college-educated, football-educated young men would become the business, professional and political leaders of the future. Forceful personalities, directed by knowledge and leadership, would become the keys to (white) manhood, christian character and the managerial manliness of corporate executive life (Oriard, 1993: 211).

Collegiate sports in general and football in particular thus became the means through which the upper-class students at schools like Harvard, Princeton, Yale and Columbia would be socialized for corporate life and national leadership. For Walter Camp, the 'father' of the sport, football and corporate life were one and the same. 'Team play' might require the sacrifice of individual brilliance in order to achieve organizational goals (Oriard, 1993). Football came to embody the same principles of scientific management in which positions were organized on the basis of status and ability. American football can be seen as an ideologically constructed group of self-interested, disciplined warriors working together to compete over property against other groups and score a victory. Teddy Roosevelt was the incarnation and cheerleader for the values that would ensure American elites would remain real men through masculine prowess in face of declining ownership and diminishing patriarchal control of the family. By the end of the nineteenth century, football, initially a sport of the 'gentlemen' from elite schools, had quickly spread throughout the country – from eastern colleges to urban sand lot (Schwartz, 1999).

Football is an alternative realm of male territorial competitive violence that stands apart from the quotidian where the disciplined nature of corporate life requires a neutralized expression of real violence. It has its own rules and regulations that celebrate a masculinity attenuated by the discipline of rational organization and threatened by the incursions of women into hitherto exclusive male realms. As a form of character ethics, 'football inculcates a virile asceticism of fortitude and discipline that will serve men well in the society at large in much the same way as does the military' (MacBride, 1995: 82). Thus football is more than an athletic competition; it is a boundary maintaining male subculture where American men can find community, dignity and agency in a mythical realm that glorifies hypermasculine identities as warrior-heroes glorify bodily violence.

No admission without a phallus

The popularity of football first grew when growing numbers of women were entering college. Such new, more assertive and androgynous women, raised questions and fostered anxieties about gender identity (Oriard, 1993). Just as football originally emerged as a response to a threatened masculinity, superbowl emerged as feminism again flourished in the late 1960s. Contrary to the 'egalitarian' claims of American politics and society, football creates a realm of traditional gender identities in which masculine power stands above and against feminine passivity. No matter how well men and women work together in the office, hospital, courtroom or university, football remains a masculine sport based on possession of the violent, intrusive phallus. This separates men from the female 'other' – with 'denigrated genitals' – who cannot enter the sacred temple of the phallus and delight in its violent rituals. Football affirms that men are not the women they fear and desire (MacBride, 1995).

Violent sports unify men in a cultural space in which male domination is assumed as normal. Football appeals to the psyche of the American male who realizes selfhood by viewing violent combat where male bonds are cemented through misogynist denigration of women and the conversion of the enemy into 'castrated pussies'. Football fandom provides solidarity and cohesion in a male nether world far apart from work or the hearth and home that must be shared by women. Typically, males gather around the television set, bond through the consumption of intoxicants and the exchange of 'sports talk' laden with frequent obscenities and a sexual imagery of phallic power and domination. Football as a spectator sport has become a basis for relaxed, easy communication between students, workers, bosses and subordinates, between salesmen and customers. Even total strangers can relate to each other. Knowledge of sports and discussions in 'sportuguese' (Rowe, 1995) or 'sports chatter' (Eco, 1986) demonstrates shared knowledge and individual expertise that provide realms of sociality, recognition and empowerment. Sports knowledge is a central trope of identity for real men which differentiates them from women.

War is hell and football is war

Walter Camp compared football to war with football armies, artillery work and generalship (Oriard, 1993). 'It is an aggressive strictly regulated team sport fought between males who use both violence and technology to win monopoly control of property for the economic gain of individuals within a nationalistic, entertainment context' (Real, 1979). Teams are like platoons, the line engages in hand-to-hand combat. The players in the trenches are directed by generals (coaches) whose war rooms (locker rooms) are just that. The groans, screams, blood and injuries, stretchers and medics simulate a battlefield – but without actual death. Winning is everything. The football player dons his armour and moves from civilian to warrior with his helmet, massive padded shoulders and extensive body armour. These icons of masculinity exaggerate male angularity and musculature as he joins with the legacy of the centurion, gladiator, armoured knight or samurai seeking power and victory in violent combat on the field of battle. Thus, football in its uniquely American form can be seen as a hypermasculine war game: 'As a metaphor for American military values, football reveals an increasing brutality in the national soul' (Rapping, 1987: 84). Moreover, superbowl is the penultimate ritual performance that celebrates the male warrior/spectator. Whatever else, it affirms that American men are 'real' men who enjoy violence and power – not sissies or pussies (MacBride, 1995).

The mystical bonding of males through the violence of war or football overcomes separation and alienation. Larger than life mythic warrior-heroes clash on the fields of war, opponents are hurt, cheerleaders dance and hierarchical gender relations that privilege powerful males are affirmed in the performances of violence. A solidarity of difference is established through a shared male gaze. Moreover, the powerful warrior elicits an erotic attraction that reproduces gender domination. Thus while most men are not overtly violent to each other, do not abuse their wives or children, domination through violence has a powerful appeal. The football player acts out in fantasy erotic/aggressive desires repressed by social dictates in general and corporate life in particular. In this way, as MacBride (1995) suggests, football acts as a cathartic event in which the castration and domination of the female other serves to displace violence from everyday life and preserve social life. At the same time, football celebrates American national identity.

Back to the political

Problematizing globalization

Every form of domination and exploitation creates resistance or avoidance. The dominated have typically sought compensation either in religious rejections of the world or in liminal anti-structures. But both fail to dislodge the political and economic system which generates their oppression. Following the Enlightenment, resistance to inequalities increasingly took new political forms as bourgeois revolutions promised popular democracy and personal fulfilment. But these 'democracies' typically served the interests of the new capitalist hegemon and so emancipatory hopes were soon thwarted. Capitalism thus generated resistance, critiques and the utopian visions of self-realization offered by marxists, socialists and anarchists. Capitalism understood these challenges and neutralized them. Nationalism further obscured class differences. The welfare state cushioned citizens from the worst abuses of capital and the hedonism of mass culture and consumerism eroded any counter-hegemonic resistances that endured. Consumerism, now globalization's legitimating ideology, offers valorized identities and lifestyles of abundance to its elites. For most people, carnivalesque identities located in fantastic realms of bodily indulgence erode the politics of resistance.

Globalization and its techno-capitalist base also recreates extremes of income. The computerization of design, manufacturing, banking and commerce, record-keeping, order-processing and so on has vastly increased productivity and eroded the number of well-paid jobs. Most workers in the industrial economies face job losses or declining wages in the 'McJobs' sectors of fast food, lower echelon routine services and security. Unemployment, underemployment and growing inequality portend major social crises and dislocations. Globalization has not only sustained inequalities and even generated new ones, but its valorization of instrumental reason perpetuates the domination of humanity and the usurpation of nature. Adorno, Horkheimer and Marcuse, among others, noted how the technological logic of capital reduced the person to a dehumanized object whose objectification was mystified by mass culture and consumerism and whose capacities for resistance were eroded. In the years since these critiques were penned, we have seen how new technologies of surveillance discipline and dehumanize. Further, globalization has accelerated the despoliation of the environment: the destruction of the ozone layer, shrinking of rainforests and the mass production of waste products, some of which are not only toxic, but will remain dangerous for 20 000 more years.

Cyberactivists to the rescue

Despite the power of huge corporations, the numbing allure of its carnival culture and an electoral politics dominated by telegenic neoliberal clones, the crises and dysfunctions of globalized capital generate resistance and, in turn, oppositional groups and coalitions with visions of genuine democracy, empowerment and self-realization. The same communication systems that empower capital and intensify information flows can also link people together and distribute information. It is now more difficult for governments or corporations to conceal information on, for example, environmental conditions, human rights or product safety because electronic access to information cannot be controlled short of making phones illegal. Cyberspace has now created new arenas where progressive cyberactivists can create networks of opposition and construct new constellations of power and mobilizations. Well-organized, progressive non-governmental organizations (NGOs) and emerging coalitions can effectively publicize information, influence public opinion and mobilize in favour of social policies for targeted progressive change (Castells, 1997). Moreover, with the decoupling of the global economy from national polities, and decentralization and dispersion of power and decision-making, it is difficult to target opposition.

From the perspective of counter-hegemonic oppositionists, however, and as Castells put it, there is no longer an obvious Winter Palace to storm. Nor are alternatives to globalization feasible, though post-capitalist forms might be possible. Turning back the clock to a 'Golden

Age' and/or smashing the machines (computers and networks), themes that once draw together reactionaries, anarchists and neo-Luddites, are neither feasible nor desirable since life would then become nasty, brutish and short. Proletarian revolution is unlikely given the legacy of totalitarian state socialism. Yet there is an alternative, or set of alternatives; globalization also creates spaces for progressive, movements that seek specific goals rather than 'overthrowing the system'. Castells (1997) cited the Zapatistas, feminism and environmentalism. I would further note the mobilizations against female genital mutilation, the Landmine Treaty, the growth of anti-sweatshop movements on American campuses and the massive rally against the WTO meetings in Seattle as harbingers of new forms of cyberactivism that will lead the battles of the twenty-first century.

Insofar as globalization transcends national territories, so too must resistance movements extend beyond the nation-state. Yet here also there are now new means for organization, mobilization and resistance. The proliferation of the Internet creates the possibilities for mounting effective, decentralized yet universal communication networks and campaigns that readily facilitate transnational political mobilizations (Dyer-Witheford, 1999). Not only have the costs of computers plummeted, but there is a growing surplus of 'obsolete' computers. While not at the leading edge of technology, these are perfectly suitable for e-mail and Internet use by the less privileged. The potential growth of networks of resistance by oppositional groups enthused with democratic/humanist agendas can empower publics to gain democratic input and control over the technologies and investment decisions that impact on people's lives. Finally, it is important to note that feminism and feminist consciousness are crucial to cyberactivism. Women in general tend to be more supportive of programmes and movements that benefit people rather than produce profits. This 'gender gap' has become a crucial moment in electoral politics. There is thus an 'elective affinity' between feminism and environmentalism. Ecofeminism represents the kind of humanistic movements now possible that can be broadened through the use of the Internet. Of course, what we are seeing here is an intrinsically pluralistic kind of progressive humanism expressed through numerous mobilizations. Moreover, many of these groups do not necessarily seek a radical transformation of the world. Yet, as Dyer-Witheford (1999) suggests, each can be considered as a beachhead and together such movements have the potential to increasingly contest globalization and move us towards a post-capitalist form of globalization.

Conclusion

Globalization must be understood as the interplay of conflicting identities. American football offers a ludic identity and implicitly celebrates a managerial capitalism in which the winners cheer as losers are castrated. Moreover, the carnivalesque identities of mass media and consumption distract people from the political concerns generated by capitalism and globalization whether in Brazil or the USA. Nevertheless, some of the utopian Enlightenment, democratic and socialist imaginary carried over from past contestations remains to inform new generations of cyberactivists. Also, despite the distractions of carnivals and consumerism and growing social fragmentation it may be that unprecedented strategic openings and organizational tools are now available for cyberactivists to employ if they so choose in order to contest the terrains of the now globalized world. Here, are the future sites where competing identities and conflicting visions of selfhood will be decided.

13
Globalization and Alternative Approaches to the Transformation of Nation-States: Scotland as a Test Case

John W. Books

While it is certainly true that many if not most Scots have never accepted English/British rule over Scotland, the current separatist movement has a very modern history indeed. The Scottish National Party (SNP) itself is only sixty-five years old. It drew together diverse cultural and political groupings in the 1930s and since then has experienced good and bad times. The breakthrough for the party came in the two general elections of 1974, when it polled 20 and then 30 per cent of the vote. Since then it has been a central factor in all elections in Scotland and its push for the related goals of devolution and independence has had to be taken seriously. The SNP was a major force behind the referendum for a Scottish Parliament in 1997, in which nearly 75 per cent of the voters supported the creation of a Scottish Parliament and 63 per cent wished for such a body to have tax-varying powers. In the 1999 election for seats in that parliament, the SNP came second behind Labour, with almost 29 per cent of the vote. From an electoral standpoint this is a very strong indication of progress towards the party's eventual goal of independence. This chapter employs and assesses four theoretical approaches to analyse why the SNP is now enjoying electoral success and whether it is likely to achieve that goal.

Throughout the post-Second World War period the principle of national self-determination has been increasingly emphasized by world bodies and important national governments. In theory this principle is rarely contested, but in reality it is not always observed. Since the collapse of the Soviet Bloc and the disaggregation of the Soviet Union new nations have been created at a rapid pace. The list of new European states includes old nations like Poland, Estonia, Latvia, Lithuania,

Hungary, the Czech Republic, Slovakia, Romania, Bulgaria and Albania. This list includes the re-establishment of old nations and the creation of new ones. The growth of regional autonomy has also been impressive, with federal arrangements being considered and even attempted. Increasingly, the European reality is one of a reassertion of local loyalties against the backdrop of a steady growth in the power and activity of the European Union (EU). This trend is reflected in Scotland, and in the aims of the SNP – a party that is keen to promote feelings of Scottish identity and use them politically. Are these trends and tendencies the result of global forces or are they idiosyncratic occurrences that could easily shift in another direction?

Comparative Politics and International Relations offer a range of theoretical perspectives on this question. These include: standard developmental theory, dependency theory, ethnonational/ethnopolitical theory and globalization. Each of these perspectives will be used in this chapter to examine the recent success of the SNP and then the explanatory potential of these approaches will be assessed. While globalization is clearly the most fashionable approach at present, the others deserve consideration and will highlight the strengths and weaknesses of the globalization perspective. Which theory best fits the Scottish reality? What does that say about the future of Scotland in this globalizing world, and about the future role of the SNP? While definitive answers to these questions are unlikely, the root theoretical questions may be addressed profitably.

The theoretical perspectives

Standard Development Theory

Within Comparative Politics, the school of Political Development known as Developmentalism cannot be said to have a uniform approach to political change. For example, scholars like Samuel Huntington (1968) and Gabriel Almond (Almond and Powell, 1968) adopt different approaches in explaining how political change is driven. However, they share enough common ground to constitute an identifiable perspective. Central to their thinking is the notion that politics is at the nub of development. Political systems control their fates, political parties and institutions respond to challenges from both their domestic and external environments. The effectiveness of their response depends upon their level of institutional development and the seriousness of the challenges they face. In this view, governments are the key actors, along with parties and groups and nations' evolution and success depends on the capacity of the governments that lead them. While Developmentalism is applied more often to what are often called Third World countries, its ideas can also be applied to political change in more advanced countries.

The concept of adaptation is vital to an understanding of the Developmentalist explanation of separatist movements. Effective governments should anticipate movements aimed at freeing peripheral geographical areas from central control and adapt or create structures to deal with them. From this perspective, the British Government's willingness to consider steps such as the creation of the Scottish Office, the development of the Scottish Committee, and more recently the creation of a Scottish Parliament with limited powers, fits the Developmental model well. This 'structural differentiation' is clearly aimed at defusing nationalist and separatist tendencies in Scotland and is a policy acceptable to both major British parties. The appropriate government strategy is to allow sufficient autonomy to prevent total separation and the fundamental restructuring of the existing political system. It must be said that this interpretation is rather derivative, since the major works on Developmentalism rarely deal with this topic directly. For instance, in his works on political decay, Samuel Huntington does not directly address this topic despite the fact that separatism is an example of this phenomenon. The implicit model involved in Developmentalism assumes that nations grow more effective over time and that the relatively developed ones cope rather well with their environments, suggesting that the disintegration of nations is unlikely. Nothing in Developmentalism envisions the creations of supranational political institutions that might make national institutions problematic or more flexible and nor does it deal well with the phenomenon of multinational corporations (MNCs). Thus, while developmental theory can be stretched to cover the case of separatism, the conceptual basis of the approach is clearly strained by emerging realities.

Dependency Theory

The most forceful challenge to developmental theory in Comparative Politics comes from those scholars labelled dependistas. Like the development school, dependency is an extremely diverse academic school – witness the differences in approach taken by Cardosa and Faletto (1979), dos Santos (1984) and Wallerstein (1980). This section relies on the ideas of Theotonio dos Santos (1984), who has generated a useful taxonomy of dependency types. Dos Santos' analysis rests on assumptions common to most dependency theory, that there are developed nations that restrain development in less developed ones by controlling them in a variety of ways. Dependency theorists talk in terms of centres and peripheries. Centres, such as colonial powers, control the resources and determine the choices available to the peripheries such as the former colonies. By virtue of military, economic or financial power, the centre exploits the periphery and is often aided in this by centres within the periphery. From this perspective, less-well-off regions within any nation can be seen as peripheries, and regional and subnational movements can be viewed as a means for local elites and people to unshackle themselves from a repressive, exploitative centre. Dos Santos (1984) suggests that there are three basic forms of dependence: colonial, financial-industrial and multinational. For dependency theorists, Scotland can be seen as a periphery that was conquered and partially colonized by England and later exploited in diverse and subtle ways by institutions supported by and including the government of the United Kingdom. This exploitation is both economic and political: the centre removes more than it gives in terms of wealth and income, and it would be unwilling to allow local power to be exercised by Scots.

Perhaps more importantly for the present situation, dos Santos' argument would indicate that the nature of contemporary Scottish dependence relates more to penetration by MNCs than to exploitation by London, the national centre. It is clearly possible to construct a scenario in which dependency arguments have resonance for Scotland and such dependency rhetoric can be found in the programme of the SNP. This is unsurprising, as any call for independence is normally grievance-driven. What is at variance with dependency theory, is that the SNP is insufficiently leftist and always has been. Communist and socialist groups in Scotland are not nationalistic enough to be seen in dependency terms. The dependency rhetoric is almost always leftist and nationalist and often isolationist. The SNP advocacy of Scottish independence within Europe does not fit this perspective. This is especially true when one considered that dependency theory in its simpler varieties ordinarily implies revolutionary outcomes. It seems that dependency theory, generated primarily to explain Third World dependence and especially Latin American dependence, is not easily adapted to First World applications.

Ethnonational Political Theory

In their recent work, *Ethnopolitics in the New Europe* (1998), Ishiyama and Bruening build a set of expectations regarding the behaviour of what they call ethnonational movements. The SNP is one of their examples. They comb the ethnopolitics literature for propositions and distill six standard expectations from it, the last five of which have some relevance for Scotland:

1. The greater the gap in economic performance amongst ethnic groups, the more likely it is that the ethnopolitical party representing the political minority group will make extremist political demands.
2. The more regionally integrated the state, the less likely it is that the ethnopolitical party will make extremist demands.
3. The broader the scope of political representation, the less likely it is that the ethnopolitical party will make extremist demands and the more the quality of representation is based on individual competition the less likely the ethnopolitical party will make extremist demands.
4. The more the current government is dominated by nationalists of another group, the more likely that the ethnopolitical party representing the minority will make extremist demands.
5. The more diverse the composition of the ethnopolitical party, the less likely it is that it will make extremist demands. (Ishiyama and Breuning 1998: 15–16)

From the perspective of ethnopolitics, what matters is how grievances develop and how they are dealt with by national governments. If an ethnic group is discriminated against economically and therefore suffers compared to the majority, it will develop a group consciousness and build organizations aimed at righting perceived wrongs. From this perspective, the existence and creation of identities is crucial. This should be true particularly in nations like the United Kingdom, in which clearly defined regions with distinctive cultural identities such as Scotland and Wales remain. In such a case if ethnopolitical parties have access to the means of political representation their demands should be moderate. Finally, to the extent that the ethnic group is internally diverse, especially in terms of its political structures, it is weakened in its effort to put forth strong claims. From this perspective, the SNP gains from being the only clear advocate of Scottish independence claims and is advantaged at times when it can claim that the British Government is dominated by non-Scots who have no interest in things Scottish. It is also advantaged by the natural regionalism in the UK. Its appeal has always been strongest among those who feel a sense of Scottish cultural identity, a consciousness of Scottishness. Its demands would however be moderated by the recent relatively small gap in economic prosperity between Scots and others in the United Kingdom. It would also be significantly weakened by the British Government's long-time willingness to tolerate and even promote Scottish institutions such as the Scottish Committee and the Scottish Office. In this view it might be argued that by consenting to a Scottish Parliament the British Government undermined the SNP's calls for independence. Ishiyama and Breuning conclude that the moderation in policy and action characterize the SNP. They are unable to say that ethnonational theory does well at explaining the progress of the SNP. While the SNP and the Scottish independence movement generally have a completely non-violent history, it is also true that they advocate the most extreme solution to their perceived problems: independence.

Globalization

In recent years the concept of globalization has been introduced into the social sciences. Anthony Giddens (1990: 64) defines globalization as:

> the intensification of worldwide social relations which link localities in such a way as local happenings are shaped by events occurring many miles away and vice versa.

Included in this perspective are all forms of social interactions: the purely social, economic and political. Much of this is spawned by technological change, especially newer forms of electronic contact and information-sharing. How then, is globalization related to separatism, especially Scottish separatism?

There are several likely links. In terms of economic change, we must expect that Scotland's economy will be increasingly penetrated by MNCS. While globalization does not require it, it is also true that Scots and Scottish institutions have encouraged MNCs to locate in Scotland in order to diversify the economy and replace failing industries. Part of the surge in investment in to Scotland stems directly from new political structures like Locate in Scotland and Scottish Enterprise. Efforts to expand the tourism industry also fit this trend and increasing tourism affects the local culture because it mean that more Scots come into contact with a diverse set of foreign visitors. It seems likely that this contact will increase the diversity of Scottish culture, a possible consequence of which would be an increasing sense of threat to Scottish identity. But here we focus on political effects.

What types of reactions to globalization should we expect in the political realm? In his *The Global Age* Martin Albrow (1997: 199) claims that small nations 'are able to locate themselves and assert a cultural identity more obviously and effectively in relation to a supranational state organization than in a modern world in which too often the alternatives have appeared to be statehood or extinction'. This seems to be true of the recent path chosen by the SNP, and would appear to indicate a very rosy future for political separatism. On the other hand, Randall Kindley (1997: 223) argues that 'globalization threatens the wealth and security once enjoyed by the small states of Europe' which causes them to choose one of two strategies: 'One way called for using traditional policies and institutions, the other for adapting existing institutions to a new policy template' (1997: 232). His analysis suggests that the latter path is the more successful. In this view the challenges of globalization are not easily met through structures designed to deal with other less complex contexts, so new institutions or reoriented ones, are necessary. From the standpoint of devolution or independence for Scotland, it would appear that this is exactly what is occurring. The new Scottish Parliament has considerable authority over what would in the past have been called industrial policy. It already has in place institutions that can be adapted to the challenge of global change. The central question may be how will this be done? Key to answering that question will be the immediate future of the party battle in Scotland. Should Labour appear to govern well and in Scottish interests, the SNP may have difficulty convincing Scots of the virtue of independence. Should economic and political difficulties overtake the new Labour regime, independence, rather than autonomy, will seem more appealing. If Kindley is right, the challenge to Labour is a very serious one, because adapting existing institutions or using new ones effectively are not easy things. The SNP's strategic position here is, in fact, an enviable one. It can watch for failure and capitalize on it and some failures, missteps and errors are certain. A globalization perspective would suggest that many, if not most, of these factors are beyond the control of the new Scottish Parliament (or, for that matter, Westminster). Globalization will continue regardless of what local authorities do (short of Cuban-style control), and it will require reaction more than action from political authorities. Adapting to the new global age will be vital to determining Scotland's future.

This approach is perhaps too broad, too vague. How do trends like increasing connectedness to the Internet lead to institutional adaptation? How much inward investment is critical in shifting the political balance? What stage of development in the European Union will lead to an increasing likelihood of successful calls for Scottish independence? Do international exchanges drive independence movements? How will increased tourism lead Scots to demand release from British shackles? Is independence-seeking really an enterprise that is driven mainly, or even somewhat, by forces like globalization? Or are other forces primary in this process? One can accept the reality of economic, social and cultural globalization without concluding that profound political changes will stem from it. That is to say, globalization theory may not be sufficiently well-specified to offer clear predictions at this time. After all, institutional adaptation would include the potential for existing institutions to adjust to these forces, and control their effects. In order to inspect more closely the options presented so far, we must look at recent economic and political trends in Scotland in more detail.

Assessing the theoretical perspectives

Economic change in Scotland

For a very long time Scotland lagged behind England in industrial development and economic progress. When industrialization came to Scotland mining and heavy industries became its backbone. Shipbuilding and other heavy industries were crucial to the industrial heart of the region. As these traditional industries waned ever more quickly following the Second World War, Scotland suffered accordingly. The period from the 1960s to the 1980s were not kind to Scotland, and the economic gap between Scotland and the southeast of England, in particular widened substantially. Recently, the Scottish economy has been more robust, and the gap has again narrowed.

While once shipbuilding, coal and steel were the foundation of the Scottish economy, now most of Scotland's output is in the service sector. Over 60 per cent of gross domestic product (GDP) is produced in the service sector, which employs 75 per cent of all Scottish workers. Manufacturing accounts for only 20 per cent of GDP, generated by 16 per cent of the workforce. Scotland produces office machinery, radio, television and communication equipment, whisky, and chemicals, items that are also its main exports. Importantly, with the exception of the whisky export trade, most of these areas are dominated by MNCs that have been attracted to Scotland in the last two decades. This growth has dramatically increased Scotland's exports, especially to Asia. Scotland's total exports doubled in the 1991–95 period, with exports to Asia growing fourfold. The bulk of Scottish exports have gone and still go to EU trading partners. Scotland has a large and thriving financial sector. The service sector, including hotel and catering, was the most important growth area in the Scottish economy in the 1980s and 1990s. Economic growth reduced unemployment in Scotland to rates similar to those in the UK in general. For a time in 1992 and 1993 Scotland's unemployment rate was actually below that of the UK average. These facts suggest that Scotland is in many ways typical of most post-industrial economies. It has responded to the loss of traditional industry and with a developing service sector. It has also worked hard to induce export-driven firms to come to Scotland and to dramatically increase its export economy. This has created new jobs and increased personal income for Scots. On the surface, at least, this is a happy tale. It should be noted, however, that Scotland has been the recipient of a good deal of European Union assistance through various structural funds. This has been a very important factor in stimulating recovery and growth, but from 2000 this aid is due to be reduced markedly.

Political change in Scotland

In the Scottish political arena, the postwar period witnessed a number of key changes. During the 1950s and 1960s the three main British parties received 95 per cent of Scottish votes between them, but the Labour Party dominated Scottish politics. In 1966 the SNP gained 5 per cent of the vote – largely by increasing the number of seats it contested. In 1970 it again contested additional seats and more than doubled its vote. Then in 1974, contesting all constituencies, it reached first 20 and then over 30 per cent of the vote. Since then it has been a force in Scottish electoral politics, arguing minimally for autonomy and maximally for independence. In the 1992 and 1997 general elections it has gained over 21 cent of the vote each time. In the Scottish Assembly election 6 May 1999 it polled nearly 29 per cent of the vote, trailing only Labour. Clearly the SNP is a major party in the Scottish context, and the only one to highlight a separate Scottish identity.

The second major shift in the postwar period has come in Scottish attitudes toward devolution and independence. The rise of the SNP in the 1970s gave rise to demands for a referendum on the establishment of a Scottish Assembly. In the referendum of 1 March 1979 Scottish voters approved a Scottish Assembly, but under the rules adopted for the referendum the majority vote was insufficient, because it did not represent the over 40 per cent of the electorate required. This outcome and the drop in votes for the SNP in the May 1979 General Election were major setbacks for those urging devolution. However, pressure to reconsider the question built through the Thatcher/Major years and the Labour Party agreed again to put the question to Scottish voters in

1999. This time the outcome was a clear vote for a Scottish Parliament with tax-varying powers. Twice in the last two decades Scots have voted for their own Assembly, signalling that the special status of the Scottish Committee and the Scottish Office was not adequate to their perceived needs. It would be wrong to interpret this as a signal that Scots want independence. The polls do not show it, and the election results cannot easily be interpreted to imply it. On the other hand, significant numbers of Scots do identify with a distinct Scottish cultural identity and want independence. Given the right sequence of events, therefore, it is easily possible to imagine a situation in which a majority could choose independence.

Confronting theory with facts

Standard development theory suggests that in response to demands for autonomy and independence, the British Government should have evolved coping strategies such as altering existing institutions or creating new ones – so-called 'structural differentiation'. Pre-existing structures include the Scottish Committee and the Scottish Office and one response would have been to give these institutions more authority, as was done during the 1970s and 1980s. Another response would be to create new institutions and the eventual granting of a Scottish Parliament fits this pattern. The problem of standard development theory is that it gives us no way to assess the likelihood that these responses will be successful. They may be, however, and this would mean that the Scottish case fits with development theory.

Dependency theorists view the world through an economic prism. For them the key is whether a dependent economic situation is being sustained. It is less important that the British Government has conceded to Scottish demands for autonomy than what economic structures dominate the landscape. The dependency perspective would concentrate on how the actions of the British Government in first creating heavy industries like shipbuilding and then closing them (and mines and other heavy industries) kept Scottish development dependent on the centre (London) working through the centre of the periphery (Edinburgh). It would then note that power has shifted away from national government centres to MNCs. In this new globalized world Scottish development is dependent on MNCs which are outside the control of Scots and their new Parliament or even that of the British Government. So, from the dependency perspective, Scotland has only traded one form of dependent development for another. The proof of this pudding, they would argue, is in the rapid and obvious shift of exports. This transition is not due to Scottish initiative but rather to the relocation in Scotland of firms who do substantial business with new partners such as the 'Asian Tigers' economies. These firms can and do leave just as quickly as they arrive. In this way it is not proper to say that Scottish exports are up, rather MNC exports from Scotland have risen. Next year they could be MNC exports from Ireland or the Philippines, but this in no way releases Scotland from dependent development. To the extent that this is true, dependency theory would predict that the political reaction would be an effort to control MNCs and moves by the new Scottish Parliament and Government to domesticate these firms. Failing this, theorists like dos Santos predict radical left-or right-wing solutions. Given the nature of the parties in Scotland, the right-wing alternative would seem most likely.

Ethnopolitical thinking focuses on the grievances that propel separatist movements. These may be physical, economic, emotional, cultural and legal. In Scotland the major grievances, such as repression of religion, education, personal and political expression, are certainly lacking. There is no occupying force, and the government has some substantial legitimacy, consequently the theory predicts moderate separationism. The SNP focuses on two elements: relative economic deprivation and the lack of local political autonomy. In the case of economics the argument has had historical basis, as the previous discussion shows. However, the difference between Scotland and England in economic circumstance is now very small – Scotland is the fourth most prosperous region in the UK. This fact does not mean that perceptions may not be different. It also does not imply that Scots would not rather have more direct control over their own economic circumstances, at least vis-à-vis London. Grievances rooted in long historical experience may continue to resonate long after circumstances change. The second major issue, the lack of local autonomy, is also changing. As the new Parliament begins to function and if it is perceived to be effective, the demand for independence may seem increasingly gratuitous. The theory of separatism promoted by Ishiyama and Breuning would suggest that autonomy would be sufficient, given the economic and political circumstances of Scotland. This would suggest that the SNP has a clear dilemma because as a separatist party its raison d'être is under challenge. It needs to push for independence now, whether that is what the population wants or not, because it has nowhere else to go ideologically. Successful separatist parties confront a crisis of direction. Their leaders wish to continue leading, but having achieved their central goal, often experience a major problem setting new ones. The SNP must now convince voters that it is actually more competent to govern than the other parties. Apparently Scots need more convincing on both the question of independence and governance. Separationist theory sets itself a limit, focusing mainly on what factors lead to separatism and more strident separatism. It says little about what happens when intermediate goals are achieved.

This leaves globalization. What insights does it provide? It is clear that Scotland is deeply embedded in the general trends that comprise the globalization phenomenon. Because of the efforts of agencies such as Locate in Scotland and Scottish Enterprise more than 600 firms from over 30 nations have been drawn to Scotland in the last decade, a period in which investment has broken all records. These firms account for over 100 000 Scottish jobs. Job creation has been overwhelmingly in the areas of office machinery, computers, radio, television, and communications equipment, and chemicals. This would seem to augur well for the future of the Scottish economy, but there are some dark clouds as well. While many of these jobs are production jobs few of them are in engineering or the design end of the process, since firms bring that with them. In fact, the 'brain drain' from Scotland continues. There is relatively little domestically generated new technology. Another negative factor is that MNCs have no allegiance to Scotland. While the government keeps statistics on how many firms are attracted to Scotland, it does not keep exit numbers. We do not know how long firms stay and what impact their leaving has. Only anecdotal evidence exists about firm exit, but it does happen, and in times of global downturn it could be a major negative for the Scottish economy. It is clear that Scots are increasingly involved in the communications revolution attached to globalization. Internet access is on the rise, information is easier to get for those with access, new friends and connections are easily made. This may dilute cultural distinctiveness in the long run, but it is as likely to provide a means for encouraging Scots to study and examine their own history and culture. Assessing the economic, cultural, social and informational effects of globalization on these factors is problematic to say the least.

This is even more so for government and political party. One effect long predicted is a weakening connection between the public and parties. The argument, well stated by Dalton, Flanagan and Beck (1984: ch. 1), is that political parties pattern information, and to the extent that new means of information transfer weaken that link they weaken parties. Television was the first enemy. The Internet is the most recent. According to this 'atomization' thesis citizens become less socially involved in parties, cease to interact in many ways with each other and become detached from organizations and available to new appeals and manipulation by media tricksters and demagogues. To date there is little sign of this in Scotland, but this outcome may have happened elsewhere. The information revolution may well inform people better about government itself, as the government creates a web presence from which citizens can find out directly about new initiatives, existing laws and outcomes. It means that citizens can contact officials directly from their homes, download information and respond to it. This may enhance government effectiveness. Should it have any differ-ential effect on particular parties? It is difficult to see how. The SNP has a very good site that it uses to disseminate information about itself, its leaders and its policies. This may well help it get its message out, but it does not make the message itself any more or less compelling. Similarly, the increased presence in the Scottish economy of international firms can also cut both ways. On one hand it weakens xenophobic arguments, as Scots interact with a wide variety of business practices and people from other lands; on the other, it may cause Scots to worry about whether they are losing control of their economy and their nation.

A related element of globalization is the growth of international organ-izations such as the European Union. This has particular relevance in the case of the SNP. The party leans heavily on the existence and utility of the EU in its manifesto to support its contention that independence for Scotland would bring benefits to Scots. Its argument is that an independ-ent Scottish government would be much more effective in bringing the benefits of EU membership directly to Scots. It claims that the British government has been unable and/or unwilling to push for the level of benefits Scots deserve. As an independent nation within the EU Scotland would fare better, because it would have direct and self-interested repre-sentation. This argument appears to have face validity and is a major part of the SNP's Manifesto for the upcoming European Parliament elections. From this perspective, the globalization inherent in the EU aids separ-ationist movements like the SNP by making small nations appear more viable. Those who argue that Scotland cannot make it on its own can be shown the examples of Ireland, Finland and Denmark. In each case EU membership can be seen to have been a good thing.

Conclusion

This chapter has assessed Scottish Nationalism from the perspective of four 'theories' of political change: standard development theory, dependency theory, ethnonational politics theory, and globalization. While each approach has some strong points, none was particularly compelling as an explanation for the rise and recent success of the Scottish National Party. It seems that the ethnonational approach and dependency theory have advantages over the other two in explaining developments in Scottish separatism. They focus on the development of grievances and their maintenance over time by nationalist organizations. They suggest that autonomy demands will not be enough, and that independence is the more obvious demand even for an organization as moderate as the SNP. Standard development theory points out the necessity of institutional adaptation, and would suggest that the chances for SNP success in achieving independence are not good given the flexible response of the British government. Finally, while globalization theory clearly relates to changes in Scotland, it does not offer a clear understanding of the types of adjustment either parties or parliaments must make to cope with the new globalism. Perhaps it is just too early to see the specific effects of these global changes. It may well be that a downturn in the global economy will demonstrate them more impressively. Such a downturn would likely mean the loss of industry and finance in Scotland and offer separationists another important reason to seek self-government.

Bibliography

Ahlstrom, S. E. *A Religious History of the American People, Vol. One* (Garden City, NY: Doubleday, Image Books, 1975).

Aho, J. A. *The Politics of Righteousness: Idaho Christian Patriotism* (Seattle, WA: University of Washington Press, 1990).

Albrow, M. *The Global Age: State and Society Beyond Modernity* (Cambridge: Polity, 1996 and Stanford, CA: Stanford University Press, 1997).

Albrow, M. 'Travelling beyond local cultures', in J. Eade (ed.), *Living in the Global City: Globalization as a Local Process* (London: Routledge, 1997) 36–55.

Albrow, M., Eade, J., Durrschmidt, J. and Washbourne, N. 'The impact of globalization on sociological concepts: community, culture and milieu', in J. Eade (ed.), *Living in the Global City* (London: Routledge, 1997) 20–36.

Albrow, M., Eade, J., Fennell, G. and O'Byrne, D. J. *Local/Global Relations in a London Borough* (London: Roehampton Institute, 1994).

Albrow, M. and O'Byrne, D. J. 'Rethinking state and citizenship under global conditions', in H. Goverde (ed.), *Global and European Polity?: Impacts for Organisations and Policies*, (Aldershot: Ashgate, 2000) 65–82.

Almond, G. A. and Powell, G. B. *Comparative Politics* (Boston: Little Brown and Company, 1968).

Ammerman, N. T. *Baptist Battles: Social Change and Religious Conflict in the Southern Baptist Convention* (New Brunswick, NJ: Rutgers University Press, 1990).

Ammerman, N. T 'North American Protestant Fundamentalism', in M. E. Marty and R. S. Appleby (eds), *Fundamentalisms Observed* (Chicago, IL: University of Chicago Press, 1991) 1–65.

Ammerman, N. T. *Bible Believers: Fundamentalists in the Modern World* (New Brunswick, NJ: Rutgers University Press, 1993).

Anderson, B. *Imagined Communities: Reflections on the Origin and Spread of Nationalism* (London: Verso, 1983 and 1991).

Anteby, L. 'Post-Zionism and Aliyah: Observations on recent immigrants from Ethiopia and the FSU in Israel', *Bulletin du centre de Recherche Français de Jérusalem*, 3 Autumn (1998) 105–16.

Appadurai, A. 'Disjuncture and difference in the global cultural economy', in M. Featherstone (ed.), *Global Culture: Nationalism, Globalization and Modernity* (London: Sage, 1990) 295–310.

Archard, D. 'Myths, lies and historical truth: a defence of nationalism', *Political Studies*, 43 (3) 1995 472–81.

Arjomand, S. A. 'The emergence of Islamic political ideologies', in J. A. Beckford and T. Luckmann (eds), *The Changing Face of Religion* (London: ISA/Sage, 1989) 109–23.

Asmal, K., Asmal, L. and Roberts, R. S. *Reconciliation through Truth: a Reckoning of Apartheid's Governance* (New York: St Martin's Press – now Palgrave, 1997).

Attias, J. C. and Benbassa, B. *Israël imaginaire* (Paris: Flammarion, 1998).

Atwood, T. C. 'Through a glass darkly', *Policy Review*, 54 (1990) 44–52.

Ayubi, N. N. M. 'The politics of militant Islamic movements in the Middle East', *Journal of International Affairs*, 36 (1983) 271–83.

Bakhtin, M. *Rabelais and his World* (Boston, MA: Massachusetts Institute of Technology Press, 1968).

Bakic-Hayden, M. 'Nesting orientalisms: the case of former Yugoslavia', *Slavic Review*, 54 (1995) 917–31.

Bakic-Hayden, M. and Hayden, R. 'Orientalist variations on the theme "Balkans": symbolic geography in recent Yugoslav cultural politics', *Slavic Review*, 51 (1992) 2–15.

Banks, M. *Ethnicity: Anthropological Constructions* (London: Routledge, 1996).

Barber, B. *Jihad vs McWorld* (New York: Ballantine Books, 1995).

Barker, C. *Global Television: an Introduction* (Oxford: Blackwell Publishers, 1997).

Barr, J. *Fundamentalism* (London: SCM Press, 1977).

Barsenkov, S., Vdovin, A. I. and Koretskii, V. A. 'The Russian nation's historical destiny in the twentieth century (The Russian question in Nationality Policy)', *Russian Studies in History*, 37 (2) Fall (1998) 13–24.

Barthes, R. 'Rhetoric of the image', in *Image, Music, Text* (London: Fontana Press, 1977) 32–51.

Barthes, R. 'The Romans in films', in *Mythologies* (London: Vintage, 1993) 27–34.

Bartram, D. V. 'Foreign workers in Israel: history and theory', *International Migration Review*, 32 (2) (1998) 303–25.

Basch, L., Schiller, N. G. and Blanc C. S., *Nations Unbound: Transnational Projects, Postcolonial Predicaments and Deterritorialized Nation-States* (New York: Gordon and Breach, 1994).

Bataille, G. *Death and Sensuality: a Study of Eroticism and the Taboo* (Salem, NH: Ayer, 1984).

Bauman, Z. *Globalization: the Human Consequences* (Cambridge: Polity Press, 1998).

Baumiester, R. *Identity, Cultural Change and the Struggle for Self* (New York: Oxford, University Press, 1986).

Baylis, John and Smith, Steve (eds), *The Globalization of World Politics* (Oxford: Oxford University Press, 1997).

Beck, U. *The Risk Society: Towards a New Modernity* (London: Sage, 1992).

Beinart, W. *Twentieth-Century South Africa* (Oxford: Oxford University Press, 1994).

Bellah, R. N. 'Civil religion in America', *Daedalus*, 96 (1967) 1–21.

Berdyaev, N. *The Russian Idea*, trans. R. M. French (London: Century Press, 1947).

Beresford, D. 'The truth won't help', *The Observer*, 11 November (1998) 19.

Berger, P. *The Sacred Canopy: Elements of a Sociological Theory of Religion* (Garden City, NY: Doubleday, 1967).

Berger, P. L., Berger, B. and Kellner H. *The Homeless Mind* (New York: Random House, 1973 and Harmondsworth: Penguin, 1973).

Berger, P. and Luckmann, T. *The Social Construction of Reality: a Treatise in the Sociology of Knowledge* (Garden City, NY: Doubleday, 1966).

Berthomière, W. 'L'épopée des Juifs d'ex-URSS', *Confluences Méditerranée*, 26 (1998) 51–64.

Bhabha, H. K. 'DissemiNation: time, narrative, and the margins of the modern nation', in H. K. Bhabha (ed.), *Nation and Narration* (London: Routledge, 1990) 291–332.

Bigo, D. 'Sécurité, immigration et contrôle social. L'archipel des polices', *Le Monde, Diplomatique*, October 1996.

Bigo, D. 'Illegal workers may pose society risky' *Ha'aretz*, 29 July 1998.

Boraine, A., Levy, J. and Scheffer, R. (eds), *Dealing with the Past: Truth and Reconciliation in South Africa* (Cape Town: IDASA, 1994).

Borowski, A. and Yanay, U. 'Temporary and illegal labor migration: the Israeli experience', *International Migration*, 35 (4) (1997) 495–511.

Bowman, G. 'Xenophobia, fantasy and the nation: the logic of ethnic violence in former Yugoslavia', in V. Goddard, J. Llobera and C. Shore (eds), *Anthropology of Europe: Identity and Boundaries in Conflict* (London: Berg, 1994) 143–71.

Bowman, G. 'Constitutive violence and rhetorics of identity: a comparative study of nationalist movements in the Israeli-occupied territories and former Yugoslavia', Paper presented at the Conference Creating the other: the causes and dynamics of nationalism in Central and Eastern Europe, University of Minnesota, 6–8 May 1999.

Boyer, P. *When Time Shall be No More* (Cambridge: Belknap Press, 1992).

Brecher, J. and Costello, T. *Global Village or Global Pillage: Economic Reconstruction from the Bottom-up* (Boston: South End Press, 1994).

Briggs, A. *Victorian Things* (London: B. T. Batsford, 1988).

Bruce, S. 'Modernity and fundamentalism: the New Christian Right in America', *British Journal of Sociology*, 41 (4) (1990) 477–96.

Burbach, R., Núñez, O. and Kargarlitsky, B. *Globalization and its Discontents* (London and Chicago, IL: Pluto Press, 1997).

Calhoun, C. 'Civil society, nation-building and democracy: the importance of the public sphere to the constitutional process'. Paper delivered to the First International Symposium on the Making of the Eritrean Constitution, 7–12 January Asmara, Eritrea (1995).

Campbell, D. 'Violent performances: identity, sovereignty, responsibility', in Y. Lapid and F. Kratochwil (eds), *The Return of Culture and Identity in IR Theory* (Boulder, CO and London: Lynne Rienner, 1996) 163–81.

Canclini, N. G. *Hybrid Cultures: Strategies for Entering and Leaving Modernity* (Minneapolis: Minneapolis University Press, 1995).

Cardoso, F. H. and Faletto, E. *Dependency and Development in Latin America* (Berkeley, CA: University of California Press, 1979).

Carrier, J. *Occidentalism: Images of the West* (Oxford: Oxford University Press, 1995).

Castells, M. *The Rise of the Network Society* (Oxford: Blackwell, 1996).

Castells, M. *The Power of Identity* (Oxford: Blackwell, 1997).

Castells, M. *End of Millenium* (Oxford, Blackwell, 1998).

Chan, B. K. 'A family affair: migration, dispersal and the emergent identity of the Chinese cosmopolitan', *Diaspora*, 6 (2) (1997) 195–213.

Chapman, M. 'Freezing the frame: dress and ethnicity in brittany and gaelic scotland', in J. B. Eicher (ed.), *Dress and Ethnicity: Change across Space and Time* (Oxford: Berg, 1995) 7–29.

Chilcote, Ronald H. 'Alternative Approaches to Comparative Politics', in Howard J. Wiarda (ed.), *New Directions in Comparative Politics* (Boulder, CO: Westview Press, 1985).

'City rises on Cape sands', *The Guardian*, 5 May (1998) 12.

Clifford, J. *The Predicament of Culture: Twentieth Century Ethnography, Literature and Art* (Cambridge, MA: Harvard University Press, 1988).

Cohen, E. *Thai Society in Comparative Perspective* (Bangkok: White Lotus Co. Ltd, 1991).

Cohen, L. *Broken Bonds: the Disintegration of Yugoslavia* (Boulder, CO: Westview Press, 1993).

Cohen, S. 'Human rights and the crimes of the state: a culture of denial', *Australian and New Zealand Journal of Criminology*, 26 (1993) 97–115.

Cohn, N. S. *The Pursuit of the Millennium: Revolutionary Millenarians and Mystical Anarchists in the Middle Ages* (London: Secker & Warburg, 1957).

Cole, S. G. *The History of Fundamentalism* (Hamden, CT: Archon Books, 1931).

Connolly, W. E. *Identity/Difference: Democratic Negotiations of Political Paradox* (New York: Cornell University Press, 1991).

Creighton, M. R. 'Imaging the Other in Japanese Advertising Campaigns', in J. G. Carrier, (ed.), *Occidentalism: Images of the West* (Oxford: Oxford University Press, 1995) 135–60.

Cummings, R. 'The Superbowl Society', in Ray B. Browne (ed.), *Heroes of Popular Culture* (Bowling Green, OH: Bowling Green University Popular Press, 1972) 101–12.

Cunningham, A. *Essential British History* (London: Usborne, 1991).

Dalton, R. J. Flanagan, S. C. and Beck, P. A. *Electoral Change in Advanced Industrial Democracies* (Princeton: Princeton University Press, 1984).

da Matta, R. *Carnivals, Rogues and Heroes: an Interpretation of the Brazilian Dilemma*, (Notre Dame, IN: University of Notre Dame Press, 1991).

Danopoulos, C. (ed.), *The Decline of Military Regimes: the Civilian Influence* (Boulder, CO: Westview Press, 1988).

Davis, G. *My Country is the World: the Adventures of a World Citizen* (London: McDonald's, 1961).

De Bord, G. *The Society of the Spectacle* (Detroit, MI: Red and Black Press, 1970).

Dieckhoff, A. *L'invention d'une Nation. Israël et la Modernite Politique* (Paris: Gallimard, 1993).

Dieckhoff, A. 'Entre citoyenneté et nationalité. Entretiens avec Alain Dieckhoff', *Confluences Méditerranée*, 26 (1998) 13–20.

Dieckhoff, A., C. Jaffrelot, 'De l'état-nation au post- nationalisme', in M. C. Smouts (ed.), *Les Nouvelles Relations Internationales. Pratiques et Théories* (Paris: Presses de Sciences Po, 1998) 51–74.

Dollar, G. W. *A History of American Fundamentalism* (New York: Random House, 1973).

dos Santos, Theotonio 'The structure of dependence', in Mitchell A. Seligson (ed.), *The Gap Between Rich and Poor* (Boulder, CO: Westview Press, 1984).

Drache, D. 'Globalization: is there anything to fear?', *University of Warwick, CSGR Working Paper*, No. 23 1999.

Dragovic-Soso, J. 'The Serbian intellectual dissidence in the 1980s: from the defence of free speech to the defence of the nation', Paper presented at the 22nd Annual Conference of the British International Studies Association, Leeds, 15–17 December 1997.

Duckenfield M. and Calhoun, N. 'Invasion of the western Ampelmännchen', *German Politics*, 6 (3) (1997) 54–69.

Dukes, P. 'Globalization and Europe: the Russian Question', in Roland Axtmann (ed.), *Globalization and Europe: Theoretical and Empirical Investigations* (London and Washington: Pinter, 1998) 93–108.

Durrschmidt, J. 'The delinking of locale and milieu: on the situatedness of extended milieux in a global environment', in J. Eade (ed.), *Living the Global City: Globalization as Local Process* (London: Routledge, 1997) 56–72.

Dyer-Witheford, N. *Cyber-Marx* (Urbana, IL: University of Illinois Press, 1999).

Dyson, K. 'The economic order – still Modell Deutschland?', in G. Smith, William E. Patterson and Stephen Padgett (eds), *Developments in German Politics 2* (Basingstoke, Macmillan Press – now Palgrave, 1996) 194–210.

Dyzenhaus, D. *Judging the Judges, Judging Ourselves: Truth, Reconciliation and the Apartheid Legal Order* (Oxford: Hart Publishing, 1998).

Eade, J. 'Identity, Nation and Religion: Educated Young Bangladeshis in London's East End', in J. Eade (ed.), *Living the Global City: Globalization as Local Process* (London: Routledge, 1997) 146–62.

Eco, U. *Art and Beauty in the Middle Ages* (New Haven and London: Yale University Press, 1986).

Editorial 'Case of nerves in Poland illustrates edginess felt by candidates for NATO', *International Herald Tribune*, 24 February (1997) 6.

Editorial 'Enlarge the European Union Before NATO', *International Herald Tribune*, 6 February (1998) 7.

Editorial 'Diplomatic dispatches: rub-a-dub-dub, 3 men on the stump', *The Washington Post*, 11 February (1998) 13.

Eide, E. B. ' "Conflict Entrepreneurship": on the "Art" of waging civil war', in the joint PRIO/NUPI project Engaging the challenges of tomorrow: adjusting humanitarian intervention to the changing nature of conflict (1997). Available: *http://www.nupi.no/un/chapter1.html*

Eisenstadt, S. N. *The Development of the Ethnic Problem in Israeli Society* (Jerusalem: The Jerusalem Institute for Israel Studies, 1986).

Ewen, S. *Captains and Consciousness* (New York: McGraw Hill, 1976).

Ewick, P. and Silbey, S. S. *The Common Place of law* (Chicago, IL: University of Chicago Press, 1998).

Falter, J. and Klein, M. (1994) 'Die Wähler der PDS bei der Bundestagswahl', *Politik und Zeitgeschichte. Beilage zur Wochenzeitun das Parlament*, B51152–94: 22–34.

Featherstone, M. *Undoing Culture: Globalizaton, Postmodernism and Identity* (London: Sage Publications, 1995).

Foules, R. B. *Unconventional Partners: Religion and Liberal Culture in the US* (Grand Rapids, MI: William B. Eerdmans, 1989).

Freye, G. *The Masters and the Slaves: a Study in the Development of Brazilian Civilization* 2nd edn (Berkeley, CA: University of California Press, 1986).

Friedman, J. *Cultural Identity and Global Process* (London: Sage, 1994).

Fromm, E. *Escape From Freedom* (New York: Holt, Rinehart and Winston, 1941).

Frost, M. 'Global civil society: liberation or oppression?', unpublished paper: University of Kent at Canterbury (1998). Available at: *http://snipe.ukc.ac.uk/international/s314/frost.html*

Gallup, G. H. *Public Opinion 1980* (Wilmington, DE: Scholarly Resources, 1981).

Gallup, G. H. *Public Opinion 1982* (Wilmington, DE: Scholarly Resources, 1983).

Gallup G. H. and Castelli, J. *The People's Religion: American Faith in the '90s* (New York, NY: Macmillan, 1989).

Gerth, H. H. and Mills, C. W. (eds), *From Max Weber: Essays in Sociology* (Oxford: Oxford University Press, 1991).

Gibbons, L. 'Coming out of hibernation? The myth of modernity in Irish culture', in R. Kearney (ed.), *Across the Frontiers: Ireland in the 1990's* (Dublin: Wolfhound Press, 1988).

Giddens, A. *The Consequences of Modernity* (Cambridge: Polity Press, 1990).

Giddens, A. *Modernity and Self-Identity: Self and Society in the Late Modern Age* (Cambridge: Polity Press, 1991 and Stanford, CA: Stanford University Press, 1992).

Giddens, A. *The Third Way: the Renewal of Social Democracy* (Cambridge: Polity Press, 1998).

Gilroy, P. *The Black Atlantic: Modernity and Double Consciousness* (London: Verso, 1993 and 1994).

Girard, R. *Violence and the Sacred* (Baltimore and London: John Hopkins University Press, 1977).

Gissendanner, S. 'Transfer or transformation? What the German social science literature has to say about unification and its systemic effects', *German Politics*, 5 (3) (1996) 460–84.

Godobo-Madikizela, P. 'Re-enactment of old identities and implications for reconciliation', Conference paper, the Institute of Personnel Management, Sun City, 21–3 October 1996.

Godina, V. 'The outbreak of nationalism on former Yugoslav territory: a historical perspective on the problem of supranational identity', *Nations and Nationalism*, 4 (1998) 409–22.

Goldblatt, B. and Meintjes, S. *Gender and the TRC*, Unpublished submission document, 1996.

Gorbachev, M. *Perestroika: New Thinking for Our Country and the World*, 2nd edn (London: Fontana, 1988).

Gorenberg, G. *Jerusalem Report* 25 May 1998.

Gramsci, A. *Selections from the Prison Notebooks* (London: Lawrence & Wishart, 1971).

Greiffenhagen, M. and Greiffenhagen, S. 'Eine Nation: Zwei politische Kulturen', in W. Weidenfeld (ed.), *Deutschland. Eine Nation – doppelte Geschichte: Materialien zum deutschen Selbstverständnis* (Cologne: Verlag Wissenschaft und Politik, 1993) 29–45.

Gumilev, L. *Ot Rossiia k Rossii: ocherki etnicheskii istorii* (Moscow: Ekopros, 1992).

Gupta, A. and Ferguson, J. 'Beyond "culture": space, identity and the politics of difference', *Cultural Anthropology*, 7 (1) (1992) 6–23.

Gupta, D. 'Between general and particular "others": Some observations on fundamentalism', *Contributions to Indian Sociology* (n.s.), 27 (1) (1993) 119–37.

Gutman, R. *A Witness to Genocide: the First Inside Account of the Horrors of 'Ethnic Cleansing' in Bosnia* (Shaftesbury: Element Books, 1993).

Gutman, R. 'The collapse of Serbia?', *World Policy Journal*, 26 (1999) 12–18.

Hall, S. 'The local and the global: globalization and ethnicity' and 'Old and new identities, old and new ethnicities', in A. D. King (ed.), *Culture, Globalization and the World-system: Contemporary Conditions for the Representation of Identity* (London: Macmillan, 1991) 19–68.

Hall, S. 'New ethnicities', in J. Donald and A. Rattansi (eds), *Culture and Difference* (London: Sage/Open University Press, 1992) 252–9.

Hall, S. 'The question of cultural identity', in S. Hall, D. Held and T. McGrew (eds), *Modernity and its Futures* (Cambridge: Polity Press and Blackwell in association with the Open University, 1992) 273–323.

Hall, S. *Formations of Modernity* (Cambridge: Polity Press, 1992).

Hall, S. 'New cultures for old', in D. B. Massey and P. M. Jess (eds), *A Place in the World* (Oxford: Oxford University Press and Open University, 1995 and 1998) 174–214.

Hall, S. 'Introduction: who needs "identity"?', in S. Hall and P. du Gay (eds), *Questions of Cultural Identity* (London: Sage, 1996) 1–17.

Hämäläinen, P. K. *Uniting Germany: Actions and Reactions* (Aldershot: Dartmouth, 1994).

Hamber, B. *Past Imperfect: Dealing with the Past in Northern Ireland and Societies in Transition* (Derry: Incore, 1998).

Hamber, B. and Kibble, S. *From Truth to Transformation: the Truth and Reconciliation Commission in South Africa* (London: CIIR,1999).

Hamilton, A. 'Rumours, foul calumnies and the safety of the state: mass media and national identity in Thailand', in C. J. Reynolds, *National Identity and Its Defenders: Thailand, 1939–1989* (Thailand: Silkworm Books, 1991) 341–78.

Hannerz, U. 'Cosmopolitans and locals in world culture', in M. Featherstone (ed.), *Global Culture: Nationalism, Globalization and Modernity* (London: Sage, 1990) 237–52.

Hannerz, U. *Transnational Connections: Culture, People, Places* (London: Routledge, 1996).

Hansen, L. *Western Villains or Balkan Barbarism? Representations and Responsibility in the Debate over Bosnia* (Copenhagen: Institute of Political Science, University of Copenhagen, 1998).

Harris, C. 'The new Russian minorities: a statistical overview', *Post-Soviet Geography*, 34 (1) (1993) 1–27.

Hayner, P. B. 'Fifteen truth commissions 1974–1994: a comparative study', *Human Rights Quarterly*, 17 (1) (1994) 19–29.

Hayoun, D. 'Haifa histadrut head: gov't has opportunity to solve illegal foreigner problem, don't distribute gas masks', *Globes*, 9 February 1998.

Held, D. *Global Transformations: Politics, Economics and Culture* (Cambridge: Polity Press in association with Blackwell, 1999).

Himmelstein, J. L. 'The New Right', in R. C. Liebman and R. Wuthnow (eds), *The New Christian Right* (New York: Aldine, 1983) 13–30.

Hirst, P. and Thompson, G. *Globalization in Question: the New International Economy and the Possibilities of Governance* (Cambridge: Polity Press, 1996).

Hoben, A. and Hefner, R. 'The integrative revolution revisited', *World Development*, 19 (2) (1991) 17–30.

Hobsbawm, E. J. and Ranger, T. O. (eds), *The Invention of Tradition* (Cambridge: Cambridge University Press, 1983).

Hochschild, A. *The Managed Heart* (Berkeley, CA: University of California Press, 1983).

Hogwood, P. *We Are One People: German Politics and Society since Unification* (Manchester: Manchester University Press, forthcoming).

Horkheimer, M. 'Authority and the family', in *Critical Theory: Selected Essays* (New York: Herder and Herder, 1972).

Hosking, G. *Russia: People and Empire 1552–1917* (London: HarperCollins, 1997).

Human Rights Watch, *Justice in the Balance* (London: HRW, 1998).

Hunter, J. D. 'Subjectivization and the new evangelical theodicy', *Journal for the Scientific Study of Religion*, 20 (1982) 39–47.

Hunter, J. D. *American Evangelicalism: Conservative Religion and the Quandary of Modernity* (New Brunswick, NJ: Rutgers University Press, 1983).

Hunter, J. D. *The New Christian Right* (New Brunswick, NJ: Rutgers University Press, 1988).

Huntington, Samuel P. *The Soldier and the State: the Theory and Practice of Civil–Military Relations* (Oxford: Oxford University Press, 1957).

Huntington, Samuel P. *Political Order in Changing Societies* (New Haven: Yale University Press, 1968).

Hussey, G. *Ireland Today: Anatomy of a Changing State* (London: Penguin, 1995).

Ignatieff, M. *Blood and Belonging: Journeys into the New Nationalism* (London: Vintage, 1994).

Ignatieff, M. 'Nationalism and the narcissism of minor differences', *Queen's Quarterly*, 102 (1995) 13–25.

Ignatieff, M. 'Overview: articles of faith', *Index on Censorship*, 5 (1996) 110–22.

Incore, Conference: Dealing with the past: reconciliation processes and peace building, 8–9 June 1998.

Ishiyama, J. T. and Breuning, M. *Ethnopolitics in the New Europe* (Boulder, CO: Lynne Rienner, 1998).

James, H. *A German Identity: 1770–1990* (London: Weidenfeld & Nicolson, 1990).

James, H. and Stone, M. (eds) *When the Wall Came Down: Reactions to German Unification* (London: Routledge, 1992).

Jameson, F. 'Notes on globalization as a philosophical issue', in F. Jameson and M. Miyoshi (eds), *The Cultures of Globalization* (Durham, NC: Duke University Press, 1998).

Janowitz, M. *Civil–Military Relations: Regional Perspectives* (Beverly Hills, CA and London: Sage, 1981).

Jenkins, R. *Social Identity* (London: Routledge, 1996).

Johns, S. and Davis, R. H. Jr., *Mandela, Tambo, and the African National Congress: the Struggle against Apartheid, 1948–1990. A Documentary Survey* (Oxford: Oxford University Press, 1991).

Johnson, S. D. and Tamney, J. B. 'The Christian right and the 1980 presidential election', *Journal for the Scientific Study of Religion*, 21 (1982) 123–31.

Johnson, S. D. and Tamney, J. B. 'Support for the Moral Majority: a test of a model', *Journal for the Scientific Study of Religion*, 27 (1) (1984) 32–47.

Juteau, D. 'Multiculturalism, interculturalisme et production de la nation', in M. Fourier and G. Vermes (eds), *Ethnicisation des Rapports Sociaux: Racismes, Nationalismes, Ethnicismes et Culturalismes* (Paris: L'Harmattan (Espaces Interculturels), 1994) 55–72.

Kanstroom, A. 'Wer sind wir wieder? Laws of asylum, immigration,and citizenship in the struggle for the soul of the new Germany', *Yale Journal of International Law*, 18 (1) (1993) 155–211.

Kaplan, R. *Balkan Ghosts: a Journey through History* (New York: Vintage, 1993).

Kasian Tejapira *Wiwata Lokanuwat [Globalisation Debate]* (Bangkok: Manager Media Group, 1995).

Kayatekin, S. A. and Ruccio, D. F. 'Global fragments: subjectivity and class politics in discourses of globalization', *Economy and Society*, 27 (1) (1998) 74–96.

Keane, F. *Letter to Daniel* (London: Penguin, 1996).

Kearney, R. *Postnationalist Ireland: Politics, Culture, Philosophy* (London: Routledge, 1997).

Kellas, James G. *The Scottish Political System* (Cambridge and New York: Cambridge University Press, 1984).

Kellstedt, L. A., Green, J. C., Guth, J. L. and Smidt, C. E. 'Religious voting blocs in the 1992, Election: the Year of the Evangelical?', *Sociology of Religion*, 55 (3) (1994) 307–26.

Kelly, D. M. *Why Conservative Churches Are Growing* (New York: Harper & Row, 1977).

Keohane, R. and Ostrom, E. (eds), *Local Commons and Global Interdependence: Heterogeneity and Cooperation in Two Domains* (London: Sage Publications, 1995).

Khasanova, G. 'Language and sovereignty: the politics of switching to the Latin alphabet in Tatarstan', *Prism*, 3 (16) 10 October 1997. Available at: *http:// www.jamestown.org/*

Khasanova, G. 'Russian identity: the view from Tatarstan' *Prism*, 4 (5) 6 March 1998, *http://www.jamestown.org/*

Kiberd, D. *Inventing Ireland: the Literature of the Modern Nation* (London: Jonathan Cape, 1995).

Kiel, T. 'Sport in Advanced Capitalist Society' (Archives of Red Feather Institute, 1984). Available at: *http://www.tryoung.com/archives/114kiel.html*

Kindley, R. F and Good, D. F. *The Challenge of Globalization and Institution Building* (Boulder, CO: Westview Press, 1997).

Kirkpatrick, L. A. 'Fundamentalism, Christian orthodoxy, and intrinsic religious orientation, as predictors of discriminatory attitudes', *Journal for the Scientific Study of Religion*, 32 (3) (1993) 256–68.

Kivisto, P. 'The rise and fall of the Christian Right? Conflicting reports from the frontline', *Sociology of Religion*, 55 (3) (1994) 223–7.

Klages, H. and Gensicke, T. 'Geteilte Werte? Ein deutscher Ost- West-Vergleich', in W. Weidenfeld (ed.), *Deutschland, eine Nation – doppelte Geschichte* (Cologne: Verlag Wissenschaft und Politik, 1993) 47–59.

Konstitutsiia Rossiiskoi Federatsii (Moscow: SPARK, 1993).

Kozlov, V. I. 'On the nature of the Russian Question and its basic aspects', *Russian Studies in History*, 37 2 Fall (1998) 69–87.

Krasikov, A. 'From the annals of spiritual freedom: Church–State Relations in Russia', *East European Constitutional Review*, 7 (2) Spring (1998) 75–84.

Krisch, H. 'The Party of Democratic Socialism: Left and East', in R. J. Dalton (ed.), *Germans Divided: The 1994 Bundestag Elections and the Evolution of the German Party System* (Oxford: Berg, 1996) 109–31.

Kroll, M. D; Seligman, M. E. P. and Sethi, S. 'A commentary on optimism, fundamentalism, and egoism', *Psychological Science*, 4 (4) (1993) 256–9.

Kuechler, M. 'Deutschland den Deutschen? Migration and naturalization in the 1994 campaign and beyond', in R. Dalton (ed.), *Germans Divided: The 1994 Bundestag Elections and the Evolution of the German Party System* (Oxford: Berg, 1996) 235–64.

Kukushkin, Iu. S. 'The destiny of the people is the destiny of the country', *Russian Studies in History*, 37 (2) Fall (1998) 9–12.

Laclau, E. *New Reflections on the Revolution of our Time* (London and New York: Verso, 1990).

Laclau, E. (ed.), *The Making of Political Identities* (London: Verso, 1994).

Langman, L. 'Identity, hegemony and social reproduction', in *Current Perspectives in Social Theory* (Greenwich, CT: JAI Press, 1998a) 185–225.

Langman, L. 'I hate therefore I am', *Social Theory and Research*, 6 (1) (1998b) 2–36.

Langman, L. 'Bakhtin and the future', in D. Kalekin (ed.), *Designs for Alienation* (Helsinki: SoPhil Press, 1998c) 341–64.

Langman, L. 'From pathos to panic: American character meets the future', in P. Wexler (ed.), *Critical Theory Now* (London: Falmer Press, 1992) 165–239.

Langman, L. 'Neon cages: shopping for subjectivity', in R. Shields (ed.), *Lifestyles of Consumption* (London: Routledge, 1993) 40–82.

Lehmbruch, G. 'The process of regime change in East Germany', in C. Anderson, K. Kaltenhaler and W. Luthardt (eds), *The Domestic Politics of German Unification* (Boulder, CO: Lynne Rienner, 1993) 17–36.

Lehmbruch, G. 'The process of regime change in East Germany: an institutionalist scenario for German unification', *Journal of European Public Policy*, 1 (1) 1994 115–41.

Leibowitz, Y., Zimmerman, M., Galnor, I. and Evron, B. *Peuple, Terre, État* (Paris: Plon, 1995).

Levinas, D. *Humanisme de L'autre Homme* (Paris: Fata Morgana, 1972).

Liebman, R. C. 'Mobilizing the Moral Majority', in R. C. Liebman and R. Wuthnow (eds), *The New Christian Right* (New York: Aldine, 1983) 50–72.

Linger, D. *Dangerous Encounters* (Stanford: Stanford University Press, 1992).

Lipset, S. and Rokkan, S. (eds), *Party Systems and Voter Alignments* (New York: Free Press, 1967).

Lipschutz, R. 'Reconstructing World politics: the emergence of global civil society', *Millennium: Journal of International Studies*, 21 (1992) 399–420.

Luker, K. *Abortion and the Politics of Motherhood* (Berkeley, CA: University of California Press, 1984).

MacBride, J. War, *Battering and Other Sports* (Atlantic Highlands, NJ: Humanities Press, 1995).

Macdonald, L. 'Globalizing civil society: interpreting international NGOs in Central America', *Millennium: Journal of International Studies*, 23 (1994) 267–85.

Magas, D. *The Destruction of Yugoslavia: Tracking the Break-up 1980–92* (London and New York: Verso, 1993).

Magatti, M. 'Globalization as double disconnection and its consequences: an outline', in P. Kennedy and N. Hai (eds), *Globalization and Identities, Conference vol 2* (Manchester Metropolitan University, 1999).

Manzo, K. *Creating Boundaries: the Politics of Race and Nation* (Boulder, CO and London: Lynne Rienner, 1996).

Marcuse, H. *Eros and Civilization* (Boston, MA: Beacon Press, 1955).

Marcuse, H. *One Dimensional Man* (Boston, MA: Beacon Press, 1964).

Marié, M. 'Introduction', in T. Allal, M. Jean-Pierre Buffard and Tomaso Regazzola (eds), Situations Migratoires, La *'Fonction-Mirroir'* (Paris: Galilée [Collection L'espace critique], 1977) 9–18.

Marsden, G. M. *Fundamentalism and American Culture: the Shaping of Twentieth Century Evangelicalism 1870–1925* (New York: Oxford University Press, 1980).

Marsden, G. M. 'Preachers of paradox: the religious new right in historical perspective', in M. Douglas and S. Tipton (eds), *Religion and America* (Boston, MA: Beacon Press, 1983) 150–68.

Marsden, G. M. *Evangelicalism and Modern American Culture* (New York: Oxford University Press, 1984).

Marsland, D. 'Nations and nationalism in sociological theory: a history of neglect and, prejudice', Paper presented to the British Sociological Association conference, University of Reading (1996).

Martin, H. P. and Schumann, H. *The Global Trap* (London: Zed Books, 1997).

Massey D. B. and Jess, P. M. (eds) *A Place in the World? Places, Cultures and Globalization* (Oxford: Oxford University Press in association with the Open University, 1995).

Marty, M. E. and Appleby, R. S. (eds), *Fundamentalisms Observed* (Chicago, IL: University of Chicago Press, 1991).

Marty M. E. and Appleby, R. S. (eds), *Fundamentalisms and the State* (Chicago, IL: University of Chicago Press, 1993a).

Marty M. E. and Appleby, R. S. (eds), *Fundamentalisms and Society* (Chicago IL: University of Chicago Press, 1993b).

Marty M. E. and Appleby, R. S. (eds), *Accounting for Fundamentalisms* (Chicago, IL: University of Chicago Press, 1994).

Marty M. E. and Appleby, R. S. (eds), *Fundamentalisms Comprehended* (Chicago, IL: University of Chicago Press, 1995).

McDaniel, T. *The Agony of the Russian Idea* (Princeton, NJ: Princeton University Press, 1996).

McFarland, S. C. 'Religious orientations and the targets of discrimination', *Journal for the Scientific Study of Religion*, 28 (3) (1989) 324–36.

McGreal, C. 'Democracy triumphs in S Africa vote', *The Guardian*, 3 June (1999) 12.

McGrew, A. G. 'Global politics in a transitional era', in A. G. McGrew and P. G. Lewis (eds), *Global Politics: Globalization and the Nation-state* (Cambridge: Polity Press, 1992) 312–30.

Mead, G. H. *Mind, Self and Society* (Chicago, IL: Chicago University Press, 1934).

Meek, J. 'Russia cracks down on minority faiths', *The Guardian*, 20 September (1997a) 20.

Meek, J. 'Kremlin faces point of conflict over identity', *The Guardian*, 27 October (1997b) 12.

Melucci, A. *Challenging Codes: Collective Action in the Information Age* (Cambridge: Cambridge University Press, 1996).

Melvin, N. *Russians Beyond Russia: the Politics of National Identity*, Chatham House Papers, The Royal Institute of International Affairs (London: Pinter, 1995).

Merkl, P. (ed.), *The Federal Republic of Germany at Forty- Five* (New York: New York University Press, 1995).

Miller, D. 'Reflections on British national identity', *New Community*, 21 (2) (1995) 135–88.

Mironov, V. B. 'Vozrozhdenie Rossii', *Kentavr*, July–August (1992) 16–25.

Miyoshi, M. *The Culture of Globalization* (Durham, NC and London: Duke University Press, 1998).

Mlinar, Z. *Globalization and Territorial Identities* (Aldershot: Avebury, 1992).

Moeran, B. 'The Orient Strikes Back: Advertising and Imagining Japan' *Theory, Culture & Society*, 13 (3) (1996) 77–112.

Moisy, C. 'Myths of the Global Information Village', *Foreign Policy*, 107 Summer (1997) 78–87.

Monama B. 'A case study on impunity: South Africa, Consultative and planning meeting for campaign against impunity in Africa', (Burkina Faso, 22–3 March 1996, Unpublished).

Muller, A. 'Facing our shadow side', *Track Two*, 6 (3–4) (1997) 22–24.

Munck, R. and Fagan, H. 'Development discourses: conservative, radical and beyond', in P. Shirlow (ed.), *Development Ireland: Contemporary Issues* (London: Pluto Press, 1995) 110–21.

Munson, H. 'Not all crustaceans are crabs: reflections on the comparative study of fundamentalism and politics', *Contention*, 4 (3) (1995) 51–166.

Myburgh, J. 'Wiser than ours?', *Frontiers of Freedom*, 9 (1996) 27–8.

Nattrass, N. 'The Truth and Reconciliation Commission on Business and Apartheid: a critical evaluation', *African Affairs*, 98 (392) July (1999) 373–91.

Neumann, I. B. *Russia and the Idea of Europe: a Study in Identity and International Relations* (London: Routledge, 1996).

Newswire – Telex Service 'Clinton takes NATO Enlargement to the Senate for approval', *Agence France Presse International*, 11 February (1998).

Nikolaev, A. I. 'Poniat' Rossiiu umom i serdtsem. Pis'ma russkogo generala 1', *Rossiiskaia Federatsiia*, 18 (1996) 52–4.

Nikonov, A. ' "Russkii vopros" sevodnia', *Svobodnaia Mysl'*, 13 September (1993) 15–26.

Noll, M. *A History of Christianity in the US and Canada* (London: SPCK, 1992).

Nuttall, S. and Coetzee, C. (eds), *Negotiating the Past: the Making of Memory in South Africa*, (Cape Town: Oxford University Press, 1998).

O'Byrne, D. J. 'Working-class culture: local community and global conditions' in J. Eade (ed.), *Living the Global City: Globalization as Local Process* (London: Routledge, 1997) 73–89.

O'Byrne, D. J. 'Citizenships Sans Frontières: Globality and the Reconstruction of Political Identity' (PhD thesis, University of Surrey, 1988).

OECD *Migrations, Libre-Exchange et Intégration Régionale dans le Bassin Méditerranean* (Paris: Conférences de L'OECD).

Offe, C. (ed.), *Der Tunnel am Ende des Lichtes: Erkundungen der politischen Transformationim Neuen Osten* (Frankfurt: Campus, 1994).

Offe, C. *Varieties of Transition: the East European and East German Experience* (Cambridge: Polity Press, 1996).

O'Hearn, D. *Inside the Celtic Tiger: the Irish Economy and the Asian Model* (London: Pluto Press, 1998).

Okojie, P. 'Migration, identity and rights in the European Union', in P. Kennedy and N. Hai (eds), *Globalization and Identities, vol 2, Conference Papers* (Manchester Metropolitan University, 1999)

Oriard, M. *Reading Football* (Chapel Hill, NC: University of North Carolina Press, 1993).

O'Toole, F. 'Unsuitables from a distance: the politics of *Riverdance*', in F. O'Toole, *The Ex-Isle of Erin: Images of a Global Ireland* (Dublin: New Island Books, 1996).

O'Tuathail, G. 'An anti-geopolitical eye: Maggie O'Kane in Bosnia, 1992–93', *Gender, Place and Culture*, 3 (1996) 171–85.

Parker, R. *Bodies, Pleasures and Passions* (Boston: Beacon Press, 1991).

Parrington, V. L. *American Dreams* (New York: Russel and Russel, 1964).

Parsons, T. *The Social System* (New York: Free Press, 1951).

Pasha, M. K. and Blaney, D. 'Elusive paradise: the promise and peril of global civil society', *Alternatives*, 23 (1998) 417–50.

Perlmutter, H. 'On the rocky road to the first global civilization', *Human Relations*, 44 (9) (1991) 897–920.

Petras, J. and Vieux, S. 'Bosnia and the revival of the US hegemony', *New Left Review*, 218 (1996) 3–25.

Pile, S. and Keith, M. *Geographies of Resistance* (London: Routledge, 1997).

Pilger, J. 'Freedom next time', *The Guardian Weekend*, 11 April (1998a) 14–22.

Pilger, J. *Hidden Agendas* (London: Vintage, 1998b).

Popov, N. *Srpski populizam* [*The Serbian populism*] (Athens: Paraskinio, 1994). Translation into Greek from Serbo-Croat.

Porat, L. *Ha'aretz*, 20 September 1998.

Portes, A. 'Globalization from below: the rise of transnational communities', Working Papers Series 1. Of the Transnational Communities Project at the Faculty of Anthropology and Geography at Oxford University 1997.

Posa, C. 'Engineering hatred: the roots of contemporary Serbian nationalism', *Balkanistica*, 1 (1998) 69–77.

Preston, P. W. *Political/Cultural Identity: Citizens and Nations in a Global Era* (London: Sage, 1997).

Ram, U 'Mémoire et identité: sociologie du débat des historiens en Israël', in F. Heymann and M. Abitbol (eds), *L'historiographie Israélienne Aujourd'hui* (Paris: CNRS Editions, 1998).

Ramet, S. 'Nationalism and the "idiocy" of the countryside: the case of Serbia', *Ethnic and Racial Studies*, 19 (1996a) 70–87.

Ramet, S. *Balkan Babel: the Disintegration of Yugoslavia from the Death of Tito to Ethnic War*, 2nd edn (Boulder, CO: Westview Press, 1996b).

Rapping, E. *The Looking Glass World of Nonfiction TV* (Boston: South End Press, 1987).

Rapport N. and Dawson, A. (eds), *Migrants of Identity: Perceptions of Home in a World of Movement* (New York and Oxford: Berg, 1998).

Real, T. 'Football violence', in H. Newcomb, *Television the Critical View*, 2nd edn (New York: Oxford University Press, 1979).

Reeves, P. 'Russia embraces the art of xenophobia', *The Independent on Sunday*, 18 April (1999) 22.

Reynolds C. J. 'Globalization and cultural nationalism in modern Thailand', in J. S. Kahn (ed.), *Southeast Asian Identities: Culture and the Politics of Representation in Indonesia, Malaysia, Singapore and Thailand* (London: I. B. Tauris for Institute of Southeast Asian Studies, 1998) 115–45.

Richter, M. 'Exiting the GDR: political movements and parties between democratization and westernization', in M. D. Hancock and H. A. Welsh (eds), *German Unification: Processes and Outcomes* (Boulder, CO and Oxford: Westview Press, 1994) 93–137.

Robertson, R. *Globalization: Social Theory and Global Culture* (London: Sage, 1992).

Robertson, R. 'Glocalization: time-space and homogeneity- hetrogeneity', in M. Featherstone and S. Lash and R. Robertson (eds), *Global Modernities* (London: Sage, 1995) 25–44.

Robins, K. 'Tradition and translation: national culture in its global context', in J. Corner and S. Harvey (eds), *Enterprise and Heritage* (London: Routledge, 1991) 21–44.

Rolston, B. 'The politics of memory: victims and truth in Northern Ireland', Open Lecture, Centre for Studies in Crime and Social Justice, 1999.

Rose, R. and Page, E. 'German responses to regime change: culture, class, economy or context?', *West European Politics*, 19 (1) (1996) 1–27.

Rosenau, J. *Turbulence in World Politics* (Brighton: Harvester Wheatsheaf, 1990).

Rowe, D. *Popular Cultures: Rock Music, Sport and the Politics of Pleasure* (London: Sage, 1995).

Rungswasdisab Puangthong, 'The quest for Siwilai (Civilisation)', *The Nation*, Bangkok, 10 January 1998.

Said, E. W. *Orientalism: Western Conceptions of the Orient* (Harmonsworth: Penguin Books, 1995).

Salecl, R. 'National identity and socialist moral majority', in E. Carter, J. Donald and J. Squires (eds), *Space and Place: Theories of Identity and Location* (London: Lawrence & Wishart, 1993) 101–9.

Salecl, R. 'The crisis of identity and the struggle for new hegemony in the former Yugoslavia', in E. Laclau (ed.), *The Making of Political Identities* (London and New York: Verso, 1994) 205–32.

Sardar, Z. *Postmodernism and the Other: the New Imperialism of Western Culture* (London: Pluto Press, 1998).

Sarkesian, S. *Beyond the Battlefield: the New Military Professionalism* (New York: Pergamon Press, 1981).

Sassen, S. *Globalization and its Discontents* (New York: Free Press, 1998).

Savel'ev, A. 'O formirovanii Natsional'noi doktriny Rossii', *RF*, 7 (1996) 53–4.

Savel'ev, A. 'O formirovanii Natsional'noi doktriny Rossii', *RF*, 9 (1996) 55–7.

Scheff, T. *Bloody Revenge: Emotions, Nationalism and War* (Boulder, CO: Westview Press, 1994).

Schlesinger, K. *Von der Schwierigkeit, Westler zu Werden* (Berlin: Aufbau Taschenbuch Verlag (AtV), 1998).

Scholte, J. A. 'Beyond the buzzword: towards a critical theory of globalization', in E. Kofman and G. Youngs (eds), *Globalization: Theory and Practice* (London: Pinter, 1996) 43–57.

Schwartz, D. *Contesting the Superbowl* (London: Routledge, 1999).

Schweigler, G. *National Consciousness in Divided Germany* (London: Sage, 1975).

Segell, G. *The Role of Military–Industrial Relations in Civil–Military Relations and Foreign Policy* (London: GMS, 1997).

Segell, G. *Whither or Dither: British Aerospace Collaborative Procurement with Europe* (London: CTD, 1998).

Segell, G. *Civil–Military Relations after the Nation-State* (London: GMS, 2000a).

Segell, G. 'Civil–military relations from Westphalia to the EU', in Stuart Nagel (ed.), *Global Public Policy: Across and Within States* (New York: St Martin's Press – now Palgrave, 2000b).

Segell, G. (ed.), 'Is there a Third Way?' (Special edition), *The European Legacy* 5 (1) (2000c).

Shaw, M. 'Global society and global responsibility: the theoretical, historical and, political limits of "International Society"', *Millennium: Journal of International Studies*, 21 (1992) 431–4.

Shaw, M. *Global Society and International Relations* (Cambridge: Polity Press, 1994).

Shlapentokh, D. V. 'Eurasianism Past and Present', *Communist and Post-Communist Studies*, 30 (2) (1997) 129–51.

Shlapentokh, V. 'How Russians will see the status of their Country by the end of the century', *Journal of Communist Studies and Transition Politics*, 13 (3) September (1997) 1–23.

Shlapentokh, V. ' "Old", "new" and "post" liberal attitudes toward the west: from love to hate', *Communist and Post-Communist Studies*, 31 (3) September (1998) 199–216.

Shohat, O. *Ha'aretz*, 21 May 1998.

Silbey, S. S. 'Let them eat cake: globalization, postmodern colonialism and the possibilities of justice', *Law and Society Review*, 31 (2) (1997) 207–35.

Sklair, L. *Sociology and the Global System*, 2nd edn (Baltimore: John Hopkins University Press, 1995).

Slater, E. 'When the "local" goes "global" in memories of the present Ireland, 1997–98', *Irish Sociological Chronicles, vol. 2* (Dublin: IPA, 2000).

Smith, A. D. *The Ethnic Revival in the Modern World* (Cambridge: Cambridge University Press, 1981).

Smith, M. P. and Guarnizo, L. E. 'The locations of transnationalism', in M. P. Smith and L. E. Guarnizo (eds), *Transnationalism From Below* (New Brunswick, NJ: Transaction Publishers, 1998) 3–34.

Smith, T. W. 'Are conservative churches growing?', *Review of Religious Research*, 33 (4) (1992) 305–29.

Smyth, G. *The Novel and the Nation: Studies in the New Irish Fiction* (London: Pluto Press, 1997).

Smyth, W. 'Explorations of place', in J. Lee (ed.), *Ireland Towards a Sense of Place* (Cork: Cork University Press, 1985) 1–20.

Sofos, S. 'Inter-ethnic violence and gendered constructions of ethnicity in former Yugoslavia', *Social Identities*, 2 (1996a) 73–91.

Sofos, S. 'Culture, politics and identity in former Yugoslavia', in B. Jenkins and S. Sofos, (eds), *Nation and Identity in Contemporary Europe* (London and New York: Routledge, 1996b) 251–82.

Solodkii, B. ' "Russkaia ideia" provokatsiia k konfliktu ili kontseptsiia spaseniia?', *Sotsial'nye konflikty*, 5 (1993) 165–86.

Solzhenitsyn, Alexandr *The Russian Question at the End of the 20th Century?* (London: The Harvill Press, 1995).

SOPEMI *Trends in International Migration: Continuous Reporting System on Migration (Annual Reports)* (Paris: OECD, 1994–97).

Sorabji, C. 'Ethnic war in Bosnia?', *Radical Philosophy*, 63 (1993) 33–5.

Sorabji, C. 'A very modern war: terror and territory in Bosnia-Hercegovina', in R. Hinde and H. Watson (eds), *War: a Cruel Necessity? The Bases of Institutionalized Violence* (London and New York: Tauris Publishers, 1995) 80–95.

Spence, D. 'The European Community and German unification', *German Politics*, 1 (3) (1992) 136–63.

Staab, A. 'Testing the West: consumerism and national identity in eastern Germany', *German Politics*, 6 (2) (1997) 139–49.

Stallybrass, P and White, A. *The Politics and Poetics of Trangression* (Ithaca, NY: Cornell University Press, 1986).

Stankevich, S. 'Russia in search of itself', *The National Interest*, 28 Summer (1992) 47–51.

Stankevich, S. 'Rossiia: mezhdu aziatskim molotom i evropeiskoi nakoval'nei', *Rossiiskoe Obozrenie*, 6 (8) September (1993) 1–2.

Steel, J. 'Apartheid of the mind that keeps South Africa in chains', *The Observer*, 4 May (1997) 11.

Storper Perez, D. 'L'impérialisme de la fonction: l'approche fonctionnaliste du phénomène migratoire', in F. Heymann (ed.), *Identités et Cultures. La Recherche Israélienne au Miroir du Centre de Recherche Français de Jérusalem* (Jerusalem: CRFJ, 1996).

Sweetman, J. *Sword and Mace: Twentieth Century Civil–Military Relations in Britain* (London: Brasseys Defence Publishers, 1986).

Swidler, A. 'Culture in action: symbols and strategies', *American Sociological Review*, 51 (1986) 273–86.

Szporluk, R. 'THE EURASIA HOUSE. Problems of identity in Russia and Eastern Europe', in *Cross Currents: a Yearbook of Central European Culture*, 9 (1990) 3–15.

Tansey, P. 'Tourism: a product with big potential', in M. D'Arag and T. Dickson (eds), *Border Crossings: Developing Ireland's Island Economy* (Dublin: Gill and Macmillan, 1995) 197–207.

Teeple, G. *Globalization and the Decline of Social Reform* (Atlantic Highlands, NJ: Humanities Press, 1995).

Thongchai Winichakul, *Siam Mapped: a History of the Geo-body of a Nation* (Thailand: Silkworm Books, 1994).

Thomas, P. N. 'An inclusive NWICO: Cultural resilience and popular resistance', in P. Golding and P. Harris (eds), *Beyond Cultural Imperialism: Globalization, Communication and the New International Order* (London: Sage, 1997).

Thompson, D. *The End of Time: Faith and Fear in the Shadow of the Millennium* (London: Minerva, 1997).

Thompson, M. 'No exit: "nation-stateness" and democratization in the German Democratic Republic', *Political Studies*, 4 (2) (1996) 267–86.

Tishkov, V. *Ethnicity, Nationalism and Conflict in and after the Soviet Union* (London: Sage, 1997).

Tomkins, S. *Affect, Imagery and Consciousness* (New York: Springer, 1962).

Tomlinson, J. *Cultural Imperialism: a Critical Introduction* (London: Pinter Publishers, 1991 and 1995).

Touraine, A. 'Sociology without society', *Current Sociology*, 46 (2) (1998) 119–43.

Truscott, Peter *Russian First* (London and New York: I. B. Tauris, 1997).

Truth and Reconciliation Commission, website: *http://www.truth.org.za*

Truthtalk, Official newsletter of the TRC, July (1998) 10.

The Truth and Reconciliation Commission *Final Report* (London: Macmillan, 1998).

Tsimbaev, N. I. 'Russia and the Russians', *Russian Studies in History*, 37 (2) Fall (1998) 53–68.

Turner, B. S. *Religion and Social Theory: a Materialist Perspective* (London: Heinemann, 1991).

Turner, B. S. *Orientalism, Postmodernism, and Globalism* (London: Routledge, 1994).

Turner, Victor *The Ritual Process* (Chicago: Aldine Publishing Co., 1969).

Vajiravudh [King Rama VI] *Prayot Hang Karn Yu Nai Tham*, [Benefits of Being in Dhama], (Thailand: Thong Seefa [Blue Flag], Undated)

Wald, K. D., Owen D. E. and Hill S. S. 'Evangelical politics and status issues', *Journal for the Scientific Study of Religion*, 28 (1) (1989) 1–16.

Wallerstein, I. *The Modern World System II* (New York: Academic Press, 1980).

Wallis, R and Bruce, S. 'Secularization: the Official Model', in S. Bruce (ed.), *Religion and Modernization* (Oxford: Clarendon Press, 1992) 8–30.

Walzer, M. (ed.), *Toward a Global Civil Society* (Providence and Oxford: Berghahn Books, 1995).

Waters, M. *An Intelligent Person's Guide to Modern Ireland* (London: Duckworth, 1998).

Whittaker, T. K. 'From protectionism to free trade – the Irish case', *Administration*, Winter (1973) 405–23.

Wilkinson, R. *American Tough: the American Character* (Westport, CT: Greenwood Press, 1984).

Wilson, B. *Religion in Secular Society* (London: C. A. Walker, 1966).

Wise, N. *Passport Thailand* (USA: World Trade Press, 1997).

Wolffe, J. 'The Religions of the Silent Majority', in G. Parsons (ed.), *The Growth of Religious Diversity: Britain From 1945, Volume 1* (London: Routledge/OUP, 1993) 307–46.

Woodward, K. (ed.), *Identity and Difference* (London: Sage and Open University Press, 1997).

Woollacott, M. 'Laying the beast', *The Guardian*, 31 October (1998) 22.

Wuthnow, R. and Lawson, M. P. 'Sources of Christian Fundamentalism in the US', in M. E. Marty and R. S. Appleby (eds), *Accounting for Fundamentalisms: the Dynamic Character of Movements* (Chicago, IL: University of Chicago Press, 1994) 18–56.

Wyatt, D. K. *Thailand: a Short History* (Thailand: Silkworm Books, 1984).

Zivkovic, M. 'Ballads and bullets in Bosnia: how dangerous are the epics of mountain Serbs?', Paper presented at the American Anthropological Annual Meeting, Washington DC, 15–19 November 1995.

Zyuganov, G. A. and Podberezin, A. I. (eds) *Rossiia pered vyborom* (Moscow: Obozrevatel', 1995).

Index of Names

Index of Subjects